Professor Leslie Thomas KC is an ⬚ civil liberties barrister and former Joint Head of Garden Court Chambers in the UK and head of JC Legal Solutions in the Caribbean. In 2020 Leslie became Professor of Law at Gresham College and visiting Professor of Law at Goldsmiths Law School, University of London. He is a Bencher and advocacy trainer for the Inner Temple. Leslie is a member of the Bar Standards Board for England and Wales, sits on the BSB's Race Equality Taskforce and is deputy chair of the Equality Diversity and Inclusion sub-committee for the Inner Temple.

Praise for *Do Right and Fear No One*

'Leslie has done more for the families of those
who die in custody or at the hands of the police
than any other single lawyer'
Louise Christian of Christian Khan Solicitors

DO RIGHT
AND FEAR NO ONE

A Life Dedicated to Fighting For Justice

LESLIE THOMAS KC

**SIMON &
SCHUSTER**

London · New York · Sydney · Toronto · New Delhi

First published in Great Britain by Simon & Schuster UK Ltd, 2022

This edition published in Great Britain by Simon & Schuster UK Ltd, 2023

1 3 5 7 9 10 8 6 4 2

Simon & Schuster UK Ltd
1st Floor
222 Gray's Inn Road
London WC1X 8HB

www.simonandschuster.co.uk
www.simonandschuster.com.au
www.simonandschuster.co.in

Simon & Schuster Australia, Sydney
Simon & Schuster India, New Delhi

A CIP catalogue record for this book is available from the British Library

Paperback ISBN: 978-1-4711-8483-3
eBook ISBN: 978-1-4711-8482-6

Typeset in Perpetua by M Rules
Printed and Bound in the UK using 100% Renewable
Electricity at CPI Group (UK) Ltd

In memory of that quiet man, my father, Godfrey.

To my mother, Pearl, and my children
Megan, Isaac and Alisa.

CONTENTS

'Where, after all, do universal human rights begin? In small places, close to home — so close and so small that they cannot be seen on any maps of the world. Yet they are the world of the individual person; the neighbourhood he lives in; the school or college he attends; the factory, farm, or office where he works. Such are the places where every man, woman, and child seek equal justice, equal opportunity, equal dignity without discrimination. Unless these rights have meaning there, they have little meaning anywhere. Without concerted citizen action to uphold them close to home, we shall look in vain for progress in the larger world.'

— *Eleanor Roosevelt*

'Is it possible that the antonym of "forgetting" is not "remembering", but justice?'

— *Yosef Yerushalmi*

INTRODUCTION

There's a line in the 1999 movie *Sixth Sense* which always gives me pause: 'I see dead people,' the boy says. Of course, no one believes him; ghosts do not exist. When people ask me what I do, I sometimes say that I represent the dead. Often this meets with confusion or a bemused, embarrassed laugh from the audience. Some ask if I am a prosecutor on murder trials; some guess that I am a wills and probate lawyer; others that I practise in the law of fatal accidents. All reasonable and fair assumptions, but incorrect. Over the years, when I have gone on to explain that I represent the dead through their families at inquests, it has struck me that most people know very little about inquests, when or why they take place, or how they function. Happily so, perhaps, because an inquest is occasioned if: the cause of death is unknown; the person might have died a violent or unnatural death; or the person might have died in prison or police custody.

When I started on this path, inquest law was to a certain extent a niche area of practice. Moreover, the area of inquests in which I practise is a narrow area of human rights law, predominantly involving deaths in custody or deaths in which an agent of the state may be implicated in some capacity. Many are incredulous that such a line of work can keep me in full-time employment. Surely, they say, there can't be so many deaths in custody in England and Wales to sustain my practice? When I outline just a few of the cases occupying my days and nights, from the Grenfell Tower Inquiry to the deaths of Christi and Bobby Shepherd by carbon monoxide poisoning in Corfu, from the Birmingham Pub Bombings to the police shooting of Mark Duggan, the next question I am asked is how and why I ended up in this particular area of law. This memoir attempts to answer both of those questions in part. But more than that, it is the story of a Black child of immigrant parents growing up and attending a comprehensive school in south London and how I became a lawyer in the first place. It is about what motivates me and keeps me fighting to do what I do.

I will be honest and let you in on a secret: I was unsure about the potential hubris of this book's title, *Do Right and Fear No One*. The truth is that in my work I feel scared almost every single day. There have been many occasions when I have been so scared that I can hardly move my feet in front of me. Today a paralysis has gripped me like I'm held in some sort of invisible vice. Every step I have to make feels like a magnetic force is pulling me in the opposite direction than the one I want to move in. Why? Simply because I will be appearing in court and, despite the training I have had and the many hours of preparation I have done, I'm not sure of what I am doing. I always feel I haven't done enough. Or that I am not good enough. Or that I will be found out as some kind of impostor who has no right to call himself a barrister at law. These are the fears that grip me before almost every court appearance I make. I suppose the real question is *why* we sometimes feel like impostors, as though we do not belong or as if we are perpetrating some kind of fraud by our presence. I will explore this feeling later in the book.

My work is more than just a job. If I mess up, it has serious consequences. I'm not talking about being sued, or coming up in front of the regulator or having complaints made against me. Yes, there is all of that, but I never think about the personal consequences that I might face. No, it's the consequences that others may face; the harm I could inadvertently do to those who have placed their faith in me to represent their cause. People could lose the opportunity to find out the truth about what happened to a loved one, or lose the right to life-changing compensation for them and their dependents, or, in other human rights cases, lose their liberty. They never told me this at law school. I was taught using hypothetical yet interesting legal problems to see how and where the law might develop and to test my legal knowledge and acumen. But I never heard a lecturer talk about the day-to-day stress of doing this job, namely the impact that getting it wrong might have on real people in their real lives. After three years of intensive studies at law school, I found out the hard way that I knew less about the law than I should have done. I didn't know how to speak to people. I was ill-equipped to deal with the grief, anger and frustrations that my clients would feel under the duress of the prevailing legal system. And now I was being let loose on the public.

The book title is also the motto of my law chambers, Garden Court: 'Do right and fear no one.' Our website explains the motto thus: 'Dedicated to fighting your corner no matter how formidable your opponent seems.' But often we lawyers do not live up to this grand ideal. Moreover, no one is completely fearless unless they are a fool. Practising law is not a science but an art. It is constantly changing and shifting. It has nebulous, muddy boundaries. What you think is right today will turn out to be wrong tomorrow. All of this makes it very difficult to give any advice with certainty. So, no lawyer will ever tell a client that they have a 100 per cent chance of success; there are too many movable factors which can alter the odds. You might have the most likable client with very sympathetic facts in your favour but the law might be against you. Or you might have an unsympathetic, horrible client who has committed the most horrendous acts, and yet all the legal precedents might seem to favour what that person has done. But still, in either situation I would not guarantee that the first client will definitely lose the case and the second will definitely win. I have known both situations and the opposite has happened.

To return to our motto, having been at Garden Court for over thirty years I now understand that, perhaps, it works best as an affirmation. It is something that I tell myself often, repeating the mantra so it sinks into my subconscious mind. Even if I feel scared, I pretend; act fearless and I can trick my mind into not knowing the difference between the real world and the imagined world. And, as I hope my story will illustrate, it works. So, today, before I started my case, I told myself again, 'Leslie, you go out there and do right, and fear no one.'

Part I

I

MUM AND DAD: PEARL AND GODFREY THOMAS

In 1943 the world was at war.

On New Year's Eve British Deputy Prime Minister Clement Attlee broadcast a message to the people of the British Empire declaring 'cold and dark is the outlook for Hitler and the Nazis. The hour of reckoning has come.' Meanwhile, as the Russians continued to inflict heavy defeats on the Fuhrer's armies in the east and Allied bombs rained down on Berlin, Adolf Hitler was holed up in his Wolf's Lair. He was preparing his own seasonal message to the German people, admitting that 1944 would 'make heavy demands on all Germans'.

On the same day, about 4,900 miles away in a small blue-and-white house on a remote Caribbean island, a young woman was giving birth to her fifth child. This island was a British Overseas Territory called Antigua, which a colonial pirate and land-grabber called Christopher Columbus named in honour of the Virgin of La Antigua of Seville in 1493.

Earlier that day, Margaret, the woman in childbirth, had been cutting sugar cane on the family's land near her home in a suburb around twenty minutes outside St John's when she felt what she recognised as contractions. But Margaret was a

7

resilient and headstrong woman and she knew it would be beneficial for her growing family if she could get one more day's crop in. She could sell the prized sugar cane in the St John's market for a few additional cents. Her fisherman husband had been at sea that day and would have scolded her if he had found out, but she was strong and healthy, happiest when out working her land. No pregnancy was going to hold her back from doing as she pleased. That evening she safely delivered her child, a healthy girl with extremely powerful lungs, whom she named Sheila. As is common in the Caribbean, all children have a pet name; Sheila was given the name Pearl.

Pearl is my mother. Her father's name, my grandfather, was Samuel Lewis, but his family called him Pa-Fred. And my grandmother was Margaret Lewis.

Antigua is a small island, a Commonwealth sovereign state in the middle of the Leeward Islands. It stretches just 14 miles long and 11 miles wide, but its location on the major sailing routes among the region's resource-rich colonies meant that it was known as Britain's 'Gateway to the Caribbean'. For most of its colonial history, Antigua's economy was reliant almost exclusively on the debilitating and dangerous work of the slaves on the sugar plantations. By the late 18th century, the slave population numbered nearly 38,000, with a single family, the Codringtons, maintaining a monopoly on the island's sugar production. When the Slavery Abolition Act of 1833 finally won the emancipation of all existing slaves a year later, Antigua had developed little or no agriculture of any other kind. The cost of living in the far-flung Caribbean colonies, therefore, was much higher than in the governing lands for the simple reason that the bulk of foodstuffs were imported; even the locally grown sugar would cost you more than in England.

In the 1940s, life on the island was hard for poor people

not only because of wartime privations, but also because – as a 1938 report to the Royal Commissioners on the West Indies observed – to all intents and purposes the British government had 'divested itself of its responsibility to the descendants of those millions of slaves who had produced the greater part of the wealth which financed the Industrial Revolution in England', adding that 'it might be as well to remember that the £20 million compensation that was paid to the slave owners remained in England, with the result that the colonies began the emancipation period robbed of much of the capital which should have been in circulation in the islands'.

At the onset of the Second World War, a century of British rule had created a local West Indian bourgeoisie without changing the living standards of the labouring class. Wages on the island were below a reasonable subsistence level resulting in mass poverty, while the British colonial owners had failed to provide basic resources for the good of the islanders. Medical care, education and housing were woefully lacking in any controls or funding, and consequently, illiteracy, disease and malnutrition were rife.

Nevertheless, the sea is all around, so everywhere along its jagged coastline, hundreds of white sand beaches (Antiguans say their island has 365 beaches – one for each day of the year), bays and coves provided harbours for a small-scale local fishing industry and so, like Margaret and Pa-Fred, most Antiguans scraped a meagre living off the land and the fruits of the sea. In addition, in 1941 the US Army built a marine and air base to the north of the island at Parham Harbour on land leased by their British allies, creating jobs in construction for the local workforce.

When peace finally came in September 1945 and the US troops departed, they left behind a rudimentary airport, and the infrastructure for a nascent tourist industry. Before long, word spread of the island's lively Creole culture with its calypso and steel drum music; the laid-back atmosphere, and the unrelenting sunshine, dazzlingly blue skies and spectacular sunsets, the clear-blue ocean and miles of untouched coastline, attracting a prosperous tourism trade as rich Americans flocked to Antigua. With its agriculture devoted to sugar cane production, the island already imported most of its food, but now, together with the American tourists, came fast-food outlets, designer boutiques and shopping malls, signalling – as Jamaica Kincaid so memorably notes in her searing and brilliant *A Small Place* – a new era of colonialism by any other name.

Like many of his fellow Antiguans, my maternal grandfather Pa-Fred owned his own plot of land on which they grew peas, guineps, okras, pumpkins, onions, tomatoes and sweet potatoes, as well as the staple crop of sugar cane. Pa-Fred also had cows in the pasture nearby, which he would tend to daily when he was not out on his boat fishing.

My grandmother's name was Margaret but everybody affectionately called her Dada. She was the archetypal strong matriarchal figure in that family. My memory of my gran is that she was not a woman known for smiling, although when you did manage to coax a laugh out of her, she had this sweet, infectious giggle. After my mum was born, Dada had five more children, each born about eighteen months or just over two years apart. My mum was number five, smack in the middle. The eldest was my Aunt Ines, then Cecilia or Auntie Cis, Uncle David (a pastor), Uncle Charles, my mum Pearl, Uncle Peter, Uncle Jonathan, Uncle Raphael, Aunt Margaret Rose and finally Aunt Veronica. One of the reasons Pearl is such a tough woman, I think, is that she was born on either side of two brothers.

The family's eldest child, Ines, was the first to leave Antigua. She went to make her fortune in the United States. Then, in 1957, when she was aged around twenty-one, Cis came up to the UK, followed shortly by my Uncle Charles. They went by boat – fourteen days on the sea across the Atlantic after stopping at other islands to collect passengers. My grandfather had wanted my mother to be a nurse, but it proved difficult to get a foot in the door. Back then in the Caribbean there was so much 'pull string' – it was who you knew not what you knew – and so he said she had better join her brother and sister in England. When Pearl was due to 'come up', Cis and Charles wrote to Dada to say that now that they were settled, they could send for my mother. But they didn't want her to come by sea: there was a lot of lawlessness on the ship and so they sent a share of the money for her to get a flight on BWIA, the British West Indian Airways. The airfare would have been a lot of money for Pa-Fred and Dada to have invested in, so there must have been a lot of hope and expectation on my mother's shoulders to continue her education and get a good job. I know that Cis, Charles and Mum would regularly send money back to Antigua to support their parents and their remaining siblings in Antigua.

And so Pearl landed at Gatwick on 14 June 1961, aged just seventeen. The train brought her to Victoria Station where her sister Cis was waiting. As the train trundled through the outskirts of London, Mum's first impression was that she would have no problem finding work – through the window stretching to infinity through the smog, she took the drab streets of terraced brick houses for miles and miles of factories. She'd never seen anything like it.

Perhaps, as I imagine her, a seventeen-year-old girl straight off the plane from her tiny island, having said goodbye to her mother, father and the six brothers and sisters she had left behind, she might have been anxious, but no. Because she was looking forward to meeting her elder brother and sister in London, she was quite cool about the whole adventure – until she got there, that is.

My dad, Godfrey Michel Thomas, was some nine years older than Mum and had arrived in the UK a few years earlier. Nobody ever called Dad 'Godfrey'; since childhood his nickname was 'Twi'. Dad and Mum were from very different Caribbean islands, from different cultures, and, in fact, were very different people in almost every way. Dad was from Dominica, a mountainous island country to the south of Antigua, part of the Windward Islands chain in the Lesser Antilles archipelago in the Caribbean Sea. To the north, Dominica's closest neighbour is Guadeloupe, and to the south lies Martinique. It is a larger island than Antigua, but much less developed.

The British took possession of Dominica from the French in 1763 after the Seven Years' War and soon after established a small colony there, importing slaves who were sold as labour in the production of sugar and coffee for trade in Europe. In a long history of European colonisation, Dominica changed hands between the two European powers, passing back to France in 1778 and again to England five years later. The French attempted to invade in 1795 and 1805 before eventually withdrawing, leaving Britain in possession. When my father left home for the first time in the mid-1950s, Dominica was still a British Overseas Territory, only finally gaining its independence on 3 November 1978.

Then, as now, the island's main resource is agriculture, and consequently its natural environment remains largely untouched, with dense, lush mountainous rainforests, home to many rare plants, animals and indigenous bird species. It is a tropical paradise on earth, known as the 'Nature Isle of the Caribbean'. It is possibly my favourite place on this small planet of ours, but perhaps I am biased. In fact, the saying goes that if Christopher Columbus was to travel through the Caribbean today, the only island that he would recognise would be Dominica. When you fly over the island it is easy to understand why: today it remains wild, rugged and entirely unspoilt, one of the most beautiful places in the world.

Dad was the youngest of four children, with two brothers and a sister. His father – my paternal grandfather Hector, or Daddy Hector – was a tall, strict man, a farmer who owned a lot of land on the mountain in the north-east of Dominica. My aunt Eula, and his older brother Hobson, or 'Bobo', stayed at home to work on the farm, while his middle brother, Uncle Philbert, or 'Tacki', became an accountant in the capital Roseau, on the western side. Dad was bright and Daddy Hector decided to send him to the UK to make his fortune, and to try to create a better life not only for the family he would go on to have in the UK, but also by sending money home to Dominica.

It wasn't cheap to send people over to the UK. Dad sailed on the banana boat, a cargo ship chartered by a horticultural company called Geest, which also carried passengers on its regular journey across the Atlantic to Preston and Liverpool. I suppose he must have decided that London offered the best chances of employment, and so it was there that he found accommodation in a rented room in Notting Hill and a job as a telephone engineer with the GPO, later British Telecom, fixing telephone lines and cables.

Pearl, Twi, Cis and Charles were part of the *Windrush* generation, the nearly half a million people from the colonies and Commonwealth countries who arrived in the UK between

1948 and 1971, many of whom were recruited as British dependents to assist with the rebuilding of the country and the economy after the Second World War. There were active campaigns in various Caribbean islands, posters proclaiming, 'Come and Help Rebuild the Motherland. We need nurses, we need bus drivers, we need engineers. Passenger Opportunity.' They were British subjects and as such they had an entitlement to come and go as they pleased, and so some travelled with the view of spending a few years in the UK, and then maybe going back and building their homes and raising a family in Antigua. My dad was certainly one of those.

Like many other immigrants who came before and after them, Mum and Dad had been 'chosen' among their siblings to come to Britain. In some ways it was considered a privilege, because the idea was that the streets there were paved with gold. That generation was expected to support the rest of the family back home, and so they had left behind parents, grandparents, brothers, sisters and friends, and travelled to England in the hope of finding opportunities for themselves and for their children. My parents' journey to new lands is not unique, poverty being a powerful driver for many people around the world in search of a better life.

My parents' early years in London played out against the backdrop of a racist backlash against immigration. This was the era of the Conservative Monday Club, Enoch Powell and the notorious Smethwick by-election in which Conservative Peter Griffiths gained his seat on the back of campaign slogans such as 'If you want a nigger for a neighbour, vote Labour'.*

This rising tide of racism soon found its expression in

---

* Although it was widely reported that the Conservatives were responsible for this racist sloganeering, later the then leader of the neo-Nazi 'British Movement' Colin Jordan proudly claimed ownership of the copyright.

legislation. Until 1962, most people from the Commonwealth, as fellow subjects of the British Crown, enjoyed an unlimited right to live and work in the UK. People from the UK itself and its remaining colonies (including Antigua) were 'citizens of the United Kingdom and Colonies', while people from independent Commonwealth countries were 'Commonwealth citizens'. Both groups were British subjects – as opposed to aliens – and both enjoyed the right of abode in the UK.

But the era of free movement ended when the Harold Macmillan government enacted the Commonwealth Immigrants Act 1962. This Act imposed immigration controls on many people from the Commonwealth. The new controls applied both to Commonwealth citizens, and to citizens of the United Kingdom and Colonies who held British passports issued by the government of a colony, rather than the UK government. This created a two-tier citizenship, with a class of people who held British passports but had no right to live in the UK.

And, before long, with the advent of Harold Wilson's Labour government, it would only get worse.

When my mum came to England, Cis was married to Uncle John and they had one child, while Uncle Charles was also married but had no children yet. The two siblings lived together in a rented house at No. 37 Bramley Road, just a few doors down from Latimer Road underground station in west London. They shared the property with a 'sitting tenant'; a white woman called Mrs Bennell and her family of five children. The Bennells had their own small separate quarters, so Mum's family had almost the whole rest of the house to themselves: two bedrooms, a big sitting room with a coal fire, a kitchen and a bathroom with a bathtub.

Charles was working for the local council as a carpenter, a profession he had trained in back in Antigua. Cis was a ward orderly at St Bartholomew's Hospital in Smithfield, and her husband, Uncle John, worked at the GPO, like my dad. Most of their neighbours were Irish and poor. That was the first shock for Mum. Until she reached Britain, the only white people she had seen were the tourists who came to holiday in the Caribbean. 'You see what happened,' she told me. 'We thought that everybody was rich. Until I first came to London, we thought people in the Caribbean were poor, but my goodness, I did not realise that you had poor white people in the United Kingdom.'

The morning after she arrived in London, Cis gave Mum three thrupenny bits and told her to gather her papers, go to Latimer Road station, take the train to Hammersmith and find her way to the labour exchange so she could register for employment. She was sent to work at the Fullers sweet factory on Fulham Road. She hated that job. Every day, she sat on the production line desperately trying to place chocolates in boxes, but before she knew it the factory belt had run away from her. She only lasted there for about three weeks, and then went with Cis to St Bartholomew's where she got a job as a ward orderly. Working in the hospital suited Mum much better. She is a great chatterbox; she likes to speak to people, and would sit on the patients' beds and hold their hands. Even now, she still has that skill. Anybody sick or dying, she is always there to hold their hand.

Within six short months of arriving in London, Mum met my dad at the local Methodist church, which today stands in the shadows of the burned-out Grenfell Tower, and they fell in love. My mum was lonely and had started to get homesick in winter when the weather was cold, and my dad didn't have anybody close to him in England and missed his family too, so very quickly they were married in that same church. Dad had just turned twenty-seven and Mum was eighteen. When my sister Janet was born (in Hammersmith Hospital) soon after, on 19 August 1962, Mum and Dad moved to new lodgings in Latimer Road where they paid thirty shillings a week for one big room. Their kitchen – a stove and a sink – was on the landing next to their room and they shared a bathroom with two other families; a husband and wife from Jamaica, and two young African brothers.

Soon thereafter they moved to a bigger room in a three-storey property on Talbot Road, just off the Portobello Road. This was at a time when rental advertisements and signs in people's windows were not welcoming: 'Room to rent. No Blacks, no Irish, no dogs.' Until the Race Relations Act of 1965, it was perfectly legal for landlords to refuse to rent to Black people, or Irish people, or any people who were different, because they were somehow undesirables, seen as trouble. Not all private landlords, however, were unwilling to let rooms to people of colour. For some, like the Polish-born self-made property baron Peter Rachman, the colour of your money was more important than the colour of your skin and so there were certain areas in London, Brixton and Notting Hill in particular, where a lot of Black people had settled.

Peter Rachman had started out working for an estate agent in Shepherd's Bush, then built up his own property empire in west London, buying up several nightclubs and many more once grand but now run-down and shabby townhouses around Notting Hill. His MO was to negotiate with, or evict, any rent-protected tenants, then subdivide the large properties into a proliferation of smaller furnished flats and bedsits in order to maximise the number of tenants he could cram into each building. Many of his tenants, like my parents, were newly arrived immigrants from the West Indies.

Many in the West Indian community welcomed Rachman as a fair-handed businessman who could be relied upon to house immigrants. But while Rachman – an immigrant himself whose family were murdered by the Nazis in the Holocaust – could not be accused of shunning a West Indian face because of racial prejudice, plenty of the properties he rented were no more than slums; dilapidated Victorian buildings that were barely fit for habitation.

With few housing rights for tenants and no rent controls, Rachman exploited his West Indian tenants by massively overcharging them. In 1950s and '60s racially biased Britain, a room that a landlord might rent unfurnished to a rent-protected tenant for £1 a week could be let by Rachman as furnished accommodation to a couple like my mum and dad for £6 a week. Furthermore, when it came to the state of the accommodation, the 'slum landlords' were happy to take their tenants' money but not to repair the property. As a vulnerable immigrant, who did not have the same protection under the law as the previous tenants of these buildings, you just had to make do. If you complained, you'd find yourself out on the street. Thus, social housing, council accommodation outside the private rented sector, was important, especially if you were a person of colour, because the market choice was limited. It became vital for families like ours. Most people would try to get their own tenancy. People weren't interested in buying their home; they were interested in *having* a home.

The lodgings on Talbot Road that my mother and father called 'home' was above an antiques shop. As before, they had one large room, with a stove and a sink on the landing as their kitchen, and one bathroom, which they shared with another family.

I was born on 29 April 1965 in that room on Talbot Road. Having felt some pains the day before, Mum woke in the early hours of the following morning and marched up and down like a watchman, looking out of the window. Around 5 a.m., my dad got up. She had kept him awake with her pacing about, but she told him not to worry, to leave her be and go to work; she would call the lady next door if she needed anything. Dad was busy giving Janet breakfast, then the next thing my mum remembers is that a new pain came. She knelt on the floor and put her head on the bed and this baby, me, flew out onto the floor. And all she could hear was my father saying, 'Oh, Sheila, you had the baby here on me.'

My father picked up the newborn me, got Mum back in bed, and put me beside her wrapped in the blankets. Then he called an ambulance, which took us to hospital. I weighed in at a healthy 6lb 12oz.

So now we were four, all living in one room above the antiques shop on Talbot Road.

The Britain I was born into was one in which anti-immigration and racist sentiment largely went unchecked. The country was in the throes of a particularly painful transition as, one by one, the last remnants of the Empire claimed their independence. As many former African colonies such as Kenya and Uganda pursued an aggressive programme of 'Africanisation', their Asian immigrant populations were forced into exile and many were choosing to find refuge in the erstwhile motherland. The consequence was a concerted campaign of anti-immigration propaganda by the right in Britain, which succeeded in striking fear into the hearts of many. In this highly charged political climate, on 27 February 1968, three years after I was born, Labour Home Secretary James Callaghan introduced the Commonwealth Immigrants Act. Supported by the opposition Conservative Party, the bill passed through Parliament in just three days. With its invented category of 'patriality', which the government crafted specifically to stop the dispossessed East African Asians of Kenya and Uganda from settling in the UK, this new legislation was racist in intent and effect. It imposed immigration controls on all citizens of the United Kingdom and its colonies unless they, or one of their parents or grandparents, had been born, adopted or naturalised in the UK. Those citizens of the United Kingdom and Colonies who were connected to the UK by birth or ancestry, that is predominantly white people, therefore, retained their right of abode. Those who were connected solely with one of Britain's current or former colonies – mainly Black and Asian people – did not. It was among the most emotive and divisive decisions taken by a British government. *The Times* called it 'probably the most shameful measure that Labour members have ever been asked by their whips to support'. Within two weeks of the passing of the 1968 Act, Shadow Defence Secretary Enoch Powell made his infamous 'Rivers of Blood' speech in Birmingham. And while at the time Callaghan publicly denied that the legislation was racist, thirty years later, in 1999, the *New Statesman* reported that the newly declassified Cabinet papers 'show beyond doubt that the legislation was intentionally aimed at "coloured immigrants" and that evidence cited to justify the legislation did not exist'.

This effectively left an estimated 60,000 Ugandan Asians, expelled from the country by President Idi Amin, and up to 200,000 Asians in Kenya with no country to call their own. Their situation was so appalling that in 1973 the

European Commission of Human Rights found that the British government had racially discriminated against them and – remarkably – that it constituted 'degrading treatment', contrary to Article 3 of the European Convention on Human Rights. Such a finding was and remains exceptional.

Despite this, the spirit of the 1968 Act lives on today. The subsequent Immigration Act 1971, which still forms the basis of our immigration laws today, imposed a single system of controls on Commonwealth citizens and aliens for the first time. Along similar lines to the 1968 Act, it divided citizens into 'patrials', who had the right to live in the UK, and 'non-patrials', who did not. A citizen of the United Kingdom and Colonies was a 'patrial' if they, or any of their parents or grandparents, were born, adopted, or naturalised in the UK, or if they had settled in the UK and been resident there for five years or more. A non-UK Commonwealth citizen was not a 'patrial' unless one of their parents was born in the UK. Again, therefore, those with connections to the UK by birth or ancestry – mainly white people – were privileged over the predominantly Black and Asian people from Britain's current and former colonies.

This racist system was reinforced by the British Nationality Act 1981, which reclassified 'patrial' citizens of the United Kingdom and Colonies as 'British citizens'. As the esteemed academic and an equality and human rights campaigner Professor Gus John said recently, 'If the 1968 Race Relations Act was geared towards prohibiting discrimination against those of us already here, the 1971 Immigration Act was about preventing more like us from coming in or claiming a right to remain.'* Non-patrials were reclassified as 'British Overseas citizens' or 'British Dependent Territories citizens' without the

* 'A Walk Down a Long Road with Ian Macdonald QC': tribute letter by Professor Gus John to Garden Court Chambers, 18 November 2019.

right of abode. To this day, Britain is one of only a few countries in the world to have two-tier citizenship – with a class of people who hold British passports but have no right to call the UK their home. The 1981 Act also abolished birthright citizenship – so for the first time in history a person could be born in the UK without being a British citizen. Indeed, as we have all too recently witnessed during the *Windrush* scandal, there are people born and raised in the UK who have faced deportation.

The story of immigration control in Britain is, more than anything else, a story of racism. The very people whose countries had been colonised and exploited by Britain were deprived of the right to live there. The *Windrush* scandal of the past few years was not an aberration, but the logical endpoint of a system designed specifically to exclude people of colour.

Eight months after the introduction of the Immigration Act, on 25 October, the Race Relations Act 1968 passed through Parliament. This essentially extended the first Race Relations Act of 1965, which had applied only to 'public' places – hotels and cinemas, for example. The 1968 Act now, supposedly, outlawed the denial of housing, employment or public services on the grounds of a person's race. A BBC report at the time suggested that this new Act was 'intended to counterbalance the Immigration Act, and so fulfil the government's promise to be "fair but tough" on immigrants.' However, the Act was practically useless. It may have paid lip service to countering racial discrimination in Britain, but it lacked any actual power of enforcement. In order to successfully fight a racial discrimination case, the victim had firstly to prove that discrimination had occurred, then demonstrate that it was *intentional* – essentially, an extremely difficult undertaking. Additionally, the 1968 Act didn't apply to government services, such as the police, as it applied only to private employers. As the Conservative MP

Quintin Hogg rather fittingly asked in the House of Commons debate, 'Why should the ordinary subject be liable to an action for damages, as the Home Secretary has decided that he should be, but the Home Secretary get off scot-free?'

2

GRANDISON ROAD, BATTERSEA

My younger brother Trevor was born on 21 August 1967. With five-year-old Janet, me barely out of nappies, and now a new baby in a big pram to lug up the stairs, Mum and Dad could no longer live in that cramped single room on Talbot Road. Mum dreaded spending another winter there. Both she and Janet suffered from severe asthma and I was affected by childhood bronchitis, which was exacerbated by living in a damp and miserably cold old house. More so, however, Mum dreaded winter because of the paraffin heater fires, which burned all day downstairs in the antique shop. With all that old junk as kindling, if a fire broke out, we would have perished, trapped upstairs.

Before his death at the end of 1962, Peter Rachman had largely divested his residential properties, allowing a new generation of businessmen to move into the seedy world of the Notting Hill housing market. The Talbot Road property, however, having simply passed into the hands of Rachman's erstwhile associates, continued to deteriorate. Little or no modernisation, maintenance or even basic repairs were ever carried out on the building.

Meanwhile, the local council was determined to rid the borough of some of the most dilapidated housing and made plans in the late 1960s to start the demolition of the slum streets and replace them with the Lancaster West Estate scheme. Some 3,000 residents in these substandard rented properties were to be accommodated in this new council housing.

Mum registered with Kensington and Chelsea council to get on the waiting list. At some point, the housing department offered her a flat in the yet to be constructed Grenfell Tower on the proposed new estate. It was at a time when local authorities had an incentive to build bigger tower blocks; the terms of the 1956 Housing Subsidies Act meant that the higher you built, the bigger the grants awarded. It was also a time when these local housing authorities were putting people of colour right at the top of these new tower blocks because they were the most unpopular floors. Mum didn't want to live on the upper storey of a high-rise building. She doesn't like heights and absolutely did not want to live in a block of flats where the lifts might be out of order and she'd have to climb however many flights of stairs with her three young children.

Auntie Cis came to the rescue. She and Uncle John had four girls and had bought a big five-bedroomed house off the Goldhawk Road in Shepherd's Bush, so we moved in with them as we waited for suitable council housing. A lot of places Mum was shown were even worse than Talbot Road. Social housing, particularly housing blocks, had a certain stigma to them. Sometimes the stigma was completely unjustified, other times it was spot on in the sense that local authorities would tend to put problem families or, I should say, who they *perceived* to be problem families together in so-called 'sink estates'. Mum did not want that for us.

As an engineer for the GPO, Dad was in a good secure job with a reasonable wage, but he wasn't interested at all in buying a house. He was dreadfully homesick. He didn't like England

and – there are no two ways about it – he had a virulent dislike of English people because of how he was treated when he arrived in the UK. His dream was to work for enough money to go back home and he was frustrated that Mum seemed set on bringing us up in the UK. I know now that he put a lot of pressure on her to pack up and take us all with him to live in Dominica, and for this reason Mum knew that she needed the security of building her own career. She had always wanted to be a qualified nurse, and having proven herself as a ward auxiliary, she was working nights at Hammersmith Hospital while training to be a State Enrolled Nurse (SEN).

One day after she had been to see a flat in a terrible block in Fulham, she gave up with the council. It was the last straw. My mum is a formidable woman. She left the Caribbean to start a new life in London at a young age with nothing to her name and only her high school qualifications but, regardless, she always had a strong drive and determination for her kids. She found out about Harding Housing Association based on Brompton Road in Chelsea, set up by a woman called Mrs Monica Mason to help house homeless families. Within a month Mrs Mason had offered us a flat in Battersea. My mum was delighted.

We had been appointed a small two-bedroom apartment on the first floor of No. 71 Grandison Road, a bright, tree-lined street of Victorian terraced houses. It was a comparatively upmarket area and, in contrast to the raucous goings on of Portobello Road Market, peaceful. The house was just around the corner from Clapham Common, so importantly for her and Janet, the air was clean. A different world. Mum and Harding Housing had come up trumps.

I was five when we moved there in March 1971. We had a tiny living room, an even tinier kitchen and a bathroom and toilet, and I shared a bedroom with my sister and baby brother.

So, it was cosy, let's say, but to us it was grand compared to our former address.

Today Grandison Road is one of those 'highly desirable' residential streets where the houses sell for seven figures. In the early '70s it was one of the most diverse and cosmopolitan communities you could imagine in south London: a mixture of different income groups, peoples, ethnicities and classes. Professional and working men and women who shared a common space; a perfect example of unity in our capital; a social experiment that had gone right.

My mum would take us shopping in nearby Clapham Junction at a lively Caribbean market with all the mouth-watering smells of West Indian street food cooking on the stalls, and rainbow arrays of Caribbean fruits and vegetables. Then there were the equally vibrant people. It was an amazing place. There was a West Indian fishmonger where you could buy fish of all different colours. Fish is a staple among Caribbean island people, so having good, fresh fish was important, and plenty of noisy bartering would go on. What I remember most clearly, though, is the sense of friendship and the laughter. It was a place where people would meet and chat. And, of course, I remember the music. There was a record shop that played reggae, blasting out from speakers onto the street, and lots of the stall owners would have their record players or cassette players to play music as well. To the west we had another Caribbean market along the Northcote Road, where there was also the towering red-brick Northcote Baptist Church.

Another reason my mum was keen to take the flat was that there were two primary schools within a short distance, Honeywell and Belleville. Most of the local kids would go to one of these, and there was a healthy rivalry between the two. It was important for my mum that from an early age Janet and I

27

could walk to school on our own along safe, residential streets, because she and Dad both worked long hours.

As soon as my younger brother was weaned, Mum started a new job doing the night shift on a mixed medical ward at Hounslow General Hospital on Staines Road. She would leave the house at about 7 p.m., finish work at about 6 a.m. the next morning and normally arrive home after we'd left for school. Then she would sleep until she got up to get our dinner ready for 4 p.m. Dad would usually get home at 6 p.m. He would either drive my mum to work in his little Toyota or she would get the No. 37 bus, which at the time was the longest bus route in London and took her an hour and a half each way. We barely saw her at weekends either; she was always doing overtime shifts because we needed the money. She must have been exhausted. But it was a small hospital, a local unit, and she had many good friends there among the staff and her fellow nurses. If she was working on Christmas Eve, Dad used to take us to see her so she could show us off to her matron and co-workers.

My mum is still incredibly hardworking. When I built my house in Antigua, she was project-managing everything. Seventy-nine years of age, and she's on the go all the time. That's what keeps her young – that and good genes, I suppose.

Dad was off at the weekends and, on a Sunday, he'd take us out to visit some of my mum's friends with kids our age, or we often went to visit our cousins in Shepherd's Bush. Occasionally Dad would take us to visit his Dominican friends because he liked to play dominos with them. He also liked a visit to the bookies. He wasn't much of a pub-goer, but he did like a flutter on the horses. This was a big part of his life on a Saturday afternoon. He would take us out on day trips to various London sights or to the zoo, and he was into photography, so he liked taking photos of us out and about against a suitably picturesque London backdrop.

In the main, though, I spent a lot of my childhood in the company of my brother and sister. Janet was a very sensible and responsible older sister and, in truth, most of the time it was she who looked after our baby brother and me. We were self-rearing; not quite latchkey kids but something close to that. Nevertheless, it was a stable family structure and the routine and the discipline of my parents' work ethic was extremely important. We all felt loved. We were fed. And I know that Mum and Dad always wanted to do the best for us. It was a case of 'Mum and Dad are working because they have to'. That's how we felt about it.

That was another reason moving to Grandison Road was such a blessing. In the holidays and at the weekend, Mum would come home from her night shift and could sleep during the day safe in the knowledge that we children could hold hands to cross the road to the Common and play outside all day on the swings or roam about having adventures in the woodland at the end of the road. When we weren't in school, we spent every second we could in the park.

I was a quiet, somewhat solemn child. I had my gang of friends, but at home I liked playing quietly, or doing my homework by myself. I was sort of the odd child, or the odd one out, in that respect. I was also extremely independent. There were many things I did as a child, and throughout my life, that I did of my own volition. Perhaps it's because I was used to entertaining myself on my own while my parents were at work and because I've always wanted to try out new things.

My sister and I started the new school year at Belleville Primary, a substantial Victorian red-brick establishment with vast arched windows and airy, high-ceilinged classrooms. It was a mixed school but at the time I went there, it was old-fashioned in that the boys were on one side of the building and the girls on the other, with Mr Harris the headmaster for the boys' school and Miss Hutchinson as headmistress for the girls. That soon changed; in fact, I think we were the last intake before it went fully co-ed in 1975.

My first friend at infant school was a white boy called Eddie Wilby, who was the youngest boy in our class. Eddie lived at the end of our street, right up near Clapham Common in a big mansion-style house. It was also a rental, in a cul-de-sac with an immense wild garden, the scene of many adventures. All through primary school Eddie and I were as thick as thieves. We were inseparable as part of a little gang at school – Eddie and me; Larry Anderson, whose folks owned one of the terraced houses near me; Kevin Bent, whose family were Jamaican and who lived opposite Larry; Savos and his siblings, who were a Greek family; Susan James, who was a couple of years younger and whose family were Irish; and around the corner was a mixed-race friend called Francis Noble. Caribbean, Maltese, Greek, Irish, English – we all knocked about together as a fantastically diverse little Battersea melting pot. I didn't even think about the fact that quite a few of my friends looked different than my family. Nor did I have much of a sense of where my parents came from, what jobs they did or how much money they had, or what religion anyone adhered to – that simply didn't enter the equation. As I progressed from infant school through to primary classes, however, the reality crept in.

People often ask what my earliest memories of discrimination are and I have to say it was probably when I joined the Cubs at the age of six. I hadn't asked my parents – Mum and Dad weren't the sort of parents who signed us up for any kind of extra-curricular lessons or activities; in this case I did it for myself. I'd seen a poster at Sunday School at our Methodist church, thought it looked fun and decided I was going to join. Broomwood Church was in the 'posh' part of Clapham; the houses were palatial, and most of the boys at Cubs came from that area.

For this reason, perhaps, I suddenly found myself in this very white environment with very privileged children. Off I'd go to Cubs all by myself every Friday evening and there I was, not privileged at all, working hard for my badges, tying my knots, reading maps, and generally having fun.

After about six months, I set off to summer camp with the rest of the Broomwood Cubs where we joined Cub packs from all over the south-east in an idyllic country setting. I was the only Black kid on this annual jamboree – and the other Cub Scouts made me know it. Six of us shared a tent, six sleeping bags on the floor. The other boys made it clear that they didn't want me in their tent; they called me a 'black shit' and wouldn't involve me in any of their games. They ostracised me in every possible way, even pushing me and my sleeping bag right over to the edge of the tent. One night we finished our activities and got ready for bed as usual, and as I went to get into my sleeping bag the other boys started snickering. As I stretched my legs down, I found that my sleeping bag was soaking wet – and it stank of urine. One of them, his name was Stephen, had peed in it. I just knew it was him because he was the one laughing the hardest.

I went to the camp leader, or the Akela as we called him, and I called it out. He just didn't want to hear it. 'But where am I going to sleep?' I complained. 'Don't be so soft. Stop whining and deal with it,' was his response. It must have become too much for me and I must have started to cry, because I poured out everything that had happened: all the name-calling and bullying. Only then did the camp leader walk back with me to the tent to investigate. When confronted, in his defence Stephen said, 'I didn't call him a black shit; I said he was a brown poop.' Of course, he said he hadn't peed in my sleeping bag on purpose; he'd been trying to get to the toilet and hadn't made it out of the tent in time. The camp leader did nothing; there was no question that the boy be punished; he didn't even reprimand him, or tell his parents about his behaviour. Nothing was done and nothing was said. And what I understood from this was that you couldn't make a complaint, you couldn't say that the other boys had picked on you, because you wouldn't be heard. I had another three days at camp with a sleeping bag, still damp with pee, and I remember thinking, 'What am I doing here?' I've never been so miserable in my life.

I never told Mum what happened. I remember the feeling of holding that hurt in for all those years and not being able to say anything. But what really stayed with me was that the person, a grown-up, who had the power to do something, had just turned a blind eye. I knew then, at six years old, that I didn't fit in: I'd been told so by my peers. And by not doing anything to help me to fit in, those in charge had plainly shown me that they, too, thought I didn't belong there. That is my first memory of being treated differently because of my colour. And there would be many more clubs which I would join and in which I would be made to feel like an outsider because of the colour of my skin.

As a child, things happened to me — inconsequential and seemingly trifling experiences — that I didn't think about much at the time or put to the back of my mind, which have resurfaced over the years. I don't know what triggers the memories, but they bubble up like a sudden jab of hurt or shame. I remember a white boy called Mark at school, for example. Mark wasn't my friend, he was Eddie's friend, but we all used to kick about together in the park, riding our bikes, mucking about. One day in the summer holidays Mark had a bottle of Coca Cola and he asked if we were thirsty. It was one of those rare sweltering afternoons and, of course, we were. Mark offered the bottle to Eddie, but he didn't share it with me. I remember pleading with him, because I was so desperately thirsty at the sight of it. I only wanted a single small sip, but he refused. He stood there right in front of me, savouring that bottle of delicious, cold Coca Cola. He waited until he got to the last mouthful, then I watched as he seemingly finished it in one final swallow. Instead, however, he swilled it around in his mouth then regurgitated it back into the bottle and offered it to me. I declined. I remember thinking, 'Why did he do that? Why had he treated me like that and not Eddie?'

Eddie and I must have been no more than ten years old when we both had a crush on a girl called Denise who was in the class below us. There was a lot of competition between us over Denise. We *really* liked her. If we wanted to play in the park with her, we had to meet her at the top of her street, which was nearer to Wandsworth Common. That was a big excursion for us at that age. One day, desperately vying for her affection, I asked if Eddie and I could walk her home. 'Oh no, Leslie,' she replied. 'It's best if *you* don't walk me home.' Her dad wouldn't understand, she said when I asked her why not. When you are that age, it's these small things and throwaway incidents that leave a mark. It's hurtful, but all you have at your disposal is to try to think the best of people. Somehow I managed to protect myself by believing that it wasn't Denise, it was her dad, and it didn't stop her from liking me. Nevertheless, as a person with Black skin, experiences like these from a very early age made me feel that there was *something wrong with me*.

Later, I had another devastating experience. Eddie and I had been good friends with another boy in our class called Anthony. Anthony was an only child, and in my eyes, his parents could only be described as rich. They lived in a huge Victorian house just off Wandsworth Common. They must have had at least ten rooms for just the three of them – Anthony, his mother and father. Eddie and I used to spend a lot of time there because his house was so much fun to be in and his parents were the kindest people I knew. Even so, I realised just how different our worlds were. Anthony's mother was the editor of a popular women's magazine. I was never quite sure what his father did, but he always struck me as some kind of scientist because he had that sort of logical brain and way of speaking to us even as young kids. Eddie and Anthony knew all my secrets and I thought they were my closest friends. Disappointment had to come.

One day, when I was probably thirteen or fourteen and already at secondary school, I called at Anthony's house on my way home. I rang the doorbell, his mother answered and told me to go on up to his room. When I went in, Anthony was clearly surprised to see me, and then I turned and saw the whiteboard on his wall. He had scribbled the N-word all over it, maybe fifty times, in big letters, small letters, along with other hateful words, such as 'coon', and 'kill them all'. I couldn't believe it. He quickly hurried me downstairs, perhaps not quite sure if I had read what he had written on this whiteboard. I did not say anything to him. I did not say I had seen what he had written. I did not confront him. After that I stopped hanging out of him.

Postscript

In the 1987 election, the Conservative Party gained power in Battersea where the once-popular Labour MP Alf Dubs was ousted. In the '8os, many of the borough's council homes were sold to private buyers, and working-class people had to move out of the streets I grew up on. Later, in my twenties, when I returned to my childhood street, the area had totally transformed. It was full of white middle-class urban professionals; it felt exclusive – the diverse community I'd grown up in had disappeared and families like mine were no longer the norm. To my mind, the lack of affordable homes in the area and the Conservative Party's big council housing sell-off was a major component in this turn of events.

3

THE BEST CHRISTMAS
PRESENT EVER

Christmas in our house was always a time of joy. We put up the same artificial tree each year, played the same two Christmas albums, *A Motown Christmas* and *Elvis's Christmas Album*. Church was always *a must*; we would go to Broomwood either for midnight mass or the Christmas Day service, sometimes both. On Christmas morning there was the excitement of opening our presents, usually small things like Dinky Toy cars, an Action Man, a toy gun that fired caps, and always socks. Every Christmas Mum bought us a Premium Bond. Then we would eat our fill of turkey, ham and roast potatoes. After Christmas dinner we would play board games, our favourite being Monopoly, and we'd all become a little rowdy, everyone speaking over each other, and that's when the usual family arguments would start. This was quite a tradition. On Boxing Day, we'd pile into Dad's tiny Toyota to visit Uncle Charles in Hackney. The next day we'd head off to see Aunty Cis and Uncle John in Shepherd's Bush. New Year wasn't a big celebration.

We didn't go on family summer holidays – not once. We would have day trips to Brighton, Kew Gardens, Littlehampton or Margate in the school holidays, but a trip abroad was beyond our wildest dreams. Then, when I was six, my Premium Bond ticket came in and the prize money paid for our first overseas holiday as a family. That summer in 1972 Mum took us on a BOAC flight to the Caribbean. Dad was still trying to persuade her to move back with him to Dominica. He was a quietly spoken man who would keep his head down and get on with his work always with the dream of returning home. Mum wanted to make her life here in the UK and was certainly not keen on going to an island which was not her own. But now that my Premium Bond paid the airfares, she agreed to take us over to see if we might be able to live there. She hadn't seen her mother and father since she had left home in 1961.

First, we went to stay with her family in Antigua. This was the first time I had flown in an aeroplane and the first time I had seen the Caribbean. Thinking back to that visit, my lasting impression was of how hot and bright the sunlight was, then how quickly night came and how dark it was when the sun sank behind the sea. The British had put little investment into the island since the days of colonialism and slavery, so at that time even the main town of St John's was relatively rural, the roads were mere dirt tracks and there was no such thing as electric street lighting. We didn't have an inside toilet at my grandmother Dada's place in Antigua and it terrified me outside in the pitch-black of night if I needed a pee.

Most people lived on small plots of land on which they kept hens and various animals and grew their own vegetables. Dada kept pigs and hens and I spent most of the day out in the yard, helping to collect the eggs and feed the piglets while she chatted to her neighbours. I got on well with my grandmother. She was a strong woman who lived to ninety-one. Pa Fred was a gentle, good-natured man who took us for rides on his donkey to the beach. I was fortunate to have got to meet him because soon after he suffered a stroke and died at the young age of sixty.

Then we went to Dominica. Now I knew why Dad was always going on about his island – it was an absolute paradise. To a young boy from Battersea's eyes, if Antigua had seemed wild and undeveloped, then Dad's family were surely living in the bush. My dad had just started to build his own place there, so on that first visit we stayed at my uncle's house on the side of the mountain in a village called Marigot to the north of the island. For miles around the land was untamed. Dusk fell around 5 p.m. under the dense, deep-green rainforest canopy from which emanated all sorts of strange sounds from the creatures that skulked in the gloom – the chorus of crickets, the rustling and rattling of snakes, the odd, low-pitched barking of tree frogs and the shocking, ear-shattering screeches of parakeets. As a child I was fearful of the dark and the perils that might lurk there, but what I didn't realise was that Dominica was a much safer place than anywhere in London. There was very little crime, everybody knew each other and nobody locked their doors. Again, I was lucky to meet Daddy Hector, because by the time I went back seven years later, he had passed at the age of about eighty years old.

4

1976, WANDSWORTH ROAD

My mum always says that I was a role model at school. I got on well with the other children and I was never in trouble with the teachers, and so when she went to parents' evenings, there were no complaints about me. I don't remember my dad coming along on those evenings often – in fact, if ever – not because he didn't care; according to Mum he didn't like going anywhere with her. Mum doesn't take shit from anybody and he was probably afraid of what she might do or say to the teachers. He knew that if a teacher told my mum any claptrap about her children, she wouldn't swallow it down easily. She would argue and insist on getting to the bottom of why they had said such and such. Dad would warn her, 'Now, Sheila, you mustn't annoy the teachers.'

When I was in my last year at Belleville, Mum wanted me to do the eleven-plus exam to get into Emmanuel, the local boys' grammar school in Wandsworth. My teacher was Mr N, and he and my mum did not get on. Mr N didn't like me and part of the reason, I think, was that I was a kid who asked a lot of questions. I wouldn't accept everything he told us as gospel and pulled him up on occasion, and so he tried to undermine me. Mum came back from one of my last parents' evenings, having talked to Mr N about my transition from primary to secondary school, and she was livid. Mr N had shouted at her when she had challenged him about why he was always talking me down. 'I can't understand what you're saying about him. He is extremely bright; he's always been bright,' she told him.

My dad's fears had been right in that respect. She was arguing for me to do my eleven-plus, but Mr N had given her the brush-off. I don't know what the criteria were for sitting the eleven-plus exam, but Mr N and the school had made the decision for me. I was destined for a local comprehensive, and the school with the worst reputation in the Battersea area at that time: Spencer Park School.

Mum was not going to take it lying down. That's my mum for you. If you say 'No', she'll go round you, over you, under you and, if need be, through you. She went to see Mr Jerry, a tall, black-haired ex-army type, who had succeeded Mr Harris as headteacher, and told him she didn't want me to go to Spencer Park. She knew I could pass the eleven-plus for Emmanuel School, but Mr Jerry was having none of it. 'Oh no, Mrs Thomas,' he said. 'You are very ambitious but Leslie will never make it.' To which she replied, 'If you think I have ambition, a lot of parents want the best for their children and that's what I want too.'

Nevertheless, Mr Jerry seemed determined not to give me a chance.

Mum kept her disappointment to herself, because as uneducated as she might be in terms of formal schooling, she knew how a person's self-esteem can be torn down, especially a quiet and conscientious boy like me who only wanted to work hard and do well. Instead, Mum has always been encouraging and always pushes my siblings and me to do the best we can. I didn't go to the grammar school, but nor did I end up at Spencer Park.

I went to Battersea County, another comprehensive, which, as it happened, would be the making of me.

Of the three primary-school friends, Eddie, Anthony and myself, our pathways couldn't have been more different. Eddie, whose parents, like mine, were working class, went to Spencer Park. Anthony, the middle-class boy with the huge house, went to Emmanuel.

The summer of 1976 was a coming of age. In April I had turned eleven, James Callaghan succeeded Harold Wilson as prime minister, and Great Britain's Brotherhood of Man won the Eurovision Song Contest with 'Save Your Kisses for Me'; I even learned the silly dance to that annoying song. It was my last term at Belleville, and as the holidays approached my parents told us that we were moving house. We needed more space; Janet was fourteen and already in her fourth year at Marianne Thornton, a school for girls just off Clapham Common. She could no longer share a room with her two younger brothers, so we would be leaving the leafy tranquillity of Grandison Road and going to live in neighbouring Lambeth.

Until that point our childhood had been quite closeted. Growing up in that oasis between the commons there had been nothing to truly unsettle our peaceful suburban existence — barring one bizarre and disturbing incident that even now seems almost like something from a bad dream. Shortly after my sixth birthday we had gone to play together on Clapham Common one afternoon. I had noticed a white freezer bag lying on the grass. I kicked it, but when my foot made contact with it, it made a heavy *thunk* as if there was something solid inside it, like meat. Being a curious child, I opened the bag. I will never forget the sight that greeted me: a severed pair of a woman's hands. They were small and delicate, and on the fingernails, it looked like there were the remains of dark reddish-brown nail varnish around the cuticles. But of course it wasn't nail varnish; it was dried blood. Janet had seen the hands too and she grabbed me by the collar and shouted at me to drop the bag, then hurried us away. A traumatic experience for any child, yet Janet and I didn't tell anyone; we had a silent pact. We never talked about it again, so as the years passed, at times when I would think about it, it was as if I had merely imagined it. It was only recently, after I described that day in a newspaper interview, that Janet and I were finally able to talk about it – it was like a relief.

Otherwise, my Battersea childhood was largely untroubled, uneventful and unremarkable, but now that chapter in my life ended. In the summer of 1976 when we moved to Lambeth, we had the hottest and driest weather on record for 350 years, with temperatures in London reaching beyond 32°C. The flat that the housing association had found for us was a three-bedroom maisonette on the great Wandsworth Road, part of the major A306 artery from south London into the capital and a busy and badly polluted bus route. Janet had her own bedroom, but I was still sharing with my brother. Our room was at the front of the building, so each night that sweltering summer I fell asleep in a fug of diesel fumes to the constant rumble of heavy traffic beneath the window.

That September I started at Battersea County. The school had a huge intake, around 2,000 pupils. In my first year I was in a class of thirty-six. My class tutor, who would remain my close friend even to this day, was Carolyn Lornie. I knew she always had my back and my best interests at heart. Indeed, the same could be said for many of my teachers, although not all of them.

My brother had just turned nine and moved to a primary school near Battersea County so that I could walk him there in the morning. To get there from Wandsworth Road along the main streets would have involved about a 45-minute walk, so I figured out the shortcut. It took us through three of the most infamous council estates in the whole of London. Doddington was the worst, notorious for all-too-frequent street robberies and rapes. Indeed, by 1983, such were its problems of crime and anti-social behaviour, it had been dubbed by a sensationalist local press 'the Estate of Terror'.

Even though many of my new friends and fellow pupils lived on these estates, walking through them in those days was a proper trial of Hercules. I found it terrifying. One of the estates seemed to be the breeding ground for several packs of marauding feral dogs. If you weren't part of the estate, you stood out like a sore thumb and were instantly the target for random attacks. If you were wearing the wrong school blazer you were asking for a beating; I was regularly pelted with eggs, various types of vegetable matter or, least menacingly, water. It was certainly character-building.

On the estates in that part of London at that time, however, there was something much more sinister at bay. The mid-'70s were a high-water mark of white nationalism and fascism in the UK, with the National Front making increasing inroads into the political landscape. Their crude propaganda exploited fears about migrants and called for policies such as an end to non-white immigration and forced repatriation. Thus, the NF was winning growing numbers of supporters among white working-class Britons, especially in those areas with a sizable Black community.

I would have been in my second term at Battersea County when I was subjected to my first violent racist attack. My brother and I were walking home from school on our usual haz-ardous route when a man in his mid-fifties approached us and said, 'You are looking at the white man's magic.' Confused but not wanting to be rude, I stood gawping at him. 'Just look at the white man's magical creation, all that we have achieved. You've come here and are enjoying it . . .' he continued. At that point, even though I still didn't really understand what he was getting at, I took my brother by the arm and pulled him away. We carried on walking, but seconds later a powerful kick to my back sent me sprawling. The man had come running up behind me and booted me violently to the ground. I was winded and my hands were grazed and bleeding but I picked myself up, grabbed my brother and ran all the way to our flat. Dad was home; he could see that I was hurt, so I told him what had happened. We went back to that estate to look for this man who had kicked me. When I saw him, my dad approached him and asked him why he had hurt his son. He denied it. I couldn't get my head round why a grown man would kick an eleven-year-old boy in an unprovoked attack. It took that experience to truly understand the meaning of the colour of my skin. I now understood exactly how different I was, and I knew that my Blackness made me a potential target.

That episode changed me. While I may not have known about due process and the law at that age, intrinsically I had a strong sense of fairness and justice. I couldn't understand how a person could just be at liberty to physically attack someone and not suffer any consequences for their actions. How was that fair or right? It also, I believe, had a huge impact on my dad. I could see how helpless he had felt in that situation. He had been unable to protect his family. This country had always been a place that was difficult for him. He was torn because he had a complete love of Dominica, and so his heart was never truly here in England. Now he disliked this country even more, to the extent that it became toxic for him. On many occasions I had to call him out, and point out that not all English people are the same, but I didn't walk in my dad's shoes so I don't know the experiences that he had. Whatever pain or trauma he had when he first arrived in the UK, he wasn't the sort of person who would share that with anyone. He just kept going the only way he knew how, which was to simmer and suffer in silence.

Dad wasn't happy at British Telecom. I heard him speaking to Mum about the prejudice and racist slights he faced in his job, how he felt he'd been badly treated, called names because of his colour; overlooked for promotion. He was a clever man, he read a lot, and had gone to night classes to study telephone engineering. He still didn't get the promotion he wanted, although he clearly deserved it. Meanwhile, he had to watch as his white colleagues, who were doing almost the same job, were promoted above him. It made him incredibly bitter and full of hate towards British people and whites. His bitterness, I think, also put a great deal of strain on his relationship with my mother, because she was happy, still working crazy hours in the NHS, but always positive, an optimist, while Dad was simply biding his time, getting through each day at his work and with his family as best as he could.

My dad and I never spoke much. He was the sort of person who would come home, put the money on the table for my mum, sit down with a paper and that was it. After the incident with my attacker, however, he became increasingly withdrawn and I watched him sink into a chronic depression. I have very little recollection of Dad doing anything with us as a family after we moved to Wandsworth Road. He would leave the house by 6 a.m. and when he returned twelve hours or so later, he'd be knackered and grumpy. I remember a time when I pushed him to the limit. We were having chips but we had no tomato ketchup. I was complaining in the annoying way that kids do, on and on. Suddenly, Dad lost it. He shouted out loud and slammed my head against the wall. I immediately felt a searing pain to the side of my head and a huge lump the size of an egg appeared behind my right ear. I screamed and screamed. Mum took me to hospital because she was so worried. When we got there, I said I'd fallen over and banged my head. I had an X-ray and was discharged. I hated my father after that and stopped talking to him for years. Which just made the situation at home even worse. After that day we knew better than to irritate him and we stayed out of his way. He went from a man who used to spend a lot of time with us, playing with us, taking us on our Sunday outings, to someone who wasn't there, although the one thing he did do was always provide for us. Watching that change in Dad taught me another lesson. It taught me that you must live life every day – you can't bide your time – because if you are biding your time day by day, you are wasting your life. You have to make the most of where you are at.

My sister was the oldest and the artistic and talented one. My younger brother was the difficult one. And I was the quiet one. As younger kids we were very close, but as we got older, I didn't get on with them at all. Janet and Trevor were both Leos and I was a Taurus – their birthdays are two days apart in August – and when I was growing up, I felt left out. They used to have joint birthday parties and treats. Consequently, I suppose I suffered from middle-child syndrome and grew up very much the outsider in this trio, with my sister and brother's allegiance being to each other. That is another reason I was so self-sufficient from an early age.

I made a handful of good friends at Battersea County. My best friend, whom I met on my first day, was called (aptly perhaps) Denis Bonafé, from the Italian meaning 'good faith', and we remained partners in crime throughout our entire school career. Denis was extremely bright, intelligent, very funny, an amazing singer and a talented actor.

When I discovered that a new karate club had started in a youth club on one of the local council estates, my friends and I signed up. Independent as usual, I never told my folks about my new hobby. It was at the height of the craze for Bruce Lee's badly dubbed late-night movies and so naturally everybody was Kung Fu fighting. We soon discovered that learning the art of karate was nothing like the movies. Learning karate under our instructor, Bob White, was hard work and somewhat repetitious. His Sunday afternoon lessons were extremely disciplined with lots of fitness training.

After six months or so, Bob put us in for our first belt. In order to compete for my white belt, I needed a Karate Gi, i.e. the traditional uniform of white, light-cotton canvas karate jacket and pants. I had to ask Mum to buy me the suit, so that's when she found out what I had been up to all that time.

The white belt proved elusive. A lot of us didn't make the grade – I didn't – and consequently quite a few of my friends stopped going. I carried on. You didn't want to get on the wrong side of Bob. At the time I thought that he was tough on me, and he could be horrible, but I understand now that he was teaching me a valuable lesson about hard work and not giving up – if you start something, you persevere and you see it through to the best of your ability. So I stayed at the club and slowly progressed through the grades.

When for some reason the karate club had to move, it relocated to Chiswick. Instead of a ten-minute jog from my house, now it was on the other side of London, an hour there and an hour back. Yet I made that trek for many years, well into my twenties, and eventually I got my brown belt, the grade just below the prestigious black belt. But for me the belts weren't the issue. It was all about the process. I thrived on the rigour of the discipline and the training for competitions. I still train in karate today; it becomes so ingrained that you can continue to practise by yourself.

By age thirteen, I was well into skateboarding, fashion, football and, like all my friends at that age, members of the opposite sex. My friend Eddie from primary school had gone to Spencer Park, but although we went to different schools, we remained the best of pals – and often still rivals in love. We always seemed to meet girls we both fancied, and so when we met a couple of girls on Clapham Common, inevitably, we both fell for the same one. Ellie was half Madagascan and each of us was trying desperately to win her heart. Again, however, I remember Ellie confiding that her dad would go ballistic if he found out that she was mixing with somebody who was Black. I couldn't get my head round that. I remember saying to her, 'But, Ellie, your dad is Madagascan and you're not white. What do you mean your dad wouldn't like me?' She didn't really respond and I didn't push it. I knew what she meant and she knew I understood her silence. It was soul-destroying. I was getting messages all the time that, because of my Blackness, I was somehow less.

A stormy and bone-chilling December in 1978 was followed by severe blizzards with deep snow drifts in the south of England. New Year's Eve was the coldest for forty years and January was grim. To this day there has not been as cold a January since that one.

On 22 January 1979, in the first of a series of industrial strikes, tens of thousands of public-sector workers took part in a day of action – the biggest mass stoppage since 1926 – in support of claims for wage increases, marking the beginning of what became known as the 'Winter of Discontent'. Hospital workers, rubbish collectors, school caretakers and dinner ladies, grave diggers, transport workers and ambulance drivers went on strike, bringing services across the country to a standstill. As rubbish began to pile up on the now rat-infested streets, London's Leicester Square was dubbed 'Fester Square'. Hospitals struggled in the absence of cleaners, cooks, porters and theatre orderlies, and without crossing patrols, caretakers or meals staff, many schools were closed. Through February, blizzards, black ice and snow drifts carried on while people spent their evenings at home in candlelight during power cuts and stocked up on tinned foods. In Parliament, the Conservative opposition, led by Margaret Thatcher, pounced on the Labour government's refusal to call a state of emergency. At the election in May, Labour lost to Margaret Thatcher. More than 300 National Front candidates stood in the election, polling nearly 200,000 votes.

As I said, I was fiercely independent. We got a small amount of pocket money from my dad, but to be honest, I didn't want anybody's money. If I had my own, I could do what I wanted with it and so I started working as soon as I could. When I was eleven, I got a paper round, and no matter how miserable and wet and cold it was, I would get up early every day and deliver my papers. As soon as I turned fourteen, I found a Saturday job in the local Fine Fare supermarket on the fruit and veg counter. I could earn more on a weekend than I had all week on the paper round, so now I felt like a king. I liked to have my own money to spend on music and going out, but I was also a serious saver. I had an incentive that summer, because my mum was paying for Janet and me to spend the school holidays in Antigua with our grandmother.

On that second visit, I fell in love with the Caribbean. I was able to appreciate it in a way that I hadn't when I was younger. I met teenagers my own age and nobody was judging me for my colour because we were all Black. It was as if I found myself there and, for the first time, I felt at one with my surroundings and my peers. That was also the summer when I properly discovered girls. My hormones must have been raging, because I fell hook, line and sinker for a girl called Cheryl who was a year older than me. The second she deigned to speak to me, I was in love and spent the whole rest of the holidays following her about, as fourteen-year-old boys are wont to do. That holiday had a big impact on me. When I got back to the UK, I felt like I was a different person.

There was another big change after the summer of '79. When I went back to school, I found that a large proportion of my classmates had undergone a radical style makeover and become skinheads – we're talking 21-hole DMs, Fred Perry shirts; proper, full-on skinheads. At first it was largely a fashion thing that went together with the punk scene. Ska and reggae were big with groups like Bad Manners, The Beat, UB40, Madness, and the two-tone artists like The Selecter and The Specials in the pop charts, and Eddie and I were right into those bands. At that time, there was a spectrum whereby you could be a rude boy, a two-tone, a mod, or a proper skinhead, and it was crazy because we all were listening to the same music. There were even a couple of Black kids in school who were proper skinheads because they were following the burgeoning UK ska and reggae scene, but then we started getting older skinhead men hanging around the front gates of the school handing out leaflets. With its increasingly uncompromising stance on immigration, the new Conservative government had won over many former core supporters of the National Front, who were focusing on schools and sixth-form colleges to peddle some nasty, racist hate propaganda. That's when things took a turn for the worse. Soon, some of my friends started saying, 'Look, it's not you, Leslie, but I can't be your friend any more.' A few of them didn't say it so blatantly, but that was the message. They stopped talking to me and started sitting away from me in class. For a Black lad, London suddenly became a very scary place. Scary for several reasons. Firstly because of the tangible presence of the National Front in our midst, secondly because of the skinhead movement at school, and finally because of the police.

Early on in that autumn term of 1979, I met up with Eddie, who had now adopted the two-tone rude boy wardrobe. Ellie was still on the scene and she invited us to a disco in a community centre with a bar just off Balham High Road. She said there was going to be live music from a ska group, so we turned up, all kitted out in our latest two-tone gear, in this dark, slightly cruddy community centre. We spotted Ellie and said hello, then, as my eyes adjusted to the gloom, I looked around and noticed all these shiny heads glowing slightly silver in the light from the stage. The place was entirely full of skinheads and it slowly dawned on me that I was the only Black person in the place. At the same time these skinheads had obviously clocked my conspicuous entrance, because then I heard, quite quietly and slowly at first, somebody at the bar saying, '*Sieg Heil, Sieg Heil, Sieg* . . .' One voice at first and then faster and louder as more and more voices joined in, and suddenly the whole room was chanting at the top of their voices. The club was a sea of skins. Eddie looked at me, I looked at Eddie, and I just said, 'RUN!' And we legged it with the whole mob of maybe seventy antagonistic skinheads chasing us down the High Road. I took off like a bullet and I've never run as fast in my life. I don't even know why Eddie was running, but there he was beside me, and we didn't stop until we managed to lose them in the backstreets of Balham. We hid in somebody's front garden until it was safe to come out.

When I next saw Ellie, I asked her why she'd invited us to a disco full of skinheads; but, of course, she'd had no idea. Like us, she'd only gone there because of the music.

Everything seemed to be stacked against kids growing up in my area, so much so that getting anywhere near where I am now would have seemed an impossible dream.

Battersea County was a comprehensive school with a philosophy of no streaming, so up until my third year, other than maths, for which we were separated by ability, we were in mixed-ability classes. I don't know what the educational thinkers behind this policy thought it would achieve by putting kids who can't read or write in the same class as other, more able, kids, but in my experience what we had at school wasn't working. I was one of the brightest kids in the class. My dad had had a grammar-school education and he taught us how to read and write before we started school. He was strict about making sure that we had lovely script handwriting. Here I was a decade later in secondary school in a class with nearly forty kids, many of whom couldn't read or write and didn't even know their alphabet.

Discipline was a real problem. If you have children in a class where they can't engage it is incredibly boring for those pupils at both ends of the ability spectrum. If you are bored, you become disruptive, so that meant we spent hours and hours sitting with our hands on our head because the teachers simply couldn't cope. There was always a struggle in trying to get by well enough to pass exams and thrive.

The difficulties in achieving our full potential didn't end there, however. In the mid-'80s most children at my school would leave after their CSEs or O Levels (as they then were) and get a job, and there were plenty of good jobs to be had. But I didn't want to do that. I didn't exactly know what I wanted to do and I can't pretend that from an early age I was certain of my vocation as a lawyer, but I did know that I wanted to do more than take the first half-decent job offer I got aged sixteen. My mum claims that I once told her I was going to be a doctor when I left school. I don't remember saying that, but apparently she quickly put me off this idea by telling me that doctors have to work round the clock before they can be a consultant and junior doctors had to do the dirty work. If this conversation did happen, then what Mum had said must have sunk in, because the next time she asked me, I said I was going to become a lawyer. Nobody in my family had done anything in law, but I saw myself as someone who liked an argument and thought I would be good at it.

When I told my teachers of this ambition, they were relatively encouraging. In other quarters, however, there was a definite sense that as a Black working-class boy from Wandsworth, I had been written off before I even had a chance to prove myself. When I was sixteen and doing my O Levels, we had a visit from the local borough careers officer. I remember clearly his advice. 'Why don't you become a mechanic, or if you are interested in the law, a police officer?' Forget my foolish dream of becoming a lawyer; to become a barrister, you had to go to Oxford or Cambridge. Firstly, so what? Secondly, it was the wrong advice. Thirdly, what this person was handing out instead of advice was a ton of discouragement. Fortunately, I had that same inner drive and determination that I'd had since my early childhood, and the independence that had made me persevere whether it meant staying on at Cubs or keeping on with karate when the going got tough. So, I didn't listen to that careers advisor. Now I think about the wasted hours, the wasted lives and opportunities, and why some kids succeed and some kids don't, and it all seems so random.

The sad thing is that there was a wealth of untapped talent in my school; there were so many kids in my class, in my year and in the wider school who were so much brighter than I was. Brilliant kids who deserved so much more. When I look back on what has happened to some of them, it fills me with an over-whelming feeling of loss. Most of them dropped out of school early, hardly any of them went to university and many ended up on the wrong side of the law. Two of my classmates died tragically early deaths. One was a close friend of mine who died driving a stolen car. That was a shocking but all-too-predictable story for lots of the kids at our school. And I don't know what was happening in the lives of these children; I don't know what difficulties they may have faced at home, or what their parents were like, or even if they lived with their family, or perhaps were in foster care. But the one thing I can think of that made my life turn out differently is the consistency and routine at home. The example of my mother and father and their work ethic imposed a kind of discipline that I guess I took for granted. Every day they'd get up, go to work, come home and provide for us, and thus maintain that family unit for us in all the chaos that was going on around us at school and in the community we were growing up in.

5

JEAN JEANIE

My sister Janet was always a grafter like me. Throughout her late teens, she worked in Jean Jeanie on Oxford Street where she was making a lot of money. When I turned sixteen, she got me a job in the dog-eat-dog world of retail, took me under her wing and taught me how to sell.

Every Saturday, and later most Thursdays for late-night shopping, I worked upstairs on the Levi's floor. My basic salary was £8 per day, but I had a sales target of £1,000, and if I hit that, I could earn a commission of 3 per cent on everything I sold. That might not sound a lot – 3p in every pound – but back in 1982, button-down-fly red tab Levi's were all the rage and they sold for £30, so, for each pair of red tabs I sold I got 30p. Shrink-to-fit red tabs were so popular we used to have people from Spain and Italy coming to buy five pairs each, so I was selling hundreds of pairs of jeans every Saturday. That meant that, on average, I ended up taking home £120 for a single day's shift.

It was hard work, though. Not everybody could do it; new staff would come in and they couldn't hack it. When you are on a sales floor and you have a target to hit, it can be highly competitive, cut-throat even, with sales people vying with each other to make sales, particularly when times are lean. I was lucky. The manager on my floor was a guy called Ian, a career salesperson a few years older than me. Ian and I got on well, and instead of competing for sales, we worked out a method of working collaboratively, and it paid off. The top management saw that what we were doing was working and they left us alone to get on with it.

The experience taught me so much. Working on commission made me understand that if I didn't work hard, didn't sell, I'd leave with only £8. It made me appreciate self-reliance. I didn't have to ask my parents for a penny.

Secondly, selling gave me confidence. I was thrown in at the deep end and had no choice but to swim. I realised that I wasn't afraid of speaking to anyone and making the pitch. I was a good salesperson and that is an important skill to master. Being at the Bar, when you are presenting a case to a court, you are essentially making a pitch: you are selling an argument, seeking to persuade. Likewise, the socialising element of customer service and ability to talk to anyone from any background is something I am forever grateful for from my apprenticeship days at Jean Jeanie.

Most importantly, it taught me that you don't need to have a scarcity mentality: you can have an abundance mentality – there is plenty to go round; more than enough opportunity, resources, wealth and success and, if you work together, *everyone* can get a share, even in sales. One of the problems, in our modern capitalist society, is the belief that for somebody to be on top, somebody must be on the bottom. I don't ascribe to that. In the five years I worked alongside Ian on the Levi's floor, I never missed my commission – not once, and that's because I was working for somebody who brought me up with him.

It was thanks to my Jean Jeanie job that I was able to move out of home when I was only sixteen. Harding, the housing association which housed us, had a policy whereby they would try to house not only the family, but also find accommodation for the children of that family when they reached the age of majority. Through Harding, therefore, Janet had been fortunate enough to get her own place, a lovely studio flat in Clapham Junction. Ironically, in the wake of the Conservative right-to-buy policy, Harding had closed the doors by the time I was eligible for housing. There was a real shortage of housing association rental properties: they didn't have the housing stock, and property prices were beginning to skyrocket.

When she was nineteen, Janet decided that she wanted to do an art degree and got into Sussex University in Brighton. She didn't want to give up her tenancy, however, so she asked if I wanted to move into her flat while she was away. Back then the housing association rent was about £15 a week, so I could cover that and all the bills with my Jean Jeanie earnings easily. I even managed to buy my first car ready to take my driver's licence: a brown Mark 3 Ford Cortina with go-faster stripes. It was a beast of a car and I loved it. I paid for my lessons and the minute I got my test when I was seventeen, I was driving it.

So, in September 1983, I moved out of the family home on the Wandsworth Road and never went back. I was happy to leave; I could no longer live under the same roof as my brother. We were constantly fighting. From his early teens, he'd been smoking and I couldn't stand the smell of his cigarettes in the house. I think Mum was happy when I moved into Janet's flat.

From that day on, I was completely self-sufficient. Most of my former classmates were already financially independent, having left school and found work, so I was no different in that respect, but not many had their own places to live. While they were working, I was starting sixth form. I was getting myself up to go to school, shopping and cooking for myself, cleaning up after myself, making sure I got enough sleep and not staying up all night watching telly. That required a certain amount of self-motivation and self-control, but then I'd had to become self-dependent at a young age. When I was eleven or so, Dad used to make us dinner while Mum was on her night shift; but he was a terrible cook. I learned to cook for myself and had been making most of my own meals from the age of thirteen.

Having my own space was a dream come true. It was *my* place and I kept it quiet – no wild parties – because I'm extremely house-proud.

Shortly after I moved to Clapham, when I'd just turned seventeen, I met Angela, who would become my first wife and the mother of my two oldest children. She was sixteen and in the year below me at school. Angela is white and, as an interracial couple, we had to be careful around the streets of London. We had to be watchful about running into skinheads, the National Front, the police, even the general public. I remember being on the street one day holding Angela's hand, and somebody drove past us and shouted out the N-word. That was *London* in the early '80s.

Things weren't easy at home with my dad either. I remember the first time I took Angela to meet my family. My father said not a word to either of us; he sat in silence the entire time. I couldn't understand why he behaved that way, why he was so rude. I had seen how he was when my sister brought her boyfriend home – chatty, laughing, engaging. My sister's boyfriends were Black, but it didn't cross my mind that it was anything to do with Angela and the fact that she was white. 'Dad's Dad,' I thought. 'He's just not being very talkative.' That was nothing out of the ordinary after all. Then my mother told me that Dad was, in fact, extremely upset with me because I had brought a white girl home. Naturally I clung on even more to my relationship. Maybe it would have fizzled out had Dad not been so against it. Who knows? But I was obstinate, and if Dad didn't approve then I was going to do exactly the opposite of his wishes out of defiance. That was my teenage rebellion. Such is the utter senseless nonsense that comes about when you allow your irrational emotions to take control, when you base your opinions not on people as human beings, but on where they are from, the colour of their skin, or their religion. You don't get to know the individual and you make ill-formed judgements.

Dad never told me to my face that he was not happy with my choice, or the fact that at a young age I settled down with my first serious girlfriend, my teenage sweetheart. I do know that it caused tension between Dad and me, to the extent that he cut me loose. Even more than before, I had no choice but to make my own way. I kept the job at Jean Jeanie in Oxford Street right up to when I went to university, and all that time I didn't ask my father for a single penny.

6

SUS

For a young Black man growing up in London in the 1970s and
'80s, there were several key moments – the New Cross Fire, or the
Deptford Fire as it was synonymously known, being one. In the
early hours of 18 January 1981, a fire broke out at a joint sixteenth-
and eighteenth-birthday house party at 439 New Cross Road in
Deptford in the London borough of Lewisham. The fire, which
started on the ground floor, spread rapidly and soon engulfed the
rest of the premises. Many of the partygoers were able to escape
to safety, but thirteen young people were trapped in the blaze and
died. One survivor later committed suicide following the trauma
brought on by the fire and became the fourteenth victim.

Margaret Thatcher had been in power for two years, and
in the days and weeks after those horrific deaths, her silence
was conspicuous. I don't think she even went to the site of the
tragedy to pay her respects. The families of the bereaved were
stricken at the seeming indifference of their government and
campaigned for public acknowledgement of their loss, as well as
answers about the tragedy. At the time, the fire was widely suspected to have been a racially motivated arson attack. However,
the police investigation was criticised as badly botched for
failing to explore that possibility, further fuelling anger and
mistrust among the wider African Caribbean community.

Friends of mine had been at the party on the night of the fire. I could so easily have joined them. At the time, I was that sixteen-year-old boy into skateboards and dancing to soul music; selling jeans in Jean Jeanie on Oxford Street and making 'loadsamoney'; thinking about my O Levels; meeting girls and snogging on Clapham Common . . . and fearing the 'sus' law, a reference to powers under the Vagrancy Act 1824* whereby the police could stop, search and arrest members of the public on the mere suspicion that they might be planning to carry out a crime, nothing else.

Back in 1981, there was real discontent on the streets and in the community; it was not safe to be a Black man in London, we believed. Throughout the late '70s and early '80s there had been a rise in the popularity of the National Front, the BNP and the British Movement party. The resurgent National Front was sending out its heinous rallying cries, organising marches and holding public meetings in immigrant areas, often resulting in violent clashes with the police, who often seemed to be on the side of the neo-fascists as they protected them from Anti-Nazi League protesters and local non-white residents. In 1979, at one such NF meeting in Southall Town Hall, excessive and aggressive policing of protesters led to the killing of Blair Peach by a police officer.

Simply being out at night was extremely difficult if you wore Black skin, not only because of the threats from the National Front or from skinheads, but increasingly from the police force itself, especially on the streets of south London – even in

---

* 'Persons committing certain offences to be deemed rogues and vagabonds: every suspected person or reputed thief, frequenting any river, canal, or navigable stream, dock, or basin, or any quay, wharf, or warehouse near or adjoining thereto, or any street, highway, or avenue leading thereto, or any place of public resort, or any avenue leading thereto, or any street, or any highway or any place adjacent to a street or highway; with intent to commit an indictable offence'

broad daylight. Throughout the previous decade, Black youths in deprived inner-city areas had become increasingly alienated, demonised in the media as a troublesome and potentially criminal problem. Street robberies were suddenly back in the headlines, stoking a nationwide moral panic about 'muggings', a term imported from America where Ronald Reagan's presidency had heralded a new emphasis on law-and-order politics.[*] Street crime in general and muggings were seen in some quarters as the domain of those so-called 'problem' Black youths. In response to this perceived menace, the policeman on the beat set about making liberal use of the old 'sus' laws to disproportionately, and often indiscriminately, subject young Black males to a random 'stop and search'.

On more than one occasion, I'd be in school uniform walking to or from school and the cops would pull me up. Once I was on my way home with a friend at about 4 o'clock in the afternoon, a perfectly legitimate time for somebody to be walking home after school, when two uniformed officers stopped us. The officers separated us and started their questioning. Mum had drummed it into me that I was never to backchat the police. 'No matter what injustice, just keep your head down, don't backchat them,' she always said. I often have to explain that this conversation is one that white parents do not have with their children; Black parents, on the other hand, do not have the privilege of avoiding it. So, whenever the police stopped me, I'd try to stay very calm and make a point of inquiring incredibly politely as to why they'd stopped *me* in particular. 'Officer, may I help you? Is there a reason why you've stopped me?' They'd ask me where I was coming from, where I was going to, then, in answer to my questions, said eventually, 'You

---

* Hall, et al., 1978.

fit the description of . . .' But they never told me, or my friends and classmates – because this was common; this was what was happening to all my African Caribbean mates, too, *all the time* – in *what way* we fitted the description of this person who supposedly had just carried out a burglary/mugging/another criminal act. And all you could do was turn your pockets out to show that you had nothing on you and hope that the officers would let you go on your way. Too many of my friends, however, would protest – and then the police would arrest them for obstruction or they would stitch them up.

It was not uncommon in those days for the police to plant stuff on you: a knife or illegal substances, for example, would miraculously be 'found' on your person. You'd also be 'verballed'; in other words, the police put words into your mouth and make up a story, which conveniently gave them grounds for arrest. A lot of people from my area at that time who previously had clean records were arrested and their good names destroyed. I don't know how I got through those years as a teenager without that happening to me, because it happened to so many of my friends: stopped and detained simply for walking home from school.

That was what we had to deal with on a daily basis – and meanwhile I was at school, trying to get to university, trying to study, and I didn't talk about it to anybody because it was simply normalised. In part, it was this injustice that I personally experienced and the injustice I saw daily on the streets that influenced me to do the work that I do.

In 1981, after two years of Thatcherism, with its programme of cost-cutting, de-industrialisation and wholesale privatisation, unemployment in Britain was at a fifty-year high, with young people in some inner-city areas badly affected by the ever-worsening socio-economic and political situation. Already poorly resourced, urban, Black and other ethnic-minority communities in areas like Brixton, Hackney, Moss Side in Manchester, Toxteth in Liverpool, and Bristol had especially high levels of joblessness. In Brixton, where 25 per cent of residents were from an ethnic-minority group, the local African Caribbean community was suffering particularly high unemployment with around half of young Black men out of work. Brixton was also beset with a higher-than-average crime rate. Between 1976 and 1980 Brixton accounted for 35 per cent of all crimes in the Borough of Lambeth and 49 per cent of all robbery and violent theft offences.

At the beginning of April 1981, the Metropolitan Police launched its 'Operation Swamp'. With its uncomfortable echoes of Margaret Thatcher's contention that the UK 'might be rather swamped by people of a different culture', this ten-day police operation saw the streets of Brixton suddenly flooded with uniformed and plainclothes patrols. Within six days police officers stopped and searched more than 1,000 people using the 'sus' law, and made 150 arrests, further heightening underlying racial tensions and complaints of police discrimination.[*] No wonder there was frustration and anger among the Black community across London. Things quickly reached a head.

The heavy-handed and excessive use of the 'sus' law, along with the perceived botched investigation into the fire in New Cross, ultimately led to a violent confrontation between the Metropolitan Police and protesters in Brixton. Two nights of rioting followed. That summer in July the rioting spread to most of the major metropolitan areas across England – Handsworth in Birmingham; Bristol; Toxteth in Liverpool (where in response police used CS gas for the first time on the

---

[*] Jefferson and Grimshaw, 1984.

UK mainland);* and Chapeltown in Leeds – inner-city areas with similarly high unemployment rates, little investment and ethnic-minority communities left feeling high and dry. So much for helping people to help themselves.

The government commissioned an inquiry led by Lord Scarman into why the riots had occurred.† Lord Scarman's report, published in November 1981, described the relationship between the police and the Black community as 'a tale of failure', and concluded that the riots were 'essentially an outburst of anger and resentment by young Black people against the police'. The Scarman Report was instrumental in changing policing in the country and getting rid of the 'sus' law. In turn it heralded the introduction of the Police and Criminal Evidence Act 1984 ('PACE). This Act gave the police new stop-and-search powers and introduced the concept of 'Reasonable Grounds for Suspicion', which, in other words, could no longer simply be based on somebody's way of dressing, their hairstyle, or the colour of their skin.

---

* In Liverpool, heavy-handed police tactics led to the arrest of Leroy Cooper, sparking street violence in Toxteth. During the riots, 'police were attacked by youths with petrol bombs and paving stones'; a man died, knocked down by a police vehicle. According to reports, 500 people were arrested, and 468 police were hurt.

† Lord Scarman, who was commissioned by Home Secretary William Whitelaw, started from the position that policies aimed at the integration of the Black community had failed. He grasped that the rioters were particularly aggrieved by police behaviour. He recommended that officers record stops (subsequently part of the 1984 Police and Criminal Evidence Act) and that mechanisms of police-community liaison to give the Black community a local voice in policing policy be implemented. More generally, he saw the Brixton community as containing 'a wealth of voluntary effort and goodwill' and said that the state must recognise the 'long-term need to provide useful, gainful employment and suitable educational, recreational and leisure opportunities for young people, especially in the inner city' (Scarman, 1981).

Scarman, however, was out on a limb. Despite the high levels of unemployment, the Thatcher government was hell-bent on a programme of cuts in public spending. The model for future urban regeneration was to attract private investment. Consequently, the inner city of Liverpool saw a multi-million-pound makeover, for example, while deprived riot-torn areas like Toxteth were more or less ignored.

7

BATTERSEA COUNTY

For good or bad, one tends to remember the teachers in one's life, and I was inordinately lucky to have some inspirational teachers at Battersea County. It was, without doubt, because of their commitment and unstinting conviction that in the end, and despite everything, I was able to thrive there.

My latter school years played out against the backdrop of industrial disquiet and political fervour. Throughout the early '80s, a long-running dispute in education over teachers' pay and work conditions resulted in intermittent industrial action involving work-to-rule and a series of three-day strikes. Undaunted, the Conservatives continued their policy of stringent public-sector spending cuts and the emasculation of the unions. In 1982, my last year at school, unemployment passed 3 million for the first time since the 1930s, Argentina invaded the Falkland Islands and meanwhile, in London, GLC leader Ken Livingstone and Margaret Thatcher locked horns in a bitter ideological battle. Everyone seemed to be taking on Thatcher.

I had already decided that I wanted to become a lawyer, to be involved in society in a meaningful way and make a difference. I had plenty of ideas about what I was seeing on the news, about social justice and my experiences of racism as a young Black man in London, but they had no structure to them. At home there wasn't a lot of political discourse between my parents. Even though Dad was quite political, I never really heard either of them talk of trades unions, employment rights, discrimination or policy.

Battersea County, however, had a slightly leftist, progressive atmosphere – and these were radical times – with most of the teachers active and vociferous members of the National Union of Teachers. So, I lived through all the political and industrial strife at school, where quite often my teachers were out on strike. When I speak to my privately educated colleagues about those years, that sort of disruption apparently was unheard of in their schools. But there was something beneficial in having an education against a background of activism. As pupils, we must have absorbed some of the teachers' politics, ideals and philosophy – to us it was the norm.

Importantly, the teachers at Battersea County really encouraged independent thinking and debate: 'Don't accept just what you are told; think for yourself.' That is what I was gifted at Battersea County and it was central to getting me to where I am today. I owe a particular debt to my sociology teacher, Linda Austin. It was largely thanks to her that I became determined to be a voice for others if I could, that this was my path.

In her early to mid-thirties, with piercing intelligent eyes and a shock of beautiful curly red hair, Linda was what I would describe as an ardent, radical feminist with a razor-sharp mind. She was a highly qualified and brilliant teacher. Her A level sociology lessons opened my eyes and taught me critical thinking. She encouraged me to ask questions, enabled me to look at things with an open mind and an analytical precision. Linda got me thinking in a radical way. Her teaching introduced me to philosophical concepts, critical theory, Marxist theory, socialism, functionalism, and to thinkers like Karl Popper. I owe so much to her because at the times when I would have given up, and when most of the other kids around me *were* giving up, she pushed me and pushed me. She was tough in terms of making me read and read, and trying to get me to a high level of understanding. I had such respect for her that I didn't want to let her down, and I suppose I did not want to let myself down either. In a way, I think I was fearful of her.

There were, of course, other influential teachers, such as Lynn Fletcher, my other sociology teacher. Lynn was soft-spoken and immensely kind. I loved being in her class and listening to how she would explain some of the more difficult concepts that Linda had introduced to me. I always found it easier to ask Lynn questions because she was so gentle. My French teacher, Miss (Huguette) Collie, always had my back, a strict but very funny woman, with a wry sense of humour and always impeccably turned out.

Then there was my English teacher, Nick Gunning. Nick had seen me through my O Level, and was now teaching me for A level. Just before I started at Battersea County in 1976, he graduated in chemistry with first-class honours from a top university. A talented musician, Nick had had the world at his feet. He could have landed any job in industry, earned a fantastic living, and been set for life, but he didn't want that. Instead, he wanted to teach English and had taken a job in a deprived part of London at a comprehensive which was recruiting dynamic young teachers. Nick took a lot of abuse from some of the students; he was pilloried by my classmates because of his appearance, looking, I suppose, a bit of a square. He was scruffy, to put it mildly, and he was a chain smoker. At first he had difficulty controlling our class, but he certainly didn't give up on any of us. He would laugh off the foul-mouthed insults and carry on regardless. In time, he won over even his worst tormentors because he taught with passion and wit. He some-how managed to bring his English lessons alive and captivated the whole class. Nick was newly qualified, so his pay must have been a pittance, yet he worked insanely long hours. He was always there if we needed help with homework or with the concepts he tried to introduce.

I came from a household where books were not a priority; there was no great library at home so I wasn't exactly a big reader. But Nick must have seen something in me because he stuck with me and helped me to prepare for my A Levels. I will never forget the kindness and service beyond the call of duty that he gave me.

Then there was the pastoral care I got from teachers. Carolyn, my long-suffering form tutor from my first year at Battersea County, continued to keep a watchful eye on me and ensured that I didn't stray. One of my best friends at school, and someone I could count on for a hug on days when things were not going well, was my PE teacher Sue Boothroyd, an incredibly kind-hearted woman. She would encourage me with my studying during my A Levels because there were so many distractions it was easy to lose focus.

At the age of seventeen, I knew what I wanted to do, but it was hard to be self-motivated because there was so much going on. I was living on my own in my sister's flat, working at Jean Jeanie every Saturday and every Thursday night, and I was in my first serious relationship. Angela wanted to become a nurse. She didn't want to go to university. Like many people at our school, she thought it wasn't for people like us. I persuaded her to take the opportunity to go to university, so she stayed on at school. Her mother wasn't happy with that decision because she could have left and got a good job.

Angela was extremely hardworking; another grafter like me.

When I first met her, she was working Saturdays in Superdrug and then she got a job at Marks & Spencer. We were both working-class kids, with our dreams and ambitions, and wanting to do good.

So, for most of the sixth form I spent evenings in Clapham snogging with Angela when I should have been in the flat revising or swotting up on essay-writing skills, or learning reams of impressive Karl Marx quotes off by heart. It was all quite innocent, but by the time my exams came round I was completely distracted.

I had coasted through my O Levels. I had a natural talent in terms of cramming, but when I tried to reproduce that for my A Levels, it didn't work. I didn't get the whole 'studying' thing. My own kids are very hardworking and when I see how they prepare for exams, there is no comparison. I realise now that I had no clue about the level of serious, concentrated, long hours of study that were required, nor did I fully grasp the method or understand the rules of examination technique. Consequently, and not surprisingly, my results were awful. I was devastated and my teachers were likewise bitterly disappointed with me because I hadn't put in the work. I felt such shame because I'd totally blown my chances in terms of university: my grades were so bad that nowhere would have me. There was nothing else I wanted to do but law. I didn't have any other plan. Good polytechnics at the time were asking for high grades: to get into Kingston, for example, to study law I needed three Bs.

In my resits, I was predicted to get a B, a C and perhaps a D, but I applied anyway to Kingston and managed to get an interview. Two of the lecturers there, Penny Darbyshire and Vera Sacks, interviewed me and, on paper, I must have seemed like a hopeless case, but they must have seen some promise in me because they made me an unconditional offer. As it happens, I didn't do much better in my resits than the first time: I got a C, a D and an E, or the equivalent of three Ds, and yet they took me on. Kingston has been good to me.

I had money in my pocket and I was into the usual things that young kids and young Black kids were into: music, the soul movement, lots of jazz funk, northern soul. I used to love dancing at the proper soul music clubs, of which there were many dotted across London – places like Cheeky Pete's in Richmond, the Lyceum on the Strand that did soul all-dayers, and Cinderella's in Wimbledon. I would get the bus all over the city to go dancing, even at fifteen or sixteen when I was too young to get in.

My look in the late '70s and early '80s was sort of two-tone meets New Romantic meets Lionel Ritchie: the tightest drain-pipe jeans worn with either a white Adam Ant-ish, pirate-ish ruffled shirt, or a two-tone, chessboard black-and-white check shirt. I used to wear these ridiculous Tucker boots (as worn by the guys in Spandau Ballet), which were made in a sort of suede-like material that folded over at the ankle. I thought I was wicked. Really sharp. My friend Eddie had a baby face and I was tall and skinny, but I didn't have a hair on my face, so we had to go to great lengths to make ourselves look old enough to get into over-eighteen films at the cinema. We used to put shoe polish on our cheeks and upper lip to make it look like we had a tash and stubble. We must have looked a real sight. This is how we got in to see the cult classic *The Warriors* when we were fourteen, despite it being an 18-rated movie.

Back then, however, they didn't often ID us at the nightclubs; it depended on the mood of the bouncer, and if I was with a white guy, they would let me in. But if I was part of a group of Black guys, they would turn us away. Even these Black soul clubs, where you went especially because they played Black soul music all night, had a racist door policy.

In my last year at school, Angela and I were a firm couple. After my A Levels I did what most kids did then and do now: spent the summer travelling around Europe by train. I planned a route through France with Angela, then I would meet up with other friends and go on to Switzerland, Italy, the former Yugoslavia, Greece, and back home through France. When I told Sue Boothroyd about my travel plans, she invited Angela and me to stay with her and her boyfriend Bob (another of the PE teachers at school) as guests on a campsite where she had a caravan in a small seaside resort called St Raphael on the Cote d'Azur.

Inter-railing was a whole new experience for us, and it was the first time I had been travelling across France without proper adult supervision. Angela's mother was worried about the two of us going off on our own. It made me nervous, because I felt entirely responsible for Angela. I was just nineteen at the time, she had turned eighteen that summer and I knew I had to look after her. However, when you are that age, adventure beckons. I thought it would be a good opportunity to see a part of the world I knew nothing about. I was in for a shock.

Our first stop was Paris. Paris in the early '80s was beautiful but, unlike London, quite segregated. We had a limited budget, so Angela and I stayed in the north of the city, which was cheaper, but I was surprised at the poverty I saw there. Many people of African descent lived in that area; it had great clubs, music and food, but there was something about it that felt unsafe, although we couldn't put our finger on it. Also, Paris was very cosmopolitan, yet there were few other interracial couples. It made me realise just how much of a bubble I had lived in growing up in London. Only by travelling to other UK cities and abroad has made me appreciate just how integrated London actually is.

If I thought Paris was bad, I had even more of a shock in store when we arrived in St Raphael. I was bewitched by the beauty of the place, the smell of pine forests, and the bright colours of the Cote d'Azur. Sue and Bob were happy to see us. It was different seeing teachers outside the school environment and it was initially awkward to call them by their first names instead of 'Sir' or 'Miss'.

After a couple of days, it became abundantly clear that I was the only Black person on the campsite. Everywhere I went, people would stare at me as if I came from a different planet. I remember being on the beach at St Raphael; my skin wasn't used to the intense sun, so I was rubbing in sun cream. Angela suddenly nudged me in the ribs and I looked up. Everyone in our immediate vicinity on that packed beach was staring at me openly, seemingly without any embarrassment that they were so plainly gawping. Even when I looked them straight back in the eye, they carried on staring; clearly they'd never seen a Black person lying in the sun before, enjoying the sea and the sand. I even heard one small girl, who couldn't have been more than three years old, ask her mother if I was burnt and why my skin was so dark. I soon realised that in this part of the world, people didn't expect a Black person to use the beach for recreation; they expected Black people to be walking up and down trying to sell them something. Indeed, the only other Black people I saw during our stay were the young men who trudged along the sand selling sunglasses and lighters. Other beach users would often treat them dismissively and disrespectfully, but as a person of African heritage I felt a bond with them, and would always acknowledge them with a smile, nod, or hello, and they would always smile back. Bob noticed this and would say that it was 'being part of the brotherhood'. I suppose he was right; it's one of those things that a Black person can relate to. I have experienced it many times when travelling to parts of the world where there are few people of African descent.

One evening we went to a casino in Cannes. I had imagined that Cannes would be full of glamour, but apart from the palm-lined boulevards and some overpriced hotels, bars and restaurants, there was nothing particularly special about it. I was even more disappointed when we got to the casino. I was half expecting something out of a James Bond movie. Then Bob did something incredibly stupid. He grabbed Sue by the hand as we were approaching the entrance and barged his way in past the security, thus evading payment. Angela and I didn't know what was going on and followed suit. It was only when we got inside that I realised that we should have paid to enter. Bob suddenly said, 'Mingle!', and he merged into the throng. As a Black man, however, and the only person of colour, I must have stood out like a sore thumb. The bouncers, whom we had hurried past, walked casually into the casino. They strolled up to me, placed a hand on my shoulder and escorted me to the front desk and demanded that I pay my entry fee. I'd never felt so humiliated in all my life. Bob thought it was hilarious. It had never occurred to him that I would be singled out, but now he thought about it, he was sorry. But that didn't stop him from repeating the story a million times during the rest of the holiday. That evening, I had learned another important lesson: white people truly do not know the privilege they have by virtue of the skin they walk around in.

8

UNIVERSITY LIFE

Back in London, I was still working at Jean Jeanie, but in order to save for university, I needed more work. I scanned the ads in my local job centre and found a position as a meal supervisor at a primary school in Balham. I had to go in at lunchtimes and at playtime to help with the children and, apart from the deputy headteacher, I was the only man in the school. Not only that, but as an eighteen-year-old Black guy working as the 'dinner man', I stood out a bit. The kids absolutely loved me and used to call me 'Mum'. I was quite a sweet, quiet, polite young man then, so the other dinner ladies became fond of me too. I picked up another job alongside as an attendant working with partially hearing kids, taking them to and from the school bus to their classroom every morning and afternoon at the end of the day. I've never met such loving kids. They taught me some sign language and I adored them.

When I started at Kingston I handed in my notice at Jean Jeanie; it was too difficult to make it on time for the Thursday late-night-shopping stint. I kept up the dinner man job during my holidays, though, for as long as I could. I even talked my mum into doing it for me during term time so that I could go back into the job as soon as my terms ended. It was crazy, but she agreed. She would get home from the hospital at nine in the morning after working all night, have two hours sleep, have a shower, and then go down to the school.

I know now that Mum did that for me because Dad had cut me loose. Later, she told me that she worked especially long hours when I was at Kingston. Dad had some funny ideas, she said, and she couldn't cope with them. I only had one suit and Mum told my dad that she couldn't have me going into court with that same single suit. Dad's response was that she could work to buy me one; he wasn't spending his money on me so that I could go and marry a white woman. So they struck a deal. Mum would work to support me at university and Dad could support Janet, and that's how they spread out the resources. Then, when Dad was fifty-five, he left the Methodist Church and became a Jehovah's Witness. After that, he couldn't care who you were married to. Mum says, 'He didn't care if you married a porcupine. Everybody was equal.'

It was hard at first when I got to university. Angela was in her last year at school and I still had my sister's flat while she was in Brighton, and so I decided to commute. This meant that I wasn't able to enjoy a normal university social life. For a long time I didn't feel like I fitted in. I must have been suffering from low self-esteem because of my A-Level fiasco and coming from a comprehensive school. I felt a bit of a fraud, as if I shouldn't really be there at all. In some ways, though, that proved to be an incentive; I'd been given the biggest break to get into Kingston and now I had something to prove. I couldn't allow myself to fail. I finally understood the point of studying, and, boy, did I work my socks off. I also worked out that the whole thing about passing exams and getting good grades was a game, and in order to play and win at that game, there were certain rules you had to understand. This is where the lessons from working at Jean Jeanie came into their own. All the opportunities that had come my way had been thanks to people with an abundance mentality: Ian, my colleague on the Levi's floor, and my teachers at school, Linda Austin, Nick Gunning, Carolyn Lornie and Sue Boothroyd. They showed me kindness and had belief in me. I realised that I wasn't going to be able to crack the whole university law degree on my own; I needed a good support network, people who were much smarter than me and would pull me along with them.

I had seen that it paid to seek out others with an abundance mentality and to strive to have that attitude myself, and at university I found that people with a similar outlook gravitated towards me and me to them. I gathered around me a small group of those who were also struggling, along with a couple of friends of mine who were A students, and we formed a kind of study group. Not everyone thought like us, though. Some of our fellow students would do things like hide books in the library to prevent others from getting hold of them. Again, that old scarcity mentality; if I take this away from you it will benefit me. But they didn't hold my group back. We pulled everybody across the line. Many in our group, the Mastermind Group, as I called them, went on to do very well. In fact, although most law students at Kingston wanted to become solicitors, most of our group became barristers and we all went up to the Bar at the same time.

In my second year, Janet had arrived back in London and reclaimed her flat. The first place that I moved to was a shared house in New Malden, living with three oil workers who essentially treated the place as a doss house. They were earning fantastic money, so they'd take me down to the pub and buy rounds. We'd be downing seven or eight pints a night, and I had to study the next morning, but the real reason I couldn't live with them was that the house was too revolting for a clean freak like me. I moved to new, more hygienic digs in Kingston where Angela could stay the night.

After we both graduated, me from Kingston and Angela from nearby Roehampton College, I moved into a flat in East Dulwich while Angela was living in Brixton. Shortly after, we decided to move in together in Honor Oak. Angela had taken a degree in modern sociology, and rather than go into nursing, she became a housing officer in west London for a women's housing charity.

In my third year at Kingston, I started working for the Brixton Circle Project, which ran the Fanon Project, a day centre and charity supporting people who had suffered mental illness and homelessness in Brixton. Janet was the director of the Fanon and asked me to sit on the management committee. It was my first job working with the community.

There were difficult decisions to be made and many of the residents were misunderstood or had problems with the police and had no access to legal advice or other social services. The work was entirely new to me and it was challenging. Little did I know that it would lead the way on many of the cases I would subsequently be involved in. Many of the former residents at the Fanon who were in and out of mental health services would have very similar experiences to those who died in police custody, whose families I would come to represent.

PART II

9

A BAPTISM IN BLACK LETTER LAW: 13 KINGS BENCH CHAMBERS

One question I am often asked is 'Have you suffered discrimination, or felt the effect of racism, in the legal profession?' It's an interesting question – but more interesting, I think, is *who* is asking the question.

When somebody I am mentoring – perhaps of the same race as me, from a similar background – asks me about racism, I can see where they're coming from. There have been many times, however, when someone has posed that question in the most random of situations, when implicit in the very asking is the problem itself. For example, when a white middle-class male has just met me and is asking me this question, it always gives me pause. For the question to be a legitimate one, the questioner needs to say to themselves, would they ask such a thing of anybody at the Bar? If the answer is no, they don't randomly ask everyone they meet if they have experienced racism in the legal profession, then why would they limit that question to somebody who is Black?

I graduated from Kingston University near the top of my year. Loosely speaking, the legal profession is composed of the judiciary, barristers and solicitors. At the time I graduated in

1984, there were roughly 38,000 solicitors and barristers in total practising in England and Wales, of which approximately 4,400 were barristers. While the two carry out similar roles – advising, negotiating, drafting – the general rule is that the solicitor is the first point of call for anyone seeking legal help or redress, calling in a barrister if a case is set to go to trial, or if more specialist advice is needed. While solicitors were granted the right to address only some of the lower courts, barristers were seen ostensibly as the experts in advocacy, and only they could advocate in High Court trials. I knew that I definitely wanted to go to the Bar, to become a barrister rather than a solicitor, but at the time I had no idea how to actually go about that. Barristers are lone practitioners, they are self-employed, but in the main they join a 'set' of chambers in which they pay rent and share expenses, but not profits. Any aspiring young barrister will need to secure a pupillage, a one-year, vocational, work-place training placement within a set of chambers. I didn't know anybody at the Bar, I didn't have any connections and, to be quite honest, I didn't even know what a pupillage was or what it involved – that's how ignorant I was.

The Head of Law at Kingston, Professor Bob Upex, had taught me employment law, and I think he must have seen promise in me because he immediately offered to arrange a pupillage. Nowadays this would be unheard of. Then, as now, competition for a limited number of opportunities was fierce and I knew enough not to look a gift horse in the mouth. So, thanks to Bob and the 'Oxbridge old boys' network', just after I'd graduated I turned up at 13 Kings Bench Walk in Temple to meet my pupil master (a term which has now fallen out of favour and been replaced with supervisor), David Richardson. David and Bob were long-time friends from their Cambridge days. That was the straightforward part and, believe me, I know how lucky I was to have had Bob land me such an opportunity.

To become a barrister in England and Wales you must become a member of one of the Inns of Court and to do so you have to eat many formal dinners. Back then you had to go to twenty-four, which you had to pay for out of your own pocket. It's called Dining and it didn't come cheap. (Today I understand that this is now more suitably referred to as Qualifying Sessions, which gives a certain legitimacy to the tradition, and rather than simply eating dinners it is more educational with lectures and talks being provided as part of the process leading to qualification as a barrister.) There are four Inns of Court, which are all located in London: Lincoln's Inn, Inner Temple, Middle Temple and Gray's Inn. I chose Inner Temple, not because I had done any particular research, nor because of its impressive list of venerable former members – including Lady Justice Butler-Sloss, Prime Ministers Clement Attlee and George Grenville, Mahatma Gandhi and economist John Maynard Keynes – but because that's where Bob Upex told me to apply. Of course, I now understand that there are better criteria, such as whether you qualify for a grant or scholarship from your Inn. But back then I knew nothing about scholarships or grants and by the time I got to my pupillage I had missed the application deadline.

The rationale of Dining, I was told, is that it is a good way of networking, to meet and mingle with practising barristers, judges and your contemporaries, and to make connections for potential pupillages and tenancies in chambers. I also learned that if you dined at the weekend it counted as three dinners, so that was my plan. The first time I went to Inner Temple, therefore, I went for Sunday lunch suitably attired according to the dress code of 'dark lounge suit, plain collar and sober tie/ white blouse', or 'genuine national dress'.

The Inner Temple Hall was a different world. Picture a long, wood-panelled hall lined with portraits of judges staring down at you, hundreds of coats of arms of various ancient past members of the Inn, high stained-glass windows, crystal chandeliers, glittering displays of priceless antique silverware, and dusty old suits of armour. Four enormous tables with pristine starched linens and complicated cutlery settings fill the length of the room: this is where applicants to the Bar should sit, but nobody had explained this to me. At the far end of the room, at a right angle, is a top table where the judges sit. One of the reasons members of the Inn, senior judges or senior barristers, are called 'Benchers', or Masters, is because they sit on long benches at this top table. I should explain that a Bencher or Master is elected by other Benchers of the Inn. The Benchers run the Inn; they are like the management committee, and they organise scholarships for new barristers, look after the Inn's estates and land, as well as its library. They are also responsible for discipline within the Inn, for diversity and the education of new barristers. Some twenty-five years after my first Sunday dining ordeal, I too would become a Bencher.

That first time, I went into this great hall, walked along the rows of long tables and straight to the top table. I took a seat on the bench and slowly the other tables began to fill up. After a couple of minutes, an elderly gentleman came in and sat down next to me. We introduced ourselves – I understand now that he was a Master Bencher. 'Which island do you come from?' he asked me. And, being a Londoner, and having that sort of south London lippiness, I quipped, 'Well, the only islands they have where I come from are called traffic islands.' I don't think he quite took to my humour, so I explained, 'I was born in the sunshine, in west London, Hammersmith, but I grew up in Battersea.' I always thought that it was obvious from my accent that I was from London. However, I also spoke extremely fast, like a typical south Londoner, thinking that the faster you spoke the more strongly you would get your point across. (That has changed over the past thirty years. Nowadays, I speak at such a pedestrian pace people are constantly trying to finish my sentences for me because they can see where my thought process is going!) That lunchtime my rapid-fire badinage was clearly going down like a lead balloon. Then this grandee asked me if I liked cricket. In Battersea we weren't renowned for our cricketing skills, so I replied, 'Actually, I prefer football myself and my team's Arsenal.' He didn't say another word to me during the rest of the meal.

13 Kings Bench Walk was a semi-commercial set of chambers. It did a lot of common law and commercial law work, including issues such as contractual disputes and negligent actions. The pupillage is normally divided into two distinct six-month periods. In the 'first six' you shadow a senior barrister, your pupil master, who in my case was David Richardson, and in the 'second six' they let you loose on the public. David, one of the most gentle, kind-hearted people you'd ever meet, took me under his wing. He was a deeply religious man and we used to have vigorous philosophical debates about politics, the nature of man, the nature of religion. He did a lot of company and corporate private client work, and I spent the next nine months or so under his supervision learning what is known as 'black letter law' – literally studying the literature on case law, looking at the statutes. And it was tough. The one thing I learned in those first months was that despite having studied law at university for three years, I knew nothing.

Every day I was churning out page after page of advice, opinion, draft applications and pleadings, one after the other, handing the pages to David only to have them handed back to me covered with his corrections scribbled in red ink. That was quite demoralising until I realised how much attention to detail was required – and slowly, slowly, I started to get it. I was, I suppose, by nature somewhat slapdash and wanted to argue the case rather than stick to the black letter. David was always encouraging, his constructive criticism delivered with his characteristic kindness. He taught me to take a step back and *think*; to look at the minutiae and be specific. It might not have been how I imagined the law when I dreamed of becoming a barrister, but the 'stiff' training I got from David in that quasi-commercial pupillage stood me in good stead. The ability to read, to pay attention to *the particular*, and to condense all the component parts clearly and concisely on paper was invaluable when it came to human rights cases.

David taught me another crucial lesson, namely that even if you are representing the Devil, you don't need to be nasty about it. On one occasion, David had the unenviable task of representing a large multinational chemical company. It had a poor record in workplace health and safety, and therefore on more than one occasion we were in the position of representing this corporation at an inquest, or a personal injury claim against them. I remember going to one settlement meeting in a claim brought by the widow who had lost her husband, an employee of the firm. David made an offer for the widow which was much more generous than it needed to have been. When questioned, he simply said, 'We are representing this corporation, but this woman's husband worked for this company for years and this is what she deserves. This is a good offer: whether she accepts it, or her lawyers accept it, or not, she would be silly to reject it because it's a fair offer.' That has stayed with me.

But to return to the question I posed for myself: is there discrimination and racism at the Bar? At Kings Bench Walk they had a very small handful of women barristers, I was the only Black person in chambers, including the staff, the only person of colour there and the first Black pupil.

In all the time I was with this set, I cannot remember David taking on a client of colour. I don't remember a representative of colour from any of the corporate bodies coming into our conferences. Often the only person of colour in the room would be me.

Let me go back to my 'second six', when I was first finally let loose on the public and given my own court cases. Like most common law sets, 13 Kings Bench Chambers had a small smattering of family work and a tiny proportion of criminal work.

In the 'second six', David thought it would be a good idea for me to gain experience under another barrister at the chambers. My second pupil master could not have been more different. He often asked me to meet him at his home and drive him around in his Bentley; he had clearly always wanted a chauffeur and this also enabled him to have a drink. He certainly took liberties with me. He was nothing like David, who prepared everything meticulously. But what I remember most vividly is the teasing and jokes he would make at my expense because I was Black. He thought it was hilarious to put on a faux Jamaican accent. 'Don't have a chip on your shoulder, Leslie, I'm only teasing you,' he would say if I objected. I never complained to anyone about this treatment because, to be honest, there was no one to complain to. I just took it. In fairness, if one wants to be fair about racism, my second pupil master was not unique in his humour. This was standard in the '80s. Still, six months into my pupillage, I longed to be given an actual court case, not least because I could escape the driving duties and the demeaning behaviour of this man.

During the first month of my second six, I would sit in my

pupil master's room anxiously waiting for a set of papers, hoping that one day the clerks would call me in to give me my first brief. For that entire month, every day was agony; I would sit and wait and leave disappointed. Then, one day I was finally called into the clerks' room. In any set of chambers, the clerks are extremely powerful. They can make or break a barrister's career. Many clerks were simply a reflection of British society in general and thus held stereotypical views on what people were capable of. Clerking in the early days, and certainly when I came to the Bar, was a closed profession, and to enter it was very much a case of who you knew, not what you knew. It was the bastion of many working-class white men who were given a shoo-in thanks to family or friend connections. There were few women clerks and even fewer of colour.

The senior clerk handed me my first set of papers. At last, I was going to court. It was a family case, an area I knew very little about apart from what I had learned at university, an application to resist an injunction brought by a woman against her husband. Our chambers did hardly any of this work, but that didn't bother me. I picked up the brief and set off to meet my client. He was a Black man who was disputing the allegations his estranged wife had brought against him. He wanted to see his children and he gave me his instructions.

In those days, when solicitors instructed barristers on a trial, sometimes both lawyers would attend court: the barrister to do the advocacy, and the solicitor to deal with the client and take notes. On small cases such as this, however, only the barrister would attend court. So, I was alone with the client and was to report back to the solicitor afterwards.

I approached the court usher to give my name and to confirm I was there representing this client, but he cut across me before I could say a word. 'Who are you? You need to fill this in. Where's your solicitor? Where's your barrister?' To the usher I was everyone other than the barrister. 'Umm,' I said, 'I *am* the barrister.'

This was my first ever case and after this exchange my nerves were even more on edge. The client and I waited outside the courtroom to be called in front of the judge. I was getting increasingly anxious as the minutes ticked past. What I didn't know at the time was that if you befriend the ushers, you generally get called upon *sooner* rather than later. We were called on last. In court the only two Black people in the room were my client and me. My opponent representing the wife of my client made the case for an injunction. When it was my turn to make my submissions, I rose to my feet. The first thing I said was, 'Your Honour, my client disputes this application and his children have a right to see their dad.' The judge's face turned red and then he erupted. 'Dad? Dad?' he shouted. 'We don't say "Dad" in this court.' I looked at my client and my client looked at me, and I looked at my opponent and I had no idea what I had said wrong. 'Mr Thomas, if you are going to address me, you do not use slang. We use the term "father" in this court.' I felt completely humiliated and belittled in front of my client. It got worse. After the judge told me never to say 'Dad' in his court, I replied, 'OK', and it seemed like my downfall was complete. 'OK! OK? OK? YOU DO NOT SAY "OK" IN THIS COURT!'

Now, I don't know whether it was because my client and I were Black, but even before I opened my mouth, I could feel the judge's cold and naked hostility, his bullying attitude towards me and towards my client. In contrast to the courtesy and patience with which the judge addressed my opponent, it was palpable: I was simply not to be afforded the same respect.

Thirty years later I deliberately make it my policy to use the terms 'Dad' and 'Mum' in court. OK?

There were times when I started at the Bar that I couldn't believe that I was there; going into court, acting as a junior barrister. Many a time I thought to myself, 'Should I be here? Is this where I belong?' I felt a total fraud. And the truth is that there are still occasions when I'm doing a big case and everybody involved is looking to me to help them and I think, 'You've got the wrong person! I shouldn't be doing this.' I sometimes imagine that I'm going to wake up, open my eyes and find myself in an alternative reality where I'm back stacking the shelves in Fine Fare. Or maybe in this alternative reality I became a police officer because I took the advice of the careers officer at school.

Gradually, though, I settled in at 13 Kings Bench Chambers and I'm eternally grateful for everything I learned under David's wing. I will never forget the fundamental lessons about justice, fairness and kindness he taught me.

Yet, while I liked and admired David immensely, I knew that commercial law wasn't what I wanted to do. I kept my head down and got on with it, but I hated every second of the work there. It wasn't me; it wasn't where my soul was.

One of the ways that I eased my hunger for creativity, instinct, dealing with people and arguing a case was to volunteer at almost every legal advice centre in my area. I was working four nights a week at either Stockwell and Clapham Law Centre, or Brixton Law Centre on Railton Road. I also volunteered as an advisor at the Central London Law Centre and wrote legal letters for the then National Council for Civil Liberties, or Liberty as it is now known. I had a pupillage, I was on a career path to becoming a commercial lawyer, so I didn't need to do any of this. I wasn't doing it because I was trying to fill a CV; I was doing it because I loved the contact with ordinary people who had what I considered to be real problems that needed solutions.

Well into my pupillage at Kings Bench Walk, practically at the end of my first year, it was at the Liberty Christmas party in 1988 that I inadvertently got my next job. I found myself making small talk with a man whose name was Tony. I didn't know who he was but he seemed interested in me. When he asked how I was involved with Liberty, I told him how fascinated I was by it and that I was working evenings at various law centres. I told him about my pupillage at 13 Kings Bench. The upshot was that he gave me his card and invited me to visit him in his chambers and meet some of the other barristers there.

The card read Tony Gifford, Wellington Street Chambers, which meant nothing to me. I didn't know that Tony Gifford, or Lord Anthony Gifford QC, was one of the foremost civil libertarians in the country, who at the time was working on the cases of the Guildford Four and Birmingham Six as well as representing miners and poll-tax protesters. I went along to his chambers and was invited into a big meeting room to speak with some of Tony's colleagues. Everyone sat down and after a relatively informal chat, Tony invited me to join them. I didn't even know I was going to an interview.

Wellington Street in those days was a collective: a group of like-minded barristers who had decided to pool their income and run a sort of welfare system whereby they took out a salary and were also entitled to holiday pay, maternity, paternity and sickness pay. They even had a collective pension fund. Wellington Street paid its pupils a salary as well. Many of the benefits it offered do not seem that unusual today, but back then it was unique. Admittedly the salaries at Wellington Street were small compared to what you could get from independent practice, but they were ensuring that everybody got a fair wage, that the highest earners were contributing to the lowest earners. They liked me and I liked them; I found the ethos of this bunch of progressive lawyers attractive; as a set they were miles ahead of anyone at the Bar at the time.

When I told David about the offer, he was devastated, and extremely worried for me. He said, 'Leslie, don't go there. I'm not convinced about them. You have a certain career here, you'll do well, you've got a good brain on you.'

I faced a real dilemma and had a difficult decision to make about whether to stay at 13 Kings Bench, or to give up a sure, steady career at the commercial Bar and take a leap of faith. I didn't think about it too long. I just knew in my heart. Everything about Wellington Street felt right. I didn't hesitate; I joined Wellington Street and never looked back.

10

WELLINGTON STREET

I arrived at Wellington Street in the summer of 1989. Wellington Street handled a lot of criminal cases, but because I had no experience of criminal law, they allowed me to have extra training under the tutelage of some of the best radical lawyers at the Bar.

On my third day, they gave me a criminal trial at Southwark Crown Court. This was my first Crown Court appearance and, apparently, when you do your first Crown Court trial in front of a jury, you're supposed to tell the usher that it's your first appearance, and the usher alerts the judge. I didn't do that. The judge was rude, vicious in fact: figuratively speaking, he kicked me around the court. Of course, I can't prove it, but I know what I sensed standing there in front of him: he didn't like the fact that I was a young Black man. He was interrupting me, pulling me up on every other word: 'That's not how you say things in my court. You don't make statements like that in my court,' and so on. But I hadn't expressed myself any differently to anyone else in the room. There was a lot of that. The racism wasn't always explicit, but I could always sense when a judge was against me because of the colour of my skin.

In that instance, I won the case on behalf of my client despite the judge's unhelpful interventions. I think the jury probably took pity on me.

On another occasion, I was representing somebody accused of shoplifting from a department store. In fact, this individual had a prolific record of similar offences. I turned up to do the trial without thinking too much about the witness list. Waiting to be called, I heard someone shout, 'Leslie!' I turned round and came face to face with one of my old PE teachers from Battersea County, Mr Turrock, AKA Bullet as he was known by the pupils. Bullet worked alongside Bob Mercer, whom I had visited in the South of France. Originally from South Africa, Bullet was a huge, smiley man, six foot four in height and a rugby player. I believe the expression is 'built like a brick shithouse'. He was happy to see me and gave me a big hug. I said, 'Mr Turrock, great to see you. What are you doing here?' And then it dawned on me – Bullet was the main prosecution witness in my client's shoplifting case. He had changed professions and become some sort of store detective or a security guard – he was big enough to be one. I had to stand down from the case. I could hardly cross-examine Bullet and call him a liar!

There was a three-month probation period at Wellington Street, and the truth is, I was having serious doubts about my tenancy. I was having a miserable time. I hated working on criminal cases. I hadn't had the training. What you learn at Bar school does not prepare you for the real world. More importantly, I wasn't particularly interested in it; in short, I didn't want to do crime. After I won that first case, however, a ton of criminal work came my way. I think solicitors found me approachable and their clients liked me, so the criminal law firms wanted to reinstruct me. I knew, though, that I was out of my depth and at some point I would hit a nail in the road.

On the last Saturday before the end of my probation, when

I knew my colleagues at Wellington Street would have to decide whether to ratify me and keep me on, I was assigned Saturday court duty. I had what's known as a 'first appearance' in Redbridge magistrates' court in the outer reaches of east London. In those days, a 'first appearance' was literally that — when the police first charged an individual and he or she went before the magistrates for the issue of bail to be determined. The case was a serious one involving the mass importation of Class A drugs. I was representing one of several East End individuals implicated in the trade who would be going in front of the magistrate at the hearing. Back then, the only mobile phones were the size of bricks and hardly anyone owned one. If you wanted to speak to your solicitor, or anyone for that matter, you had to go to a telephone box with a pocketful of coins. I was instructed on the case late on the Friday evening, and when I say I was instructed, my clerk Suzie at Wellington Street handed me what is called a 'back sheet'. This is literally a piece of paper with, on one side, the name of the client, the name of the court, the name of the solicitor and the solicitor's office telephone number, and on the back, some extremely rudimentary instructions: 'Counsel is instructed to go to X court, to represent the defendant on the first appearance and make a bail application.' That was it. If it was within office hours, you'd pick up the phone and call the solicitor to glean a few more details. But what did you do on a Friday evening at a time when there were no mobile phones?

I looked at the back sheet and my instructions read, 'Client wants to turn QE.' Remember, I hadn't done crime. I didn't have a clue what 'QE' meant. Offices closed at 5 p.m. and everyone had disappeared for the weekend.

I had to get up at the crack of dawn the next morning to take buses and trains across London to this far-flung outpost. I was still in the dark about what 'turning QE' meant, so I did what I usually did at court when I didn't know something: I asked my fellow barristers for the defence. Before they could answer, a senior detective in the case came over wanting a word. I told him that I understood that my client wanted to turn QE, and asked him what it meant. He explained that it stood for 'Queen's Evidence': in other words, my client wanted to give evidence for the prosecution against his fellow co-defendants. In my ignorance, I had just told one of his co-defendants' counsel. He may have felt really bad for me, but his duty was to defend his client and he would, of course, also have a duty to tell his client that my client was planning to give evidence against him.

The detective was one of those real old-school DIs from an east London station and could have been right out of the television show *The Sweeney*. I'll never forget his response: '*You fucking idiot. If your client's fucking dead by midnight you'll have it on your fucking conscience. What's your fucking name, you incompetent idiot? I'm going to report you.*'

And that's why I hate abbreviations. As lawyers, we assume that everyone knows what they mean, but they don't. I didn't know what QE meant. I do now. I'll never forget that, and now when I talk to clients or junior members of my team, I always try to keep my language clear and free from jargon.

I then had to go into court and make the bail application for this guy in the full knowledge that if I was unsuccessful, he would be remanded into custody with his co-defendant, the guy he was planning to rat on. I was shaking so much I could barely walk or indeed talk. I was close to tears. We spent all morning in court with this DI eyeballing me and giving me the daggers. I tried my best and made the most impassioned plea for bail. At one point I thought I might have swung it, but right at the end the magistrate refused my client bail. As I walked out of the courtroom, the senior detective inspector came up to me and said, 'Which chambers are you at? Give me your fucking name.'

The reality is that I shouldn't have been doing that case in the first place. I was inexperienced and on a steep learning curve. After that I lost a lot of cases to the point where I didn't know whether I'd ever cut it. But I kept going, I won some cases and lost others, and with each one I learned a bit more and became a slightly better lawyer.

In early 1990 the government pressed ahead with its Community Charge, dubbed the poll tax, the central policy of the Conservative Party's winning general election manifesto in 1987. The proposed and now-notorious poll tax was to replace the old domestic property rates system, which was based on the worth of one's house, with a fixed charge levied on each adult resident in any household. It was roundly criticised as being unfair and particularly punishing for low-income households with hundreds of groups calling for mass non-payment. The poll tax had already been rolled out in Scotland, but throughout the early months of 1990, in the run-up to its 30 April implementation in England, anti-poll tax demonstrations grew in frequency and intensity of feeling. After years of mass unemployment under a Conservative government that seemed only to care about helping the rich get richer, resentment was reaching a tipping point. A number of protests across the country culminated in violence, notably in London on 31 March, when a demonstration descended into violent skirmishes between protesters and the police. As the marchers converged on Trafalgar Square, the police had moved to contain the crowd and prevent its progress down Whitehall towards Downing Street. With the demonstrators effectively corralled, the situation quickly escalated into a full-blown riot during which hundreds were injured and many more hundreds of arrests were made. In attempts to break up the demonstration, mounted police charged at the protesters, while 'snatch squads', a group of two or three officers in riot gear and armed with shields and batons, would run at the crowd and grab an individual who would be dragged out of the melee and handed over to other officers. The protester would be detained at the scene, perhaps herded along with others into the back of a meat wagon. Only later would they be taken to a police station where they would be processed and learn the reason for their arrest and the charges against them. The snatch squad officer, meanwhile, would go straight back into the crowd to grab their next supposed 'offender'.

In the aftermath of the riots, I was called to represent a lot of those who had been caught up in the poll-tax disputes. The solicitor on many of these cases was a forthright radical young solicitor called Louise Christian of Christian Fisher, and latterly Christian Khan. Louise had an incisive legal mind, and was one of the most fearless and fierce solicitors I have met in all my time at the Bar. You would definitely want her on your side if you got in a legal fight. Despite my relative inexperience when she first instructed me on these protest cases, she had faith and confidence in me, and I became very good at them. Many people were being convicted based on false evidence and lies, because the snatch squad had picked them out of the demonstration seemingly indiscriminately. Only when they were in front of the custody sergeant would they hear the arresting officer claim that it was for disorderly conduct, or assault, or whatever. But none of that was true and, what is more, the arresting officers had no idea why these people had been handed over to them, and had therefore been making it up on the spot.

When I went along with my clients for the first magistrate's hearing, the officers tended to give their evidence in pairs. It was at a time when you didn't have disclosure of officer's notebooks, but when listening to the police officers' account of what my client had done to warrant an arrest, it was clear to me, and perhaps to everyone in the court, that they tended to support each other. Once I started to question them on the periphery, however, they couldn't tell the court any of the *detail*, nor could they corroborate each other because they hadn't witnessed the so-called 'offence' leading to arrest. Indeed, when I looked at the officers' notebooks, half the time it was clear that they had either put their heads together and written up their reports side by side, or their reports had been copied and post-dated.

I won a lot of cases on behalf of poll-tax protesters and, consequently, many of them wanted to sue the police for wrongful arrest. Louise Christian suggested that I might act for her clients on these civil actions. Similarly, while most of the barristers at Wellington Street were handling criminal cases, the subsequent civil actions were given to me. I had a strong foundation in civil litigation from my first commercial pupillage, so in principle, that didn't frighten me at all. Only one person at Wellington Street was working on police cases at the time and that was James Wood QC, now of Doughty Street Chambers. James taught me everything he knew about doing civil actions against the police. At the time, nobody else at Wellington Street had time to concentrate on them, so I became the go-to person. Within the space of a few months my practice at Wellington Street, which had predominantly been criminal law, became a civil actions practice. I became Mr Police Action and I relished the role.

Shortly thereafter, two junior lawyers started at Christian Fisher around the same time: Sadiq Khan, an impeccably dressed, calm and eloquent Asian man from Tooting (I remember thinking to myself: this man would do well in politics), and a woman from the north of England called Sarah Cleary. Both would become close friends of mine and would instruct me over the next few years. They were bright, talented, articulate and vocal solicitors. I had never met lawyers like Sadiq or Sarah before. They were the new breed of racial lawyers, young and keen. Sadiq, Sarah and I spent a great deal of time together working closely on cases for Louise and on their own caseload.

While I was still a relatively untested junior barrister, both Sarah and Sadiq were trainees and as such they had confidence in me. Together we had a string of excellent results in civil actions. One of the reasons for my success in these cases, I think, was the fact that I got on well with clients. I could relate to them: the very things that had happened to them had happened to me. Often, the only difference between us was that I'd never given the police any lip on the frequent occasions when they'd stopped me.

Early in my career at Wellington Street, I had many dealings with Stoke Newington police station. At that time the station had a reputation for stitching people up. Not only was there a problem with racist officers; there was also a lot of corruption in the ranks. The Metropolitan Police in general, and in certain other police stations – Brixton, Battersea, Clapham and Streatham in particular – didn't have a particularly good reputation among Black people either. Indeed, Brixton and Streatham were also notorious. However, the truth is that bad apples were employed across the board in the Met. The Black community had always known that there was a problem, but it wasn't until the inquiry into the Metropolitan Police's handling of Stephen Lawrence's murder in 1993, and the subsequent publication in 1999 of the Macpherson Report, that the nature of systemic and cultural racism in the police was finally out in the open.

Up until the Stephen Lawrence Inquiry, I was acting in these police actions involving corrupt police officers, and I was getting justice for my clients in plenty of cases, but it was a huge battle. When I went into my first police action in 1990, three years before the murder of Stephen Lawrence, I didn't have a clue as to what was in store. As an impassioned and idealistic young barrister working in a progressive set like Wellington Street, I thought that I had entered a gentleman's profession; that we all played fair, nobody took shots, we all abided by the Queensbury Rules, so to speak. My understanding was that if there was evidence, then you had to disclose that evidence to the other side, even if it was unhelpful to your case. When I did that first police action, I couldn't believe how wrong and utterly naive I had been – there were so many things on so many levels that completely messed with my head.

Firstly, in the late '80s and early '90s, there weren't that many police actions. There have always been false imprisonment, malicious prosecution and assault claims in civil litigation, and they have been in our common law for at least a century. But at the time I started out on this path, people were just beginning to use civil litigation as a tool to challenge corrupt policing. There had, of course, been pioneers in the early '80s, but by the early '90s, actions against the police became politicised. Nowadays police action work is a specialism in itself: there are lawyers who practise in this one area of law and can make a living. There are police forces up and down the country who have police action specialist defence teams doing only this work. Thirty years ago, however, when I started, there were only a handful of us who were engaged in these proceedings, and because this area of law was so new, the process had not been standardised.

My first police action case was tried in the old Westminster County Court, now the Central London County Court. I was in front of a judge who patently hated the fact that I had the temerity to bring an action against the police on behalf of my client. I was representing a woman who had been arrested for allegedly having altered her car-tax disc. She had denied the charge, claiming that she didn't know how her tax disc had been altered, but regardless of what may or may not have happened, on her arrest the police had gone right over the top. My client had been manhandled and racially abused and was making a claim for assault and false imprisonment. She was a businesswoman and she was Black. In court, she gave her evidence well. Then my opponent produced a bundle of witness statements relating to a completely different incident, to do with a school, my client, and a dispute relating to her child. It was alleged that my client had been aggressive to school staff. These witness statements had not been 'disclosed' to us as part of the compulsory sharing of documents by each party to an action. I made a complaint to the judge asking for them to be disallowed. The judge summarily dismissed my complaint. Today that could never happen. There is full disclosure beforehand and an exchange of witness statements. Each side knows ahead of time what the witness will say in the witness box.

It was shocking then, to see how the rules, as I understood them, could be bent in such a way as to render them immaterial. Back at chambers, I told Liz Woodcroft, one of my supervisors, what had happened. 'Leslie, that's what it's like,' she told me. 'The whole thing about the Bar being a profession for gentlemen is nonsense.'

At the same time, Tony Gifford was working on the cases to appeal the convictions of the Guildford Four and the Birmingham Six, in which, as we now know, there were serious miscarriages of justice. In both cases, the defendants had been saying all along that they had been forced into making confessions under intense intimidation and coercion by the police, and that passages of their interviews had been overwritten. With the introduction of the ESDA test, this was subsequently forensically proven. At that time, these police interviews were not recorded; they were written out by hand. The ESDA, or electrostatic detection apparatus, allowed forensic scientists to examine the indentations on each page, to see if there had been tampering of the police documents: whether the written pages were contemporaneous transcripts, if the pages were written in order, if bits had been added or pages were missing. The Guildford Four spent sixteen years in prison before their conviction was finally declared 'unsafe and unsatisfactory' and reversed in 1989. In 1991 the six men who had been tried and convicted for murder in the Birmingham pub bombings had their sentences reversed and walked free. Each had been sentenced to twenty-one life sentences, of which they too had served sixteen years. No longer could anyone remain in any doubt that police officers could be bent. So, on the one hand, at Wellington Street my senior colleagues were fighting a whole other level of police corruption in these heavy cases involving alleged IRA terrorists and murderers and, on the other, there was I, fighting corruption and bent coppers on a very small scale – cases involving PCs on the beat who were verballing and stitching people up.

I was happy at Wellington Street. I had found my feet doing the police action work, and everything was going right; I was at one with life. Wellington Street was a tiny set of chambers, there were only eleven of us when I went there, about a quarter of us were people of colour, and it was like a family.

In the summer of 1989, I was invited with several others in

chambers to a boat party on the Thames. For whatever reason, I didn't go, but one of our colleagues, Linda Webster, did. She was on the *Marchioness* when it collided with the *Bowbelle*, a larger and heavier dredging barge, and sank. The following day at chambers, I got a telephone call from someone asking if I'd seen Linda. She hadn't come in and no one could contact her. Everyone was asking, 'Where's Linda? Where is she? Linda's not been home.' Later that night we heard that she had died on the *Marchioness*. It was like having a death in the family. Part of the soul of the place had gone. Linda was a rising star and would have gone on to be one of the great advocates at the Bar.

Afterwards, there was a change at Wellington Street. There was a real sorrow among us, and then unexpectedly our leader and leading light, Tony Gifford, who was to the outside world our head of chambers, gave an indication that he was planning to go to Jamaica to form a set of chambers to represent people on death row there.

With Linda's death, it was as if the spirit of Wellington Street had died a little too, and when news of Tony's imminent departure sank in, everyone began to question whether the chambers could survive. Tony was one of the biggest earners in the set, and once he said he was going, others started to talk about leaving. Wellington Street collapsed. Quite a few of my colleagues were, in fact, in talks to form a new set at Doughty Street. However, there was a lot of secrecy about the plans and I wasn't included in the discussions.

It was devastating. Wellington Street had been my home, and now I found myself potentially homeless. It made me question my judgement. The words of David Richardson came back to haunt me. He did not trust these radical lawyers. I felt I had made the biggest mistake of my career. I didn't know what to do or where to go. It was, however, easier to move sets as a

barrister, as opposed to a complete junior, because I had solicitors behind me, and I was doing some good work at the time,
work way beyond my call.

There were two sets of chambers with a similar ethos to
Wellington Street: Tooks Court, where Mike Mansfield QC
worked, and 2 Garden Court, which was then situated in the
Middle Temple. Tooks Court was predominantly a criminal
law set, although it handled some civil work. I went to talk
to the team there, but I was hesitant. Still scarred from my
experience at Redbridge Magistrates Court, I didn't want to
be pushed back into doing criminal cases. I knew that most of
the juniors at Tooks were expected to do crime. I decided that
I would talk to the senior clerk to see what sort of pressure he
would put on me and whether he would have my back. What
would he do, I asked him, if a solicitor declined to instruct
me because I was Black. The clerk's response shocked me. 'It
depends,' he said.

Once I heard that, there was no way I was going to that set.
Mike Mansfield called me to say there had been a misunder-
standing; the clerk was wrong. But it was too late; the damage
was done and I had made my mind up.

The other progressive set of chambers had the motto 'Do
right and fear no one'. This was 2 Garden Court, started by
six young, radical, politically committed lawyers led by a hippy
activist-type Scotsman called Ian Macdonald. A barrister notable as a pioneer of committed anti-racist legal practice, Ian's
reputation as a successful trial lawyer was forged in the 1970s
and '80s in the Black Parents Association and students' association cases in London and Manchester and the notorious Angry
Brigade, Balcombe Street siege and Mangrove Nine trials, the
latter of which was recently dramatised in Steve McQueen's
acclaimed *Small Axe* series for the BBC. These noteworthy

and hard-fought trials which challenged, among other issues, the unrepresentative composition of juries, unjust trial and prosecutorial procedures, police harassment of the Black community, racial injustice in housing, policing, prosecution and immigration decision-making, led to numerous key reforms within the criminal justice system. Alongside solicitor Gareth Peirce, his tireless work and campaigning on behalf of the Birmingham Six led ultimately to their acquittal and release in 1991. Ian also represented the families of the bereaved at the inquest into the New Cross Fire in 1984 and in 1998 he was leading counsel for Duwayne Brooks in the ground-breaking Lawrence Inquiry.

A kind, generous and straight-talking man, Ian loved recounting his battles with the establishment – particularly the story of when he applied to become a QC when the then Lord Chancellor, Lord Hailsham, is reputed to have said, 'Over my dead body!' Lord Hailsham died in 1987 and Ian finally took silk in 1988.

Garden Court could be a good home for me. So, I applied and interviewed successfully, and started there in July 1990. The rest, they say, is history. I celebrated thirty years here in 2020. Back in 1990, however, my career was about to take off in a way I could not even imagine.

I I

GARDEN COURT

'Civil liberties, from a working-class point of view, are
about having the space in which to engage in political
struggle – to organise alternative bases of power which
can lead to the transformation of society, to record the
struggle as it progresses and to express, in theory and
in practice, an independent class position. This space
is always contested and the occupation of any part of it
carries no security of tenure.'

Ian Macdonald QC, founding member,
Garden Court Chambers

Article 3
No one shall be subjected to torture or to inhuman
or degrading treatment or punishment.

Article 5
Everyone has the right to liberty and security
of person.

Like any person in a position of public authority, we expect
police officers to work within the law, to uphold impeccable
professional standards, treating everyone equally with fairness,

dignity and respect. For some, therefore, it can be a shock to realise that the people we trust to keep us safe are often guilty of abusing the most basic of our human rights.

I started at Garden Court as a junior barrister in July 1990. Here my police action practice took off in earnest. There are any number of reasons that a person may be compelled to take out a civil action against the police, but early in my career I was dealing most commonly with cases ranging from allegations of assault by a police officer or officers; instances of wrongful arrest and false imprisonment and malicious prosecution — where an unjust and inappropriate charge is made by the police against an individual for an improper motive; and with other forms of police misconduct leading to claims under the Human Rights Act.

In cases such as these — where a police officer has behaved in a way that breaks the law and/or has infringed a person's fundamental human rights, or does not meet accepted professional standards — there were and remain limited means of redress. Firstly, then as now, making a complaint to the police had little practical effect. Such complaints were an internal police matter, investigated by other police officers (then the Police Complaints Authority). Even today with the Independent Office of Police Conduct (IOPC), formerly the Independent Police Complaints Commission (IPCC), although it is overseen or investigated by an independent body, there is still little faith that those investigations are effective. Very few complaints resulted in criminal charges being brought against offending officers or with police officers being disciplined because the procedure is heavily weighted in their favour. In a few cases complainants have even been sued for libel by named police officers.

Secondly, on the rare occasion when criminal proceedings

were pursued against a police officer, it hardly ever resulted in justice. The simple fact is that, historically, in cases involving a member of the police force, juries are highly unlikely to return a guilty verdict leading to a criminal conviction. This is the case even today. For this reason, the Crown Prosecution Service (CPS) is reluctant to pursue a criminal case against a member of the law enforcement agencies.

Finally, a civil action for damages can be taken out against the commissioner of the Metropolitan Police for police claims brought in London, or against a chief constable for police claims brought against other police forces. In other words, the individual officers alleged to have committed police crimes are not personally held legally or financially accountable for their actions.

In cases where members of the public suffered unwarranted and unprovoked assaults by police officers, often those who were assaulted were arrested and subsequently charged with a criminal offence, most commonly that of assaulting a police officer or obstructing a police officer in the course of his/her duty. As *victims* of criminal assaults, they themselves have ended up in handcuffs, and often found themselves defending criminal charges in court. Rarely in such cases, however, was there any independent evidence of the alleged crime. It was the word of the police officers versus that of a member of the public, often an entirely innocent individual who has no idea why they were arrested, or perhaps had simply found him- or herself in the wrong place at the wrong time.

It may be hard to countenance or understand why any member of the police force would behave in this way, but, perversely, it seems likely that some arrests are made in order to justify the use of excessive and unreasonable force or violence against members of the public. Most commonly the charges brought against these individuals would be summary offences, i.e. minor offences that would most likely be tried by magistrates rather than in a Crown Court in front of a jury. Due to the close working relationship between magistrates and police officers, magistrates are generally more disposed to believe police officers than are juries. Thus, in essence, the police would use magistrates to draw a veil over their crimes by convicting the victim. Through this cynical process of criminalisation, the police deftly justify *their* unlawful conduct and simultaneously deflect public censure from themselves.

Understandably, people who have been wrongfully arrested, and/or subjected to an unprovoked assault by a member of the police, want justice. *They* are victims of a crime and, rightly, they expect that the person alleged to have committed a crime, police officer or not, will be charged, investigated and tried in a court. In reality the criminal justice system makes it exceptionally difficult to hold police officers to account.

Consequently, a civil action, in which a case for damages will be heard in a civil court in front of a civilian jury, can be the *only* form of justice for the often entirely innocent individual. Even then, civil actions against the police are far from straightforward and often the chances of making a successful claim are pitted against the claimant.

One of my earliest police cases after I started at Garden Court was 'an all-too typical story', so to speak. My clients were two young Black men. Late one evening, after they had been out together in north London, they were driving home when, for no good reason, they were flagged down by two police officers. The driver stopped, at which point the officers grabbed both from the car, pulled them over to the side of the road and separated them. My clients were fully compliant and were not being disrespectful to the police. Confused and unsettled at this turn of events, one of them asked the officer who was holding him – let's call him Officer A – why they had been stopped.

'Look, you don't get to ask us questions. We ask the questions, you answer them,' he was told.

Officer A then announced that he was going to perform a search, and he moved as if to put his hand in my client's pocket. Knowing all too well that it was not unheard of for the police to plant evidence on young Black men, my client objected, saying, 'I'll empty my own pockets.'

When he insisted on turning out his pockets unaided, a scuffle duly ensued, and Officer A promptly drew his colleague's attention to a small packet of cannabis lying nearby on the ground. Officer B then approached and wrestled my client to the ground. Observing this, my second client approached the police officers. It was all a big mistake, he told them, the cannabis had not been in his friend's pocket; it had nothing to do with them. Meanwhile, my first client was being subjected to a full search, all the while protesting his innocence. Nevertheless, the officers arrested him for possession of cannabis and his friend was summarily arrested for obstructing the police. During the course of the arrests both my clients were roughed up and handcuffed. A police van arrived soon thereafter, they were bundled in and driven to Edmonton police station, and the client's car was left at the side of the road.

On arrival at the station, the custody sergeant decided that he had sufficient evidence to charge my clients; in the early '90s you could be charged simply on the word of an arresting officer *just like that*, within moments of arrival at the police station.

My clients were detained for several hours before being

released on bail, given a charge sheet and given notice to attend the local magistrates' court the next day. In England and Wales, when you are arrested and charged for any criminal offence, your case is almost always heard in the first instance in the magistrates' court in front of two or three magistrates, or a district judge; this is your 'first appearance'. Most cases will be completed there, with less serious cases, or summary offences, such as minor assaults or motoring offences, being tried and sentenced by the magistrates. Only the more serious offences are passed on to the Crown Court, either for sentencing after the defendant has been found guilty in a magistrates' court, or for full trial with a judge and jury.

In my clients' case, at their first appearance they pleaded not guilty. The magistrates sent the case off for exchange of evidence against them, and set a date for a full trial some months later in the magistrates' court. My clients appointed solicitors, continued to insist on their innocence, and awaited the date of their full trial.

If you have never come into contact with the police and experienced an arrest, apart from the glaring fact at the heart of this case of the plain illegality and injustice of planting drugs, this might sound straightforward. But put yourself in the shoes of these two young men who had been driving home one evening in north London. Both were in their early twenties, one in a full-time job in IT, and neither had ever had any previous contact with the police.

Imagine going to bed that night, knowing that you would have to call into work the next morning to tell your employer that you wouldn't be in, and presumably have to give an account of the reason for your absence. Then, as in the case of my clients, imagine the further requests for time off work to attend meetings with lawyers or to report to the police station on bail conditions. Think of the disruption this will cause. Imagine then telling your family and your workmates that you are being sent to trial, the inevitable stress that you will experience in the weeks or months before the trial date, the worry and distress about what will happen should you be convicted.

At the ensuing trial at the magistrates' court, my clients were acquitted of all charges. Following the court case, they appointed me via their solicitors to take civil action against the police for wrongful arrest and false imprisonment, assault and malicious prosecution in that the original grounds for arrest were unfounded. It is possible to take civil action in the court against the police for damages or compensation as a result of any unlawful act, or omission, on the part of a police officer. However, this course is not to be entered into lightly. You are not guaranteed to win the case; indeed, successful actions against the police are rare.

Therefore, you should always take legal advice from a solicitor to establish whether the costs involved would be worthwhile. Legal aid might be available, but you might have to pay a contribution towards the expenses of the case.

However, the evidence was pretty clear: the young men had good records; neither had ever been in any trouble before; one of them had a position of some responsibility in a decent job; they were both reasonable and articulate in describing their experience. The legal basis for my clients' claim was airtight. In the UK, the burden of proving that an arrest and detention is justified falls on the police, once the fact of the detention is admitted. So, interestingly, a claimant does not have to prove that they were unlawfully arrested and detained; it is for the police officer to prove that he or she lawfully arrested and detained the individual. In that respect, civil actions are totally different to a criminal trial.

Secondly, assault: a police officer 'may use reasonable force, if necessary, in the exercise of the power',[*] but given that my clients were claiming a wrongful arrest, i.e. there were no reasonable grounds for suspicion in the case of their arrest, then it followed that the use of *any and all force* by the police officers was unlawful.

Finally, malicious prosecution (in other words, a criminal prosecution brought against someone without any proper or lawful reason). My clients' case fulfilled all the criteria needed to pursue this claim: that there had been a prosecution; that it had been determined in his or her favour; and it had caused him or her damage. This was undeniably true. To be successful in a malicious prosecution action, however, the claimant must *also* prove that the prosecution was brought *without* reasonable and probable cause, *and* that it was motivated by malice. This is less straightforward to prove, nevertheless I was confident that my clients would be successful.

Civil actions are tried in front of a jury who decides whether the complainants' claim for damages is upheld. Back then I thought, naively, that if they went into the court and gave their evidence well in the civil hearing, my clients would be believed, as they had been in the magistrates' court. However, even if you are rightly acquitted in the criminal court, it doesn't necessarily follow that you will win in the civil courts, for several reasons.

When it came down to weighing up and deciding where the truth lay, particularly in my clients' claim for a wrongful arrest, I believed – again, naively – that the jurors would bear in mind that we live in a free society. In that respect, it should have been easy for my clients who simply had to state honestly

---

[*] Police and Criminal Evidence Act 1984, Section 117.

what happened, *ergo* they were deprived of their liberty for no reason, or, indeed, for an improper reason.

The police trial was a real eye-opener. In this and many of my subsequent early police actions, what I repeatedly experienced was the unconscious bias of the judges to simply accept without question the evidence of police officers, particularly if they were in uniform when testifying. Furthermore, inevitably in most cases, the jury is influenced by how the judge sums up the case. As a young and idealistic lawyer, that was a devastating realisation for me, particularly in this case, because in his summing up the judge made these two young men look like liars, if not outright drug-crazed violent criminals, who had cynically pursued their case against upstanding police officers simply for the damages. I was shocked at how partisan the judge was. My clients lost their civil action. They left court not believing they had a fair crack at the whip for justice. It's one thing to lose and put that down to a jury not believing you; most clients can accept that. It is entirely another thing if you think the judge, who is meant to be a fair and impartial referee, blatantly took sides and then, as it were, steered a jury in a direction when they summed up the evidence.

Unfortunately, this was typical of the cases I was doing in the early '90s.

I2

MOVING HOUSE,
MARRIAGE AND MEGAN

They say three of the most stressful events in life are moving home, getting married and the birth of a child, particularly your firstborn. Angela and I did all three in 1992.

By the summer of 1991, we had been together for nearly a decade. We had reached the stage where we both had our careers, but were still living in different homes and really only seeing each other at weekends. Something needed to change. We would either go our separate ways or make a commitment to be with one another. If I am honest, I was scared and did not know what I really wanted at the time. We decided to take a break from each other, and during that short period, my work was as intense as ever and doing this very stressful job I felt incredibly lonely. So, towards the end of that year, I asked Angela if she wanted to resume our relationship. I took her away on a surprise holiday to Portugal and there I proposed to her. She accepted.

Back in London, we decided to set up home together. I put my flat on the market and started to look for a house in the Honor Oak area. Surprisingly, things happened much quicker than I expected. Within a week someone made an offer on my flat and a week later we found a beautiful old Victorian house nearby. It was in a poor state of repair, but we were young and I was excited by the big makeover challenge. (In some romantic and, I can now see, slightly naive way, I thought I was going to be like my childhood hero, TV lawyer Petrocelli, who was always building or repairing his house while working on knotty, high-stakes cases.) The reality was far from the Hollywood TV series, however. Everything in the house needed to be pulled out or repaired, from the death-trap electrics to the antediluvian plumbing, to the rotting roof. On top of that, the crumbling internal walls had to be replastered and decorated throughout the entire house. It was a veritable money pit and, despite working at Garden Court, where the money was now beginning to come in, I felt poorer than ever. I decided that I would live in the house while all these works were being done; I couldn't afford to live anywhere else and I certainly couldn't face the prospect of going back home to my parents after living independently from the age of seventeen. Utter madness when I think about those decisions now. We had also acquired two kittens (Tom and Queenie), which Angela had obtained on our relationship break and were now living with me among the chaos of house repairs. The cats didn't seem to mind the mess and I suppose it wasn't too bad for me either as I was away from home a lot, travelling up and down the country on cases. But it was a nightmare for Angela, who had discovered she was pregnant in February 1992. She was suffering terribly with morning sickness – actually a misnomer as she was suffering all day and night. This continued throughout the entire pregnancy, with some respite in August for a few weeks before the sickness resumed. It was so bad that by the time we were ready to properly move into the house in April 1992, she decided to move back home to be with her mother.

As we had agreed to get married before Angela's pregnancy, I thought that we may as well do it before the baby was born. Old-fashioned thinking, but this is what we did. So, between working hours, travelling to and from cases, I was supervising the building works at the house *and* organising our wedding as Angela was too ill to do so. We got married on 14 August 1992. It was a small affair with just close friends and family. I took a break from the house repairs and work and organised a honeymoon weekend retreat in an old country manor house in York. Then we returned to London life and the madhouse with the cats and the builders.

Things only became more complicated. Our builder turned out to have a serious drinking problem. This came to light when we started to discover countless empty cans of Tennent's Super 14% proof lager all over the house. We then witnessed how he would start the day with a can of Tennent's instead of the habitual mug of builders' tea. In the end I had to end the contract because it transpired that all the work he was doing was unsafe and would have to be re-done. It was a real pity as I liked him and at that stage in my life I hadn't had to fire anyone for anything. Shortly afterwards, in early 1993, we learned that the builder had been suffering with depression and had taken his own life.

Megan Amy Thomas was born on 10 November 1992. In fact, we both thought she would be a boy. I hadn't wanted to know the sex of our child beforehand as I thought it would be a lovely surprise, but because of the shape of Angela's tummy and how big she was, in my head I had convinced myself that it must have been a boy inside her. I got that wrong.

The day Angela went into labour was stressful. She was giving birth in the maternity suite of St George's Hospital in south London, the nearest hospital to her mother's house.

I travelled over to the hospital with a stereo cassette player, scented candles and a selection of music tapes to play during the birth. I had to do an urgent advice on a judicial review emergency application for some clients and because I did not know how long Angela would be in labour, I also took with me my huge and very heavy laptop computer together with piles of papers to read. I would be the first to admit I had my priorities completely wrong. I realised that I too had an addiction – not to alcohol like my builder, but to work.

Megan was born, all of 6lbs with a head full of beautiful black curls and the loudest set of lungs you could imagine. We had not really thought about just how much our lives were about to change. When we three arrived home, Angela and I soon discovered two key things about babies: firstly, they sleep when they are good and ready to sleep. They have no concept of *your* schedule. And secondly, some babies suffer badly from gripe pains. Megan did not sleep to routine and she was an incredibly gripey baby. No amount of rocking, singing or walking with her would send her to sleep. The sleepless nights would continue for the next two years. Angela and I were struggling to function with barely an hour's sleep every night. It was incredibly tough on us and our fledgling marriage. Eventually I discovered that Megan would fall asleep if she was driven in the car, so at times at 2 or 3 o'clock in the morning I would be out driving with her in her car seat. She would be fast asleep, but as soon as I got home and was lifting the baby seat out of the car, her eyes would pop open again and she would start crying and I would have to get back in the car and drive some more. But such are the joys of parenthood and, as difficult as those times were, I look back at them with love and a smile to myself.

13

THIS COURT IS NOT A GAME OF *THE PRICE IS RIGHT*: CIVIL ACTIONS AND THE CASE AGAINST THE POLICE

By the time Megan arrived in 1992, my caseload had grown exponentially. Now I was used to the pressures of a seemingly unending stream of civil actions against the police. With each case, as I was honing and flexing my advocacy skills, I was growing in confidence too. In order to win a case and obtain the best possible compensation for my client, I found that the more outrage I could muster in my speeches, and the better I could convey to the jury that this could happen to any one of them, the higher the damages awarded. And, more importantly, the greater the chance (hopefully) that the police would not allow such a wrongful arrest – or false imprisonment, or inhuman assault, or other misconduct in a public role – *ever* to be repeated again. This was my aim.

On the defence side, the barristers for the police would tell the members of the jury to keep their feet on the ground: that the claimant was only taking the civil action because they were after the money, that any award of high damages would equate to taking a police officer off the street. They would say things like, 'Ladies and gentlemen of the jury, if you are going to compensate the claimants for the wrongs they suffered, think of an appropriate sum. For example, think of the price of a new television or the cost of a good holiday.'

I remember talking to the late Tony Jennings QC about his civil actions against the police. Tony was a former colleague in Garden Court, and later at Matrix Chambers, and one of the best and funniest advocates I have known. He was a criminal brief but did the occasional civil police action. I was always interested in hearing the techniques of a successful litigation, and Tony had recently secured an award of hundreds of thousands of pounds for one of his clients. I asked him how he'd managed it. In his charming Irish brogue he said, 'Well, Leslie, I listened to the police barristers telling the jurors to think of the price of a top-notch colour television, and a good foreign holiday and so on, and then I looked the jurors in the eye and said, "Ladies and gentlemen, this court is not a game of *The Price Is Right*. Remember that we are talking about serious police misconduct here."'

That year, I was instructed by a firm of solicitors in Hackney to represent an elderly Jamaican couple. In this case, I was led by one of my mentors at Garden Court, the great Courtenay Griffiths QC. Courtenay is regarded as one of the most revered criminal briefs of his generation and an outstanding advocate, but he hadn't done a police trial before. As his junior I was the civil litigator and he was the jury advocate. I, therefore, was the one to teach him everything I had learned about how to approach the summing-up address to the jury in this case.

In January 1989, Marie Burke, a 73-year-old great-grandmother, and a family friend, George Edwards, had been involved in a minor accident in the Burkes' car. No one had been injured and they returned home to alert the police to the incident. Shortly thereafter, police officers arrived at their home, pushed past Mrs Burke and wrongly arrested her 79-year-old disabled husband Edgar, dragging him outside in only his long johns, vest and socks. When Mrs Burke ran outside with a water jug and a diabetes pill for her husband, she was wrestled to the ground by a female officer. Two more officers arrived to pin her down. As Mrs Burke lay sprawled, held down by three police officers, her dress had ridden up over her head. A passer-by had witnessed the incident and supported Mrs Burke's account, saying that the officers seemed to have 'deliberately tried to inflict as much pain as possible'. Putting aside the rights and wrongs of what had happened, look at the optics of it: insensitive policing, or subjecting two frail, vulnerable, blameless individuals to rough and degrading treatment?

Mrs Burke was taken to Hackney police station, searched and prosecuted for assault. The charge was dropped two days later and our claim was that it had been brought maliciously by the female police officer and that the police conduct had been calculated to humiliate and distress. As Courtenay said in his speech to the jury, 'These officers behaved in an arbitrary, oppressive and unconstitutional way.'

The jury decided by a majority of seven to one that Mrs Burke had indeed been assaulted, falsely imprisoned and maliciously prosecuted. However, the jurors dismissed the civil action brought on similar grounds by Mr Burke and the claim that police officers had entered Mr and Mrs Burke's home without permission.

When the result came in, Courtenay and I were of course delighted that we had won in relation to Mrs Burke's case, but shocked that the claim by Mr Burke had been denied, and that may have shown on our faces. I don't know if the jury felt guilty about not finding in favour of both clients, but they announced that Mrs Burke should be paid £20,000 by the Metropolitan Police commissioner in compensation for the assault, another £15,000 for false imprisonment and £15,000 for the malicious prosecution. At the time, that award of £50,000 was one of the highest awards of damages in history, and now it was the turn of the police and their defence barristers to be in shock. The jury had done the right thing by this couple.

This case opened the eyes of the juries on police civil actions and during the 1990s the awards of damages against the Metropolitan Police commissioner and other police forces across the country went through the roof. One of my clients was awarded £75,000 for a relatively minor wrongful arrest and malicious prosecution case. Another of Courtenay's clients, who had been assaulted and incurred head injuries from a baton strike, received damages of £325,000. Courtenay was on a roll, but this level of damage awards wouldn't last.

Later, when I had more experience in conducting civil actions against the police, I was instructed on a claim of false imprisonment, wrongful arrest, malicious prosecution and assault involving a young blind woman, Ms B. This was one of the first cases on which I was instructed by Andre Clovis, a young Black solicitor a couple of years older than me, from a Brixton law firm, Hallmark Atkinson Wynter. Over the course of the following decades, he and I would frequently team up together.

I have been involved in cases involving some real inhumanity over my career, but this is one that I can never forget. At the time of the incident in 1996, my client was twenty-five years old, living within a stone's throw of Peckham police station with her three young children. Ms B had sole responsibility for her children's daily care, with the help of her mother, her sister and other members of her family and friends. Ms B's brother had died in 1994 of cancer. On the afternoon of Saturday 6 July 1996, a man calling himself 'P' had come to Ms B's house, along with an unnamed female, saying that he wanted to pay his condolences to her mother. The woman had not introduced herself, nor spoken to Ms B, who was with her children in the living room watching TV, and after a short while had asked if she could use the telephone to order a taxi. In due course, a mini cab arrived and the woman left the house. The following morning, Ms B's mother came to tell her that the cab driver had called at the house to say that the woman from the day before had run off without paying her fare. Ms B wondered why he had not returned the same day, then thought nothing more of the matter.

Later that day, the doorbell rang again. Ms B opened the door to two police officers, a male and a female. They were there to investigate the incident of the woman and the unpaid cab fare. Ms B explained that the woman had come to her house with a man, she was not known to her and had not introduced herself. The police officers did not believe her and became more insistent that she provide them with the woman's details. Their tone was becoming ever more aggressive and my client was frightened. Her children were distressed. She finally told the police officers that there was nothing more that she could say to assist them further, and she tried to close the door. However, the door flew back in Ms B's face and she heard her daughter scream as though she had been struck. Her right bicep was suddenly held in a tight grip, she was pulled out of the house and, flailing, she felt what appeared to be hair in her hand. Instantly, intense pressure was applied to her wrist and forearm by the male officer, who was screaming at her to let go of the other officer's hair. My client's mother and her sister were crying out that my client was blind, that the officers should let go of her. Nevertheless, the male officer continued to bend her wrist back painfully.

Ms B was pulled into the street and dragged in her bare feet to a police van, while her children stood crying in the doorway. When her sister pleaded to be allowed to go with her, she was refused. Ms B had not been told that she was under arrest, nor the reasons for her being dragged from her home and taken into custody. On arrival at the police station, she was half-pulled, half-walked into the police station. Around her, she heard police officers laughing, but none of them spoke to her nor helped guide her in any way.

At the station, she heard a female voice telling her that she was under arrest for assaulting a police officer. Now very scared and crying, when she tried to give her account of the incident, she was told to be quiet. I think that's when they actually realised that my client was blind, despite the fact that both she, her mother and her sister had been telling the police officers that she could not see since they arrived at her door.

After an hour or more, her sister arrived at the station. Eventually an officer informed my client that they would not be pressing charges. Before she could be released, however, she was asked to sign a document declaring that the whole incident was her fault. Ms B remonstrated and asked for a solicitor, but was told that if she did not sign the document and admit to the allegation, she would have to wait for the paperwork to be completed and for her legal representative to attend, in which case she would be detained for a further forty-five hours. Frightened and in distress at being separated from her small children, Ms B agreed to sign the document. It was, in fact, a police caution for the claim of assault on an officer.

One can barely imagine the distress and fear of being

manhandled out of one's home and into police custody for no good reason. But given my client's blindness and physical frailties, the actions of the police on that Sunday afternoon seem all the more unconscionable. The experience took its toll on the whole family. Ms B suffered chronic post-traumatic stress disorder. She was frightened to be left alone, had recurrent nightmares and trouble sleeping. Her youngest boy developed behavioural problems and anxiety counselling.

After two years, in spite of a letter to my client's solicitor from the CPS admitting that 'the arrest was unlawful and therefore constituted an assault and false imprisonment', no disciplinary action was taken against any of the police officers, nor did Ms B receive any form of apology. Subsequently, I was instructed to represent her in a civil action case. I wanted the case to be heard in front of a jury so that the officers would be held to account, but in the end, we didn't go to court; somebody saw good sense and the civil action was settled.

This case opened my eyes. It led me to believe that if this blind young mother could be arrested and detained – somebody who is vulnerable, who is in her home with small children – it could happen to any of us. You just have to be in the wrong place at the wrong time.

Mrs B never did find out who 'P' and that woman were, nor why they had come to her house on that fateful day.

I 4

POLICE AND THIEVES IN THE STREET: BRIXTON POLICE

In the '90s, a large proportion of my work consisted of hearings arising from stop-and-search incidents involving the Brixton police. Almost a decade on from the Brixton Riots, Lord Scarman's report, and the scrapping of the 'sus' laws, little had changed to improve police community relations in Brixton, especially with an over-policed Black community. In 1989, the new Prevention of Terrorism Act, introduced specifically to combat Irish terrorism, had granted even greater stop-and-search powers to the police.* It could be used to search anyone, *without* specific suspicion, and again, the police had been using it to stop and search Black and Asian youths. The police in Brixton had a poor reputation for playing fast and loose with their interpretation of 'reasonable grounds'. My client, Mr H, was just one of many young Black men to experience this first-hand.

At about 4 p.m. on the afternoon of Wednesday 12 December 1990, Mr H, who worked as a clerk for Lambeth council, was travelling through Brixton in a two-door Volkswagen Golf

---

* Under the Terrorism Act 2000, these became 'Section 44 powers'.

convertible car with four other Black men. Back then, being in a car with a group of young Black men would in itself be enough to rouse the suspicion of the police and, sure enough, as they turned off Brixton Hill they were followed by plain-clothes police officers of the Territorial Support Group (TSG) on burglary patrol in an unmarked van. Mr H and his companions pulled up at the address of Mr H's fellow back-seat passenger, who went into his house to collect some videos. The driver also got out and was then approached by one of the TSG officers. Another officer rapped on the car window and said he wanted a word with Mr H's friend in the front seat, but was given the brush-off. At this point, the officer talking to the driver grabbed hold of him and, with the help of a third officer, forcefully searched him. Seeing this, Mr H and his friend got out of the car and protested, 'There's no need for that.' They did not physically intervene; they were not aggressive, nor did they use abusive language. Ten more police officers arrived at the scene. Mr H kept his cool, even when one of the police constables pushed him against the garden wall and told him that he was going to search him. He gave no reason for the search, nor did he state his name or his police station – the first in a series of breaches of the provisions of the Police and Criminal Evidence Act. When the PC made to reach into Mr H's pocket, Mr H objected. He would turn out his own pockets. 'You might try and fit me up,' at which he was told, 'You're nicked.' When Mr H asked why the officer replied, 'You'll find out later.' Another breach of the Police and Criminal Evidence Act.

On arrival at Brixton police station, Mr H was taken into a cell and strip-searched. They found nothing. He was held for almost three hours before being charged with threatening behaviour and obstructing the police.

At the trial in front of the stipendiary magistrate the police officers said, under oath, that their reason for following Mr H and his friends that afternoon was because the car's number plate had been flagged as suspicious on the police radio earlier in the day. When pressed by the magistrate to corroborate this claim, the police officers were unable to produce the police log. As for the grounds for Mr H's arrest and subsequent strip-search, they cited obstructive, aggressive and threatening conduct. According to the officers, Mr H had thus rendered a search in the street impossible. They said Mr H had taunted them, 'You're only doing this because we fuck all your white women.' Having heard the police evidence, the magistrate acquitted Mr H of both charges without hearing the defence.

Mr H wrote to the Police Complaints Authority. He received no apology and none of the TSG officers nor those involved at Brixton station were disciplined. Subsequently, I represented Mr H in his civil claim against the Metropolitan Police commissioner for false arrest, wrongful imprisonment, assault and malicious prosecution. His case finally went to trial in 1997.

In the past, Black clients would likely have been told that they had no chance going up against so many white police officers. I never took that position. In Mr H's case, despite the odds, I was prepared to believe in him, particularly given the fact that the police had failed to provide the log to justify the initial reason for the stop. Nor could I believe the police officers' account of his behaviour. A slightly built, quietly spoken and unassuming council worker, Mr H was instantly likable. More importantly, as his subsequent strip-search demonstrated, he had nothing to hide. As I told the jury, the police case was 'nonsense'.

When Mr H gave his evidence, the jury were faced with two extreme versions of events. They believed my client and effectively found that the police officers had repeatedly lied under oath – in two different courts – and awarded damages of £45,000.

At the time this was a significant award, sending a clear message to the Metropolitan Police – and they knew it. Sir Paul Condon, then commissioner of the Metropolitan Police, appealed the decision in the Court of Appeal. In his judgment, Lord Justice May concluded:

> The amount of exemplary damages was high. [. . .] I am nevertheless persuaded that there are exceptional circumstances in this case, such that this court should not interfere with the jury's award [which] showed beyond any doubt that they took a poor view of the conduct of the police. They had heard evidence in a contested trial, [and] they were invited to conclude that the conduct of the police had the added aggravation of being racially motivated. They certainly thought that high awards were justified.

The Met lost. My client kept his award for damages.

15

A DEATH IN POLICE CUSTODY

'Police Deny Failing to Help HIV Prisoner'

Portsmouth News, 30 April 1996

In late April 1996 when I did my first inquest involving a death in police custody, I was a very junior counsel. It was a real baptism of fire. I was instructed to represent the mother of a young man who had died in a police station in Hampshire. At that time, it was generally thought by many in the profession that inquests were not 'important' cases. If one was representing the interest of the family, inquest work was not lucrative, since there was no legal aid for the clients involved. I did this first case pro bono, and I believed this was why such work was readily available for junior members of the Bar.

I had a couple of days to prepare for the hearing at the Portsmouth Coroner's Court and I didn't know where to start. There was no disclosure of evidence before the commencement of the hearing: I received nothing beyond the back sheet from the solicitors and a witness statement from the mother of the deceased. My clients' son, M, had died while being restrained by the police. He was a drug addict and had taken a significant amount of drugs on the day of his death. He had been arrested, struggled with several police officers, suddenly gone limp and died. Other than these bare details, I had absolutely no information about the case. I had no post-mortem report. There was no disclosure of police witness statements: I therefore did not know what the police officers would say about M's death. Nor did I have any idea about what to expect in an inquest hearing, least of all what was expected of me.

I asked various members of my chambers for guidance and they pointed me to the textbooks on the subject, but there were only two reference books at the time. I tracked down a heavy black-letter tome called *Jervis on Coroners*. This, I was told, was the leading text on inquest law. A daunting volume written in the complicated language of legal theory and arcane case law, I found it impenetrable. Jervis told me all about the great history of the coroner's court and the finer aspects of coronial law, including treasure. Yes, treasure: traditionally, coroner's courts deal with treasure troves, so if somebody finds some ancient Viking gold buried in their field, that is dealt with in a coroner's court. But although I had discovered that fascinating snippet, Jervis was anything but a practical guide. I was none the wiser about how to actually do an inquest case.

My colleagues advised me that the inquest proceedings would be a short matter and so I turned up in Portsmouth thinking it would be a simple affair. It was not. My first impressions on entering the courtroom were daunting. The hearing was presided over by the deputy coroner. There were three police officers to give evidence and they were represented by very senior counsel. The chief constable was separately represented, again by a very senior barrister. Immediately, I felt heavily outnumbered. I noted that, although they had different clients, both barristers acting for the police interest sat alongside each other and were constantly conferring. I was excluded from all their discussions. Despite the fact that I had read in the books that the inquest was not like a usual trial, that it was not adversarial and so there were no parties, it certainly felt that way. It was me and the bereaved parent against them.

I looked around the court. I saw that the police chief constable's barrister had a big bundle of documents; the barrister representing the other officers had a big bundle of documents; the Portsmouth coroner likewise. This was no small quick hearing. It was intense and complicated. I sat empty-handed, beside me a grieving mother. I didn't know how to deal with such grief. I asked her what had happened and what she knew about her son's death. She told me she hadn't been there, so she couldn't say anything for certain, but she did know there had been a number of independent witnesses and she did not see them at court. Where were they?

I approached the coroner and asked to see his witness list. His manner, I felt, was instantly cold and hostile towards me, but he reluctantly handed me the sheet of paper, muttering: 'If you must, Mr Thomas.' The independent witnesses and bystanders at the time of the police arrest were not listed. I couldn't understand why the coroner wouldn't want to call these witnesses to give evidence in front of the court and so I queried this. But the coroner simply said he wasn't going to call them. He had reviewed their witness statements and had decided there was not much they could add to the evidence, so he was going to read those out himself. I obviously hadn't seen their witness statements and so asked if I could do so. Again, reluctantly, the coroner grumbled, 'If you must, Mr Thomas.' I remember thinking that the law was supposed to be a gentleman's game, and, well, it just seemed to me that this was not playing fair; I was handicapped from the get-go.

The jury was sworn, the witnesses were called. When the hearing got underway and I heard the evidence for the first time, I was shocked. M had died in the police station a year earlier in May 1995; he was thirty-nine, unemployed, had a serious illness (he was HIV positive) and had a heavy drug habit. On the night of his death, police officers had gone to an infamous housing estate in the area to investigate reports of a flasher on the prowl in the area. Seeing M on a bicycle, which they suspected him of stealing, the officers gave chase. When cornered, M had kept riding straight at the senior officer, the two collided and ended up sprawled on the ground with M struggling to make his escape. The sergeant immediately jumped on M's back to restrain him, but he had continued to violently struggle. Other officers arrived and they dragged M to a grass verge at the side of the road, laid him face down and cuffed him with his hands behind his back. When a police van arrived, the officers asked him to turn on his side and bring his knees up to his waist, but M did not respond and made no movement. The officers lifted him and put him face down inside a cage at the back of the vehicle. He was no longer struggling and lay motionless on the floor of the cage.

On arrival at the station at about 2.30 p.m., when officers went to take M from the van, no pulse was found and an ambulance was called. A paramedic later told the inquest that he had found M lying on his front and he showed no signs of life. When he turned him over, his face was bloodied. Finding no pulse or heart activity, the paramedic made an attempt to resuscitate him before deciding to take M to hospital, where he was pronounced dead.

The cause of death in this case was uncertain and there was

a complicating factor in that prior to his arrest and restraint M had taken a large amount of drugs. The question which the inquest would consider, therefore, was whether this was a drug-related death or if M had died as a result of being restrained.

The family believed that not only had the officers used unnecessary and unreasonable force in the arrest, but that the police had also been guilty of negligence and misconduct by failing to check M's health and to administer vital first aid. They also suspected that the reason they had neglected to do so was because the officers involved clearly knew M from previous incidents and were aware of his HIV status.

On the first day of the inquest, the Home Office pathologist Dr Roger Ainsworth told the jury that M had died from acute heart failure which he believed had been caused by an overdose, the effects of long-term intravenous drug use, but also partly by a stress-induced adrenaline surge as a result of the arrest. The pathology evidence was equivocal, therefore: the drugs had played a part, but the struggle was also a factor. However, the pathologist did not consider the manner of restraint used by the police. And at this point in my career, I didn't yet know that people could die as a result of being forcibly restrained in the wrong position. I hadn't even heard of the concept of positional asphyxia. This first case was one of the reasons I would later become an expert in the field.

The coroner called the three police officers in turn to give their evidence. When each went into the witness box, he produced a notebook. Before I questioned them on their evidence, I asked the coroner if I could see the police officers' statements and their incident report books. The police barristers objected. The coroner was exasperated, puffing, 'Oh, Mr Thomas, you are really being awkward.' Clearly in mind to uphold their objection, the coroner reluctantly allowed me to see the note-books, but only while the officers were already in the witness box, so that I had to read them then and there. When I asked my questions, I was repeatedly hurried by the coroner: 'Do get on with it, Mr Thomas. You are really making life very difficult for us.'

It was awful. And on top of all that, I was dealing with a bereaved mother who could not come to terms with the sudden and unexplained death of her son. As inexperienced as I was, I was totally unprepared for how to cope with her grief.

In giving evidence, the senior officer in charge on the night of M's death denied that he, nor anyone else, knew who the suspect was at the time of the arrest and so could not have known that he was HIV positive. All the police officers involved denied any mistreatment of M or the use of any unnecessary force when they tackled him to the ground. 'The force needed to be used because he was violent and struggling,' one police constable testified. He also said in evidence that he thought M might have been pretending to be unconscious when he had placed him in the back of the van, that another had checked for a pulse in M's neck and nodded, which the officer had assumed meant that he had found one. He said, 'When he was on the ground I was not conscious of any time that he was not wriggling until I asked him to roll on his side and put his knees to his chest. When this has happened on previous occasions with prisoners, they have been bluffing [. . .] and then trying to make their escape. I didn't think there was anything wrong with him at that stage.'

Most crucially, however, this police constable's evidence discredited that of his senior officer: he said that having become concerned about the suspect's wellbeing after the van arrived at the police station, he had been handed a pair of rubber gloves with which to handle him because it was known that M was HIV positive. The officers were all too familiar with M; indeed, they referred to him by his pet name which was often used at the station.

When I questioned the senior officer, I accused him several times of lying and earned myself yet another stern reprimand from the coroner for my accusations. But it was clear there were multiple contradictions in the police officers' evidence and the facts about M's arrest and death, and that one of the police officers, I suspected, was lying to cover up the potential gross negligence and misconduct which had arguably led to the unnecessary death of my client's son.

In most of the other cases I had acted in at that point in my career, at the close of evidence, the lawyer representing each interested party had an opportunity to address the jury. And so, at the end of the hearing, I stood up and asked the coroner if I could now deliver my arguments to the jury. With yet another ill-tempered *harrumph*, I was told to sit down and that, of course, I couldn't! I was only permitted to address the coroner on matters of the law and make my case to him as to why he should leave this verdict as opposed to another. Then as now, the coroner had the sole discretion to direct the jury on which verdicts they may deliver. I sat down without another word.

The jury returned an open verdict attesting that they were unhappy with the evidence presented for them and that there was an indication that M's death may have been avoided had not the police used the excessive restraint methods during the arrest. In the end, all my awkward questions, which had so greatly exasperated the coroner, had perhaps managed to convince the jury that the police were implicated in the death.

It was a significant victory, but it had been a horrible experience from the outset. I hadn't had the benefit of seeing crucial evidence in disclosure; the other barristers had been hostile; the coroner had been condescending, rude and unsympathetic. It seemed to me that the police barristers and the coroner saw their roles as just to shut everything down. 'How was this justice?' I thought. It wasn't. It was an experience I will never forget and I was determined it was one that would never happen again.

That said, while I learned so much through error in Portsmouth, to do an inquest in the mid- to late '90s was horribly difficult and dispiriting. At that time, and until the introduction of the Human Rights Act 1998, the coronial system in England and Wales was governed by Section 8 of the 1988 Coroner's Act. Under this authority, the inquest was purely a fact-finding process in which the role of the coroner, or the coroner's jury where there was one, was limited. Their task was to say *who* the deceased was and *how*, *when* and *where* the deceased came by their death. They were to decide 'by what means' the deceased came by their death, but not 'in what circumstances'. Their verdict was to be a brief, neutral, factual statement. In other words, the role of an inquest was not to apportion guilt or attribute blame. It was not a means to hold the state to account.

Although, then as now, the inquest was a non-adversarial legal case, as the representative for the family, my role was to fight for an open, fair and rigorous investigation and to ensure that the relatives learned the truth about how their loved one had died. Back then, the most demanding aspect of an inquest for both the clients and for me as their advocate was undoubt-edly the coroner's broad discretion to deny any disclosure of witness statements or material prior to the hearing. Inevitably, I had to spend a lot of time and energy in securing disclosure, then in carefully identifying gaps in such evidence. Another hurdle, as I was to discover time and time again, was that under the 1988 Coroner's Act, there was a lax interpretation of the disclosure of evidence. The police were not legally obliged to produce evidence that the family and I might have considered vital in a timely fashion – indeed, if at all. A lot of time also had to be spent preparing the family for both these problems and the possible agonising revelations that such disclosure might produce, especially when often they might be learning for the first time painful details of the last hours or moments of their loved one's life.

Often, as in the case of M's death, the stress for the family was only exacerbated by the attitude of the coroner. For some of the more conservative coroners, there was an abhorrence of the notion that a family would directly seek to politicise their bereavement. As a result, they were the coroners most likely to want to place limits on the scope of the inquest: they didn't seem to understand the benefit for the family of considering the wider context of a death, often believing wrongly that it served only to make things worse for the family. I therefore often found myself preparing families for the frustrations and anger that might arise when faced with the potentially negative, defensive and obstructive stances that some coroners would adopt. This could be incredibly stressful, because generally bereaved families felt entitled to have a more assertive participation in the process. As far as the etiquette and formalities of the old-fashioned and fusty coroner's courts were concerned, my clients were often as ignorant as I was of the rules of the game. Furthermore, given the shock and grief at the tragedy that had befallen them, and given that they had no material remedy to gain from the inquest proceedings – only the truth – they were sometimes, understandably perhaps, less willing to play by those rules.

Hardest of all, though, was learning how to manage the family's grief and their anger. In an inquest where the stakes are high, there is always the danger of the family being too verdict-centred. Even if an inquest does manage to expose unlawful, inhuman or unfit treatment of the deceased, because of the limitations of the verdicts a jury or coroner can return, the verdict may not reflect such findings. Further, even if an unlawful killing verdict *is* returned, more often than not the people responsible are unlikely to face any further sanction.

When a lawful killing, misadventure or open verdict is returned, the families can feel bitterly betrayed. And even though I may feel that I have failed, then as now, a big part of my job is to counsel the family against judging the success of the inquest on the basis of that verdict. It is only through experience that I have understood that perhaps the primary role of any lawyer representing a family at an inquest is to put them in a position where they are able to make their own judgement on how their loved one met his or her death.

16

THE QUESTION OF RESTRAINT

'. . .but until that moment I had never realized what
it means to destroy a healthy, conscious man. When
I saw the prisoner step aside to avoid the puddle,
I saw the mystery, the unspeakable wrongness, of
cutting a life short when it is in full tide.'

George Orwell, 'A Hanging'

Nearly fifteen years after the 1981 riots, there was new unrest
in Brixton, again triggered by the death in custody of a young
Black man and anger at policing in the community. In the early
hours of 5 December 1995, following reports of a break-in
and burglary at knifepoint of a young couple in bed, Wayne
Douglas had been pursued by police through the streets near
the scene of the alleged crime. At around 2.30 a.m. Brixton
police officers succeeded in making an arrest and Wayne was
taken to Brixton station. One hour later, lying handcuffed in a
cell, his heart stopped beating. On arrival at hospital, Wayne
was declared dead. He was twenty-five years old.

No contact was made with Wayne's family. The following
evening his sister, Lisa Douglas-Williams, saw a report that a

man had died at Brixton police station. Unable to get in touch with her brother, Lisa rang the station and asked the custody officer if Wayne was in custody, but was told no straight away. The following afternoon a police inspector called to tell her about the robbery and Wayne's death. When she went to formally identify Wayne's body, Lisa discovered that the post-mortem had already been completed: it indicated that he had died of heart failure due to an underlying condition. But Wayne was young, fit and healthy: it didn't add up.

By December 1995 I'd been at Garden Court for about five years. When I heard the news of Wayne's death, I was working on a number of police trials and police actions, busy doing paperwork and also getting ready for the usual hectic Christmas holidays at home with a toddler. My life at the time was chaotic. It was a mixture of juggling childcare, getting up very early each day working on briefs, crazy dashes across London to take trains to other parts of the country, and then travelling back home often very late into the evening for the madness to start all over again. On those days I was working in London, I was extremely grateful because it allowed me to spend a bit of time with Megan. She was growing quickly and I realised I was missing this and important milestones in her life. But the cases, especially the controversial ones, just kept coming. Moreover, if the case was particularly interesting, I found it difficult not to accept the new instructions. Wayne's case was one such instruction and, more importantly, his death took place in south London, more or less near where I lived. I felt compelled to act for his grieving family.

The circumstances surrounding the death of another young Black man at the hands of the police and the statements issued by Scotland Yard in the days following were hugely controversial and once again sparked riots in a community where grief was so often coloured with outrage. Not only were the police not mounting proper investigations into the deaths of Black people, but now they were also killing us.

A week after Wayne's death, a hundred or so family members, friends and people from the local community gathered outside Brixton police station in a peaceful demonstration in protest at this latest police-related death. Emotions were running high and when the protesters began a march down Brixton Road, some were chanting 'Killers, killers, killers' at the police in full riot gear lining the route. The police presence at the demonstration was later described as 'incredibly heavy-handed'. The standoff between the police and protesters quickly escalated into violence. Shops were looted and several cars were set on fire.

The inquest in December 1996 into Wayne's death was my first really big case, and my second involving a death in custody following restraint by the police. It would also be the first of several similar cases I would work on involving the Brixton police.

In light of the outcome of a number of recent high-profile inquests and inquiries into the deaths of Black people in custody, which had been attracting especial cause for concern, we knew that Wayne's inquest might be the focus of heightened media attention. Just months earlier, in August 1996, in the same week that the inquest in front of Southwark Coroner Sir Montague Levine into the killing of Brian Douglas returned a verdict of death by misadventure,* we learned that the Crown Prosecution Service had decided not to pursue a criminal prosecution against any of the officers connected with Wayne's death.

---

* Brian Douglas (no relation to Wayne) died in May 1995 after being struck by a new American-style police baton.

A month later, the Home Office published for the first time numbers of deaths in custody for all police forces in England and Wales in the year 1995–96, and had provided information retrospectively on the numbers of deaths over several years. It had risen sharply: fifty deaths in custody were recorded from March 1995 to April 1996;* nineteen people had died in police stations, of which thirteen were in London. The new report also shed light on police complaints and discipline in police forces in England and Wales: in the same period, ninety-eight officers had been dismissed; sixty-three had resigned following disciplinary hearings or suspensions from duty; and charges had been brought against 410 officers, 117 of which were as a direct result of complaints by members of the public. Nine police officers implicated in a death in custody had faced either disciplinary or criminal charges as a result of Police Complaints Authority investigations, but none so far had been found guilty.

After my first inquest into the death of a young man in police custody – in which the question for the coroner was whether his death was restraint-related or drugs-related – I had vowed that never again would I be bullied or pushed around in a coroner's court. Wayne's inquest was held at Southwark Crown Court in November 1996 in front of Sir Montague Levine, or Sir Monty as he was affectionately known, and this time I was ready.

The inquest was extremely contentious from the outset. In Wayne's case, given his actions in robbing a couple at knifepoint while they lay in bed, there is no doubt that the jury's sympathies were likely to lean towards the police. However, as in many of the cases I work on, the fact remained that in this country we pride ourselves on our trust in due process,

---

* In the calendar year 1995 there were thirty-nine deaths in custody; in 1994 there were thirty-eight deaths.

we do not have the death penalty, and Wayne did not deserve to die as a result of his arrest. Three members of the jury had to be replaced after two said they had links with police and later one said she 'could not cope'. Furthermore, early in the proceedings, Sir Monty made a point of addressing the court to warn against harassment of witnesses. 'I am mindful that emotions and feelings have been running extremely high concerning the demise of Wayne Douglas,' he said. This was given as a general caution, yet who exactly was he warning off? The police pathologists? The police officers or the police surgeon? The only reasonable assumption was that he had directed the admonition at the family and friends of the deceased, and while he might not intentionally have meant to cause offence, it was undoubtedly insulting and hurtful for them to feel singled out as potential firebrands. Remember, this was the first and perhaps only opportunity for Lisa and the rest of Wayne's loved ones to hear exactly how he had died, and in those circumstances the least they could expect was to be treated with compassion and dignity.

Over forty witnesses were called to give evidence, including three medical experts as to the cause of death. According to the police officers' evidence, shortly after giving chase, they cornered Wayne in a children's playground. He was still holding the kitchen knife, which he had taken from the site of the burglary, but the officers quickly disarmed him and tackled him to the ground. The officers arrested Wayne and restrained him in a prone position, handcuffed with his arms behind his back. They put him in the back of a police van, face down, and he was driven to Brixton police station. Eyewitnesses painted a somewhat different story, however. One had told the *Caribbean Times* newspaper that he'd seen Wayne immediately drop the knife when confronted by the officers. As soon as he did so, 'they all jumped on him. They dragged him to the park and beat the shit out of him. [. . .] I could hear the guy screaming. They were jumping on him, kicking him, hitting him with their batons.' Another said, 'You could hear the sound of their batons on his bones.' At the inquest, another eyewitness described how one police officer had knelt on Wayne's head while he was being handcuffed and four officers had pinned him face down on the ground. It is unlikely that either of these accounts were totally accurate as the injuries on Wayne's body did not fully accord with either description, but there are often problems with eye-witness testimony, one of which can be exaggeration.

On arrival at Brixton police station, one of the police witnesses giving evidence said that Wayne was carried into the custody suite where he was placed on the floor in a prone position then put in a cell. There he was stripped and searched; while officers carried out the search, they again turned him onto his stomach. At this point Wayne had complained of having difficulty breathing, so after they finished their search they turned him onto his back, and left him alone in the cell. Not long afterwards, the officer stationed outside his cell noticed that Wayne had rolled onto his front and seemed to be struggling to breathe. On entering the cell, he found that Wayne had, in fact, stopped breathing. He attempted to give medical assistance and called for help. An ambulance was called, but Wayne's heart had stopped.

In evidence, Lisa told the jury that while Wayne's actions leading up to his arrest were not to be condoned, her brother had been unwell and depressed following the stillbirth of his first child two weeks previously. He had worked as a postman but was now unemployed and living in a hostel, and had wanted simply 'to get away from everything' with his girlfriend.

One of the pathologists called to give evidence was Dr Freddie Patel, who would later become infamous for other reasons and was struck off following complaints made against him. Dr Patel argued there is no such thing as positional asphyxia and I will never forget his words: 'It's a myth.' Louise and I had instructed Dr Nathaniel Cary as an expert witness. Nat Cary was a relatively young forensic cardiac pathologist from the world-renowned Royal Papworth Hospital, a specialist heart and lung unit, and he had produced an independent report on Wayne's death. He was a breath of fresh air in the pathologist community. He rubbished any suggestion that young Black men could suddenly drop dead. He strongly refuted the idea that it was purely coincidental that Wayne should have died during the course of his arrest and that his death had nothing to do with the fact that, on four separate occasions, he had been held face down with his hands cuffed behind his back.

This myth was based on the suggestion that Black people in general had bigger hearts, and bigger hearts came under more pressure. But one of the reasons that a lot of young Black men had big hearts was because they were strong, fit men who worked out. If you exercise, your heart gets bigger, a fact that is completely unrelated to race. Wayne Douglas, a big, fit man, died under restraint, not suddenly, for some unknown reason. Nat Cary helped to debunk that myth.

Another myth was Adult Sudden Death Syndrome, similar to cot death or Sudden Infant Death. Some pathologists would have us believe that there are those who are predisposed to dropping dead, totally ignoring the fact that at the time they suddenly died, they were under restraint, face down, with pressure being applied to their back, preventing the mechanics of breathing. This has since been proven and is now accepted in the forensic and police lexicon as positional asphyxiation or restraint asphyxiation, but in the late '90s this was relatively new for British police forces.

Although the jury concluded that Wayne's death by heart failure was an accident, they soundly rejected Dr Patel's medical testimony and accepted that police restraint and positional asphyxia had played a part. Indeed, Sir Monty had said in his summing up that he had been 'appalled' to learn that the police were given only a few minutes' training on methods of restraint, especially face down. It was a landmark decision. A string of cases followed in which there were findings against police officers on death by asphyxia caused by restraint in a prone position.

The verdict on Wayne Douglas was nevertheless of an accidental death. More importantly, the coroner had made errors in his summing up by failing to give adequate or clear directions on two possible forms of unlawful killing – gross negligence manslaughter and unlawful act manslaughter. He had arguably misdirected the jury on what they needed to find before they could consider an unlawful killing verdict (he muddled the two different types of manslaughter). An unlawful killing verdict, we argued, would have been appropriate in a case where there had been gross negligence in the way the police had treated Wayne during or after his arrest, or if a 'deliberate, unlawful dangerous act' had resulted in involuntary manslaughter. The verdict of accidental death was unjust. There was no reason for Wayne Douglas to have died that night.

Wayne's sister did not stop fighting for justice on behalf of her brother. In July 1998 she sought to quash the verdict of accidental death and again I worked with Louise Christian on the case, but we were unsuccessful in the Court of Appeal. The Master of the Rolls, Lord Woolf, accepted that while there may have been 'just enough sufficient evidence' for unlawful manslaughter to be a possible finding, he didn't overturn the verdict and refused the call for a fresh inquest, stating that 'little more could be achieved by subjecting all concerned to the considerable expense and stress of a further inquest.' Lord Woolf also denied the possibility of gross negligence on the part of Brixton police. The family were distraught. They felt that they had been denied justice in their struggle to hold the police to account for Wayne's death. Particularly upsetting to Lisa was Lord Woolf's comments about the cost of a fresh inquest: 'A proper verdict on my brother's death is far more important than money.' That was a low point, but it taught me an important lesson: even where the law is clear-cut, the decisions of judges certainly are not.

In her statement after the hearing, Louise issued a statement on behalf of Wayne's family in which she accused the Metropolitan Police of failing to implement seven recommendations for improved police training and research on methods of restraint made by the coroner at the conclusion of the December 1996 inquest: 'The importance of this case is that it was not just Wayne Douglas who died because of positional asphyxia following an arrest,' she said. 'Other young men, in particular Black young men, are dying in custody for the same reason. After Wayne Douglas, there have been two more inquests involving men whose deaths were due to positional asphyxia. But still there is no implementation.'

Louise's words would come to haunt the British establishment and police forces on both sides of the Atlantic for years to come. Two decades later young Black men are still dying as a direct consequence of this kind of restraint, and despite all the learning about the condition of restraint/positional asphyxia, these deaths continue apparently unabated.*

---

* George Floyd, who died in May 2020, is arguably the most infamous death by restraint, relighting the Black Lives Matter protests in the summer of 2020.

17

MY FIVE PRINCIPLES

In the late 1990s most of my caseload involved either civil actions against the police, or inquest work.

One of the key themes running through many of my police cases is the issue of collusion. It's not unusual in death-in-custody inquests or claims for assault, wrongful arrest or malicious prosecutions, to discover on examining the evidence that so similar, or nigh-on identical, are the written incident reports that it seems as if a number of police officers must have got together and had briefings before composing their accounts. This doesn't make the police officers, or the institution, look good to the jury if individual officers are seen to be copying or relying on other people's evidence to give an officially sanctioned, 'squeaky clean' version of events. But it works both ways. Not all cases of collusion amount to justice even if they are exposed.

I did a case in Leeds where exactly this happened. It seemed obvious to my client and me that an officer had copied passages from another officer's notebook, to the extent that spelling errors, grammar mistakes and incorrect punctuation were replicated.

In turn, I took both of them to task, but the jury wasn't having any of it. In that particular case, it seemed that no matter how much malpractice and collusion I illustrated to the jury, they had decided to support the police's counterclaims. Why? In short, the jury simply didn't like my client, a troubled woman who had suffered various setbacks in her life and came across as hostile in the witness box.

Often the client is their own worst enemy. You can take them through their evidence, but there is no rehearsal. There are strict rules in that regard; you are not meant to prep or coach your client in any way. In fact, it is in breach of the Bar Code of Conduct to do so. There's nothing wrong, however, in giving your clients guidance as to what is going to happen in court, and telling them what to expect and how to behave in giving evidence and on cross-examination.

I've learned what sort of things can turn a judge or a jury against a client, and, conversely, how the model client should behave in giving evidence and dealing with questioning. So, I have formulated five principles, which I've distilled from observing poorly-given evidence over the years. The giving of evidence is a very unnatural thing to do. I understand that it can be stressful and anxiety-inducing, but if the witness or client breathes, tries to relax and remembers these five simple tips, hopefully it will help their cause.

RULE NUMBER ONE: *Listen to the question you are being asked.*

In all my preliminary and subsequent meetings with clients, I state that it is crucial that they *listen* to the questions they are asked. Often, when clients step into the witness box they want to tell *their* story, and are so busy thinking about what they want to say that they don't actually listen to or hear the question. I will say to a client, for example, 'So, on the Saturday night when you were leaving the pub, which route did you take?' The client will seemingly hear that question and then give me a totally unrelated answer. Politicians often do this when they want to change the narrative, but you can't do that in court. You will irritate the judge or jury or the person asking the questions.

RULE NUMBER TWO: *Answer that question, and that question alone.*

So, *listen*, breathe, think and *answer the question you have been asked*. It's simple, but often ignored or breached.

RULE NUMBER THREE: *Keep your answers short.*

You will be surprised how many questions just require a 'yes' or a 'no' answer. There are of course occasions when an open question is asked, to which you should simply say as much as you need and then stop. People don't do that. They will add all sorts of unnecessary detail. Some clients will say highly damaging things when, in reality, they simply need to answer the question. When you are prosecuting or bringing a claim, as the claimant's counsel, generally speaking you open the case proceedings and give evidence on behalf of your client first. So there is little for the client to say other than what has already been laid out by his or her barrister. As their barrister, when I am asking them questions in the witness box, they can trust me to elicit from them the information they need to get across to the jury. Clients don't seem to always grasp that I am trying to steer the questions and answers in order to back up their claim. In cross-examination, the only rule is to destroy or undermine the testimony that has gone before. So, when my client is being cross-examined by my opposing defence barrister, the less said in response the better.

RULE NUMBER FOUR: *If you don't know the answer to a question, then you simply say, 'I don't know the answer to that question.'*

The last thing you do is speculate. There is no shame in saying that you don't know the answer to something, or that you don't remember. In fact, oftentimes that is a genuine response. There are going to be times when people use ignorance as a ruse to hide the truth, but in many of my cases the clients are afraid to say they don't know, perhaps because they think that it will make them look unreliable or foolish. I always stress that if they don't know, they don't know. That's all there is to it. And if you don't understand or didn't quite catch the question, ask the questioner to repeat it, or to rephrase it.

RULE NUMBER FIVE: *Be patient and respectful – and don't argue.*

Don't argue with the person who is asking the questions – don't be cute, don't be sarcastic, don't be ironic, don't answer a question with another question.

That's the theory anyway. The reality is, alas, often very different, and the worst clients are the ones who, having told you they are going to be the best witnesses, break all five rules. Sometimes, though, I can still be surprised at how brilliantly some of the most unlikely clients or witnesses cope under the pressure of a trial situation.

18

A RUN-OF-THE-MILL CASE

In the late 1990s juries in civil police actions were becoming more and more appalled at accounts of police misconduct, and as a result the jury compensation awards for false imprisonment, assault and malicious prosecution cases were increasing – indeed, over the previous decade, awards of damages against the police had increased eightfold. And yet, of the hundreds of officers implicated in cases brought against Scotland Yard between 1993 and 1996, which had cost the force approximately £4.5 million, only nine had incurred any disciplinary action.

Quoted shortly after the latest record payout from the Met, Louise Christian explained that jurors were awarding higher damages because of police unwillingness to crack down on culpable officers. 'Jurors are disillusioned with police doing this again and again, with no action taken against the officers involved. If it's the only way to register their concern, juries will go on increasing compensation awards,' Louise told the *Voice* newspaper.

Failing to recognise that police behaviour was itself outrageous, however, the right-wing media launched a campaign to rein in the level of damages awarded by juries. I remember some of the headlines following the case of Daniel Goswell, for example, on which my colleague, friend and mentor Courtenay Griffiths QC acted for the claimant. In 1990, Mr Goswell had been struck on the forehead with a baton causing a wound which required five stitches. While the injury he sustained wasn't life-changing, it could have been; indeed, it could have killed him. In 1996 a jury awarded compensatory damages to the amount of £120,000 for his injuries, £12,000 for false imprisonment, and £170,000 in exemplary damages for the 'arbitrary and oppressive' behaviour of the police. Instead of expressing disgust at the conduct of the police and asking what measures could be taken to improve the service that the Met was providing, the headline on the front page of the *Daily Mail* screamed '£60,000 for Each Stitch! Fury at staggering £302,000 payout to man with minor head cut after row with the police'. Dubbing the damages award 'a Mickey Mouse payout', the article continued: 'The award, the highest ever against the British police, is three times what a victim of crime would get for losing both legs,' thus minimising the impact and importance of those injuries and the problems of the Met Police's behaviour and focusing instead on the compensation.

The Commissioner Sir Paul Condon was getting nervous. In civil actions against the police at that time there was no limit on the damages that a jury could decide. Jurors would base their awards on what they thought was not only fair recompense for wrongful treatment at the hands of the police, but also awarded exemplary damages, appropriate to and reflective of the gravity of the individual police officer or officers' misconduct in each claim, as a punitive sum against the police authority.

The case that compelled the judiciary to think twice about the level of damages that the police were having to pay out was the case of Mr Hsu v Commissioner of Police of the Metropolis. Kenneth Hsu, a hairdresser, represented by a former Wellington Street colleague of mine, Ben Emerson QC, and Sadiq Khan at Christian Fisher, brought the civil case after he was set upon by Metropolitan Police officers in July 1992 when they had called at his home in south London over a dispute involving a former lodger. When Mr Hsu refused to let the officers into the property without a warrant, he had been arrested and violently assaulted. He was held in a neck lock, handcuffed with his hands twisted up behind his back, punched in the face and struck with a set of keys, then kicked in the back and the kidneys. He was also subjected to racial taunts both in the police van and while being detained at Streatham police station. The police's justification for Mr Hsu's arrest and charge was that he had shoved a police officer in the chest. When he was eventually released from police custody, he was turned out onto the street barefoot wearing only a vest and a pair of jeans. Mr Hsu had previously made two unsuccessful approaches to the Police Complaints Authority to investigate the three constables involved, and in March 1996 was successful in his civil claim. The jury by its verdict rejected the police's version of events which they clearly deemed to have been deliberately concocted and falsely reported in the officers' notebooks, in order to back up their evidence in court, and awarded Mr Hsu damages of £220,000. The barrier had been broken and we knew the sky was the limit in terms of civil action damages. The police knew this too. Something had to give.

Thirty-year-old Claudette Thompson had been lawfully arrested in the early hours of 28 September 1991 for a drink-driving offence, to which she later pleaded guilty. Matters had taken a turn for the worse when officers had decided to place her in a cell. Five officers, including two female officers, were involved and 'considerable and unnecessary force' was used.* She was jumped upon, smothered and a chunk of her hair was pulled out after a sergeant suggested that officers 'chuck her in the bin'. In Ms Thompson's words, 'it was like I was being abused physically and sexually by all of them'. The police alleged that force had only been used after Ms Thompson had refused to be searched, and that during a struggle she had bitten an officer's finger, causing bleeding, and physically assaulted several others present. She was consequently also charged with assault causing actual bodily harm, and taken to the magistrates' court in handcuffs. She was acquitted on the assault charge and in June 1995 was successful in a civil action against the police for false imprisonment, assault and malicious prosecution, the allegation being that the police had fabricated the assault claims and falsified evidence relating to the bitten finger. The jury awarded her £1,500 for the assault and her injuries and £50,000 in exemplary damages.

In December 1996, Patricia Wynn Davies reported in the *Independent* that over the course of the previous decade, 'damages awarded against the police had increased eightfold'. In the three years since 1993, cases brought against Scotland Yard had cost the force £4.5 million.† In light of these spiralling costs, and deeming the award granted to Ms Thompson in particular 'plainly unreasonable and excessive', the Metropolitan Police went on the offensive in a campaign to limit damages and a week later, *The Times* reported that Scotland Yard had instructed lawyers to challenge the large exemplary damages awards in the case of Claudette Thompson, Danny Goswell and Kenneth Hsu in the Court of Appeal. Quoted in the article, Commissioner

---

* Transcript of Thompson and Hsu v Commissioner of the Police of the Metropolis (Appeal) 19 February 1997.
† Of the hundreds of officers implicated in these civil actions in this period, only nine had been disciplined: Patricia Wynn Davies, 10 December 1996 www.independent.co.uk/news/police-seek-limits-on-jury-awards-1313851.html

Sir Paul Condon claimed that lawyers had switched their focus from pursuing complaints against the police to civil litigation in which their clients received legal aid, stating – disingenuously, I would argue – that, 'What we have had is cases five, six, seven years old, some of which had very little significance at the time. There were no complaints against police, no action', adding: 'These are old cases, exploiting the different burden of proof between civil and criminal cases. They were minor incidents which have speculatively been given a run-on legal aid. In some cases, the police have been seen as a soft touch.'

The press campaigns were successful, because while in February 1997 the Court of Appeal ruled against the police in the case of Claudette Thompson, in the case of both Daniel Goswell and Kenneth Hsu, damages were reduced significantly. In his ruling Lord Woolf, Master of the Rolls, said that 'juries when assessing damages awarded to members of the public for unlawful conduct towards them by the police should in future be given guidance by the judge with a view to establishing some relationship between such awards and those obtained for personal injuries.' Furthermore, he added that 'the jury in such cases should be told the only remedy they had power to grant a successful plaintiff was damages. Save in exceptional circumstances, damages were to compensate the plaintiff, *not to punish the defendant*.'

I felt the changes take immediate effect, both in terms of my day-to-day practice and my caseload as the police work began to diminish. This was not because awards of damages thereafter were significantly smaller and so there were less claims against the police, nor because the police had simultaneously stopped committing egregious misdeeds or beating people up. Rather it was because of a significant blow to access to justice. The legal aid system, created through the 1949 Legal Aid and Advice Act by Clement Attlee's post-war Labour government, had become highly politicised and was constantly under threat.* Eligibility for civil legal aid had been eroded by the Conservative government when in 1987 it became available to only those on the lowest incomes, and the new rules meant that almost 10 per cent of those who used legal aid now had to pay towards it.

In the mid-'90s, at the same time as awards of damages were shrinking beyond recognition, the press was mounting a sustained attack on so-called fat-cat legal aid lawyers. Granted, there may have been a tiny handful of legal professionals doing big criminal or financial cases who were milking it, but I don't accept that the vast majority of publicly paid lawyers abuse the system. In my experience, in terms of civil litigation legal aid, there are very few fat-cat lawyers in evidence – if at all. Nevertheless, the media campaign had succeeded in undermining the tax-paying public's trust in the system.

There was even greater inequality in access to justice and an ever-growing unmet legal need among the poorest sections of society. Yet when Tony Blair became prime minister in 1997, he was intent on maintaining the previous government's limits to legal aid. In October 1997 the Labour Lord Chancellor Lord Irvine announced that while family cases would stay within the legal aid schemes, the means test would be tightened, and most civil cases would be replaced by Conditional Fee Agreements, known as CFAs, which are essentially 'No Win, No Fee' agreements. If the claim was successful, however, then the lawyer acting for the claimant would be entitled to a 'success fee', to be paid by the defendant who had lost the case. In a big case,

---

* Devised at the same time as the welfare state, the white paper preceding legislation states that the aim of legal aid was 'to provide legal advice for those of slender means and resources, so that no one would be financially unable to prosecute a just and reasonable claim or defend a legal right; and to allow counsel and solicitors to be remunerated for their services'.

when you had been working on it for two or three years and your fees could thus be fairly significant, that uplift could be considerable, sometimes as much as 100 per cent. There was a real incentive for people to do CFA agreements, therefore, particularly if you could justify doubling your fee because it was all coming out of the defendant's pocket.

Unsurprisingly, defendants including the Police and other state agents complained about how unfair this was. There was a review, and in 2012 the coalition government abolished the uplifts. If there was no uplift, a barrister had to take the very real risk of potentially not earning a penny for weeks, even months, of work. I've been in that position, and gone unpaid. This applies not only to police actions, but also housing disrepair, personal injury, and clinical negligence cases, for example. Lawyers simply can't afford to take on an unlimited number of CFA cases. Do too many, and you could go bankrupt. So, one might well ask, who *does* take on these cases and what benefit is there in taking that risk? (Answer: Lawyers with a social conscience.)

Coming back to the question of unmet legal need, and access to justice, what I've witnessed in the past three decades amounts to a constant attack, both in reducing legal aid, and in the consequent reduction in the number of lawyers willing to take on cases unless they are publicly funded or very high-value legal actions. Indeed, the next big thing that the present Conservative government is currently considering is the introduction of fixed fees. Not only will barristers not be paid according to the hours they work, but they will be paid a fixed flat fee which the government will decide. One could argue that bringing down the fees is another way of allowing for a more affordable legal system for the consumer. That might be true, but here's the rub: these changes won't really affect large commercial cases. The big corporate work is going to happen anyway. What this amounts to, therefore, is an attack on the work being done by the majority of barristers working for private individuals, undermining our ability to ensure that human rights cases involving ordinary citizens be heard. It's scary. I can see a time coming when lawyers will simply refuse to do this work and ordinary people won't be able to enforce their fundamental rights in an effective way because there will not be sufficient skilled and decent lawyers to run those cases. Who wins with these proposed changes? The establishment, of course.

THE LONDON LEGAL ELITE V ME

Police work has not been easy. In the very early days, the vast bulk of the civil actions and inquests I was instructed on were in Manchester and Liverpool, and I also did a ton of work in Yorkshire, especially in Wakefield and Leeds. When my children were young, for long periods I was away from home, travelling to cases up and down the country.

In fact, my practice and success in this field was not built on the elite civil liberties law firms in London. In my experience, back then there was a tangible snobbery among some of the solicitors in terms of who they would instruct on cases involving abuses of police powers and deaths in custody. Only a handful of the high-profile London firms instructed me. One of my closest friends and confidants was the aforementioned Andre Clovis at Hallmark Atkinson Wynter and, later, after 2007, at Tuckers. Andre and I were so close that at times it was like a marriage. We would constantly bicker and argue with each other about case strategy. But we could do that and not offend the other. We were partners in fighting crime. We did a slew of cases where we were invincible. Andre is undoubtedly one of the best police action solicitors in the UK.

The obvious irony in this: there I was, a working-class Black man, working for a particular client group, i.e. working-class

Black people. And yet, in terms of this specific type of civil liberties and human rights work, I simply wouldn't be instructed by most firms. It was very frustrating and I did not know why.

Here is just one example. In the late '90s, when I took on the highly controversial inquest into the death of Ibrahima Sey in Newham, I worked pro bono. At that time there was effectively no legal aid for big and serious inquests like these. If a family member couldn't afford representation, they either found lawyers prepared to act pro bono, or they did it themselves. I started practising in 1989, and essentially in the 1990s the bulk of my paid work was in civil claims against the police. In turn the police actions funded me and allowed me to act pro bono on these important inquests in which the police and the state were held to account. In other words, there was a general understanding that, if you had worked on the inquest pro bono, the family's solicitor would instruct you to work on any ensuing civil action to compensate you for the pro bono work.

And yet I didn't do the civil action on Ibrahima Sey. I wasn't asked. I wasn't even told that it was taking place. Months after I'd finished the inquest, I bumped into one of my opposite numbers on it, a friendly adversary of mine, a police law barrister called John Beggs QC. He told me that he had just done the defence on Amie Sey's civil claim and was surprised not to see my name on the claimant's pleadings. Then he had let slip that Amie's solicitors had instructed someone else. It was like a punch to the stomach when I heard this. It felt as if I wasn't valued, I wasn't *seen*; and I had to learn about it from John Beggs. It was one of the most humiliating things I've ever experienced. It was never explained to me why I was never instructed by that firm. But this was not an isolated incident; back then, many of the large London civil liberties firms refused to send me any regular work. I might receive the occasional one-off case, but never from any of the established practitioners, only from very junior solicitors.

At the time I was maybe one of a tiny handful of Black barristers doing these police cases. Even today there aren't that many Black barristers working in this area. Although I can't prove it, and can only speculate, I feel that it may well have been a class thing. Had I gone to a different school, a different university, had a different skin colour and accent, maybe I would not have been treated that way. I sometimes think that there's an unconscious bias at play, or plain bias; that some people think that if you are a Black man representing a Black client in an action against the police, the jury might conclude, 'Well, of course he would be on their side.' To think that is to not see me as a lawyer, a skilled, competent advocate. It is to see only the colour of my skin, or perhaps listen to my working-class south London accent, and to suspect, or believe, that because of these attributes I am incapable of securing a good and fair result for their client. This is all supposition on my part. Perhaps the solicitors and these firms didn't like me because I tell it as it is and fear no one. Or perhaps it was simply that they did not think I was any good. And, of course, the irony is that these very solicitors, who for whatever reason never once instructed me, were working for civil liberties firms which represented clients of colour, and whose raison d'être was exactly to fight unconscious bias. I think there is a real hypocrisy in all of this.

Nevertheless, in spite of all those setbacks, my inquest and civil action practice did take off. And there is no doubt that this is down to one man: Gilly Singh Mundy. Gilly was the case worker at INQUEST, the charity organisation which grew up as a result of a number of campaigns at the beginning of the 1980s surrounding deaths in custodial settings. Often castigated as the author of the politics of modern inquests by those who oppose it, INQUEST is the only non-governmental organisation in England and Wales that works directly with the families of those who die in custody. It primarily serves to support families by giving independent free legal advice to the bereaved on inquest procedures and their rights in the coroner's courts, while helping them to secure good legal representation. The dedicated staff also provide much-needed emotional support for the families throughout. Over the years INQUEST has campaigned endlessly to raise awareness of the whole range of different types of death in custody, such as heart attacks and asphyxiation while subject to 'approved' methods of control and restraint; alcohol-related deaths in police custody; suicides and deaths of vulnerable inmates, both young and old, while sentenced to segregated prison cells; and the disproportionate number of deaths of Black and ethnic minority people in custody. Over the past forty years INQUEST has been critical in bringing attention in coronial courts and beyond to these unnecessary and preventable tragedies.

Gilly was at the heart of some of the most important and controversial cases, and was instrumental in helping me gain experience in this field. I owe him so much; he had faith in me. He would tell me that there is no reason that these families shouldn't have somebody who understands where they are coming from. Someone like me acting for them. And he would tell the families that they should make sure their solicitors instructed me.

They say that good people die young, however, and Gilly was only in his late thirties when in March 2007 he suffered a heart attack and died at his desk at INQUEST's offices. It was such a shock. He was so loved. Gilly's funeral had the biggest turnout you could imagine. I miss him more than I can say.

However, some of the struggles I've had to overcome are not

necessarily those that are lost in the mists of my early years at the Bar. In June 2017, by the time of the opening of the public inquiry into the fire in Grenfell Tower on the night of 14 June 2017, which claimed seventy-two lives, I was Legal Aid Lawyer of the Year, I was Queen's Counsel, I had won diversity awards, and had undertaken some of the biggest inquests and inquiries in this country. Yet, despite all this, and even though this is what I am known for, the first solicitor who instructed me on Grenfell, who is a woman of colour, told me that when she went to the initial meeting of the Grenfell lawyers, my name wasn't on the list of barristers to be considered, and she had to push hard for me to be instructed. Many of the candidates who *were* on the list didn't have as much experience as me. That's not to say that they are not good lawyers, many of them are, but in terms of simply being given a chance to be included for instructions, my name was not even there in the running.

In short, as a Black barrister in this field, and one from a working-class background with a comprehensive-school education, it doesn't matter how good people *tell* you that they think you are; it doesn't matter how good you *think* you are. It *does matter* how good and capable you *actually* are *as a Black man*. And the truth is I still have a lot more barriers to surmount.

PART III

2 0

THE PROBLEM WITH THE POLICE
AND GUNS: MY FIRST POLICE
SHOOTING CASE

For over 150 years, the use of force by the police in the UK has been informed by the notion of the rule of law and restraint. Unlike in the majority of European countries, in the UK, with the notable exception of the Northern Ireland Police Service, police officers are *not* routinely armed. Law and order are maintained on mainland Britain, the thinking goes, not by a militant, tooled-up constabulary, but rather through 'policing by consent', in which the principles of compromise, respect and the use of 'no more than reasonable' force are paramount. For the status quo to be preserved, and our continued consent to being policed, our trust in the police to do the right thing is vital – think the sage and avuncular Dixon of Dock Green, for example, or the wily yet all-too-human Detective Inspector Morse.

Of course, the truth is that since the early 1990s, policing in the UK has become increasingly dependent on the use of force. With the introduction of CS spray, American-style batons and the latest addition to their armoury, Taser guns, some might even say it has undergone a militarisation by stealth. Furthermore, police forces up and down the country have Armed Response Vehicle teams on hand, whose specially trained armed officers are charged with tackling armed criminals and are authorised to carry and discharge a firearm while on duty. While these Armed Response Units typically respond to spur-of-the-moment firearms incidents, other Specialist Firearms Officers routinely carry out authorised planned operations against criminals suspected of being in possession of firearms. In such operations, by apprehending armed and dangerous criminals before they can carry out a potentially fatal robbery or attack, the aim of the police firearms team is to *prevent* the loss of life.

As a state agent, no police force in the UK adheres to a shoot-to-kill philosophy and no individual officer *sets out* to kill the suspect. However, simply through the act of arming a police officer, the risk of loss of life, inevitably, is heightened. In even the most meticulously planned operations, when confronted with a potentially armed and dangerous criminal, in that split second, if the firearms officer believes that there is a threat to his or another's life, he will pull the trigger. If his hunch was wrong, he shoots an innocent person. Conversely, if he misjudges the situation, fails to react and is mistaken, the officer gets shot. As journalist Nick Davies pointed out in an article on police shootings for the *Guardian* in 2001, 'The truth about armed police which the politicians have never understood is that if we give guns to our police officers, they will use them; and if they use them, then from time to time, as a matter of certainty, they will shoot the wrong people.'

James Brady was one such innocent victim. James died on 24 April 1995 from a single gunshot fired by a Northumbria Police marksman during a bungled robbery at a working man's club in Newcastle. He was twenty-one. In the words of his father,

James was 'a lad with a love for life' who had left school at sixteen and joined the army, serving for three years as a motor mechanic and also played with the military band. 'Everybody he knew liked him. He was too easily led by his peers.'

The circumstances of James's death were highly controversial. On the night of the shooting, James and three accomplices, armed with an imitation handgun, CS spray and a chair leg, broke into the Westerhope Excelsior Social Club with the intention of tying up the steward and robbing the safe of the takings. The police had, however, received a tip-off about the planned robbery and a team of officers were lying in wait inside the darkened social club. As James turned to face them, the marksman mistook a small black torch James held in his hand for a gun, and shot him dead. He died almost instantly. His mother and father contended that the death of their son could have been avoided; he should have been arrested outside the club.

While unlimited public funds were available for the chief constable's lawyers to represent him and legal representation for the police officers was funded by their union funds, James's family did not have the benefit of any resources or legal aid, which is not available for inquests. I therefore agreed to work on this case for a modest fee. I felt unhappy about accepting money for a family's pain, but James's father Kenneth Brady was a good man who wanted to get justice and insisted on paying me.

Representing the family of James Brady at the inquest into his death at Newcastle Coroner's Court in September 1998 was a landmark case in my professional life. It was the first inquest ever in which officers had successfully applied for anonymity. Consequently, the police marksman known only as Officer A gave his evidence behind a screen. It was also my first case in

Newcastle. I had to navigate and understand a Geordie accent, which my clients found amusing, when I kept asking what local terms meant.

The key issue in this inquest was whether the shooting was reasonable and proportionate: whether, honestly believing that Mr Brady was holding a gun, the police marksman had acted in self-defence. Or, as we argued, was the operation itself ill-judged from the outset.

The jury heard that the informer had provided the police with the date and location of the planned robbery and the names of two of the suspects, including Mr Brady, along with the following: the number of intruders to expect; the approx-imate time of the burglary; the point of entry to the premises (a downstairs kitchen window at the rear of the club); that one of the intruders would be carrying an imitation firearm, i.e. a starting pistol; and the sum they hoped to steal (£15,000).

The firearms operation was intended to apprehend the intruders and thereby protect the proprietors and clientele of the club, and the officers were told to treat all firearms (including 'imitations') as genuine unless and until proven to be otherwise. It was decided that the officers would ambush the intruders as they entered the club through the window, which involved placing five armed officers hidden at various vantage points.

The most disturbing thing that we learned, late in the pro-ceedings, was that two of the armed officers involved, who had since retired from the force, were suing their own police force for psychiatric injury as a result of negligence. They had issued a writ against the chief constable of Northumbria Police claiming that James and his associates should have been tackled outside the club and James should not have been shot. I don't know whether there had been an attempt at a cover-up, but this was highly significant and what some might consider to be crucial evidence, which did not come to light until *after* these officers had already given evidence at the inquest during which they had failed to mention their civil action and their own criticisms of the drastic operation. It also transpired that the Newcastle coroner David Mitford had known about the impending civil proceedings prior to the start of the inquest, but had not deemed it relevant to inform me as the Brady family's legal representative. As soon as we found out – when the barrister for the chief constable mentioned it to the Bradys – I made an application for the officers to be recalled for further questioning. I felt that the system of coronial justice was fundamentally flawed and dishonest, and the players were able to get away with things because they were acting within the rules. I had no doubt in my mind that the rules needed to change.

In his summing up, the coroner explained to the jury that they had a choice of three possible verdicts: lawful killing, unlawful killing or an open verdict. In a case like this, where a police officer has deliberately shot an individual because they say they were justified, the police want a lawful killing verdict. Anything less is not a vindication of their actions. The decision hung on the jury believing that Officer A had discharged his weapon in the honest belief that James was armed and dangerous and his own life was at risk. An open verdict should be returned, the coroner said, only if the jury felt there was not enough evidence to make a decision. After nearly five hours' deliberation, the jury returned an open verdict. The police were shocked. On behalf of the family, I felt elated. As an outsider, I had gone to Newcastle and taken on the establishment there, faced a difficult hearing, listened to James being referred to as a criminal, and learned of crucial evidence that had initially been withheld from the family. Although we had not secured an unlawful killing verdict, I considered this a victory against the odds.

The Police Complaints Authority inquiry was reopened and the case papers were referred back to the Crown Prosecution for a second time. A year or so later, having re-examined the evidence for a third time, the chief constable decided finally not to prosecute Officer A, or any of his colleagues, over the killing. Kenneth Brady and I decided to challenge the decision in the European Court of Human Rights in Strasbourg, but we were unsuccessful.

Shortly after the James Brady ruling, Sadiq Khan instructed me on my second police shooting inquest, this time involving Bedfordshire Police. It was one of the most memorable inquests of my career – for all the wrong reasons.

On 26 February 1998, following the erroneous report of a break-in at the property, Irishman Michael (Mick) Fitzgerald was shot dead in his home by a police marksman as the culmination of a siege situation. Mick, a former railway worker, was thirty-two years old. Friends and family described him in news articles at the time as a big, gentle man, a huge John Wayne fan who collected imitation guns and had even bought a pair of cowboy boots in homage to his hero. Since the death from cancer of his mother five years earlier, however, Michael, who was unemployed, had suffered from depression and had a chronic alcohol problem, with a tendency to binge drinking. Indeed, his only brush with the law had been a conviction for drink-driving in 1997 when he was placed on probation and banned from driving.

On the night of his death, Michael's girlfriend had driven round to his flat at around 6.30 p.m. As she drew up in the car park, she had seen a pair of legs disappearing through the ground-floor kitchen window. Mistaking this person for an intruder, and fearing for Michael's safety, she reported a burglary in progress to the police. Two officers arrived at the scene and when one of them went to the kitchen window and identified himself, a man appeared in the shadow of the room. It was Michael, adopting a John Wayne-like extended arm stance, pointing what appeared to be a gun at the officer. The police officers and Michael's girlfriend moved to a safe distance from the house, and assistance, including an Armed Response Vehicle (ARV), was summoned. Michael's girlfriend had told the officer that Michael owned a replica firearm – she was unaware of him owning an actual firearm – and he had a drink problem. However, at this point neither she nor the officers had identified the 'occupant', i.e. the supposed intruder, as Michael.

Fifteen minutes later the ARV with two armed officers and further unarmed back-up were on the scene. As they stood at the front of the building, the occupant appeared in the doorway of the flat. In response to a shout of 'Armed police. Drop the gun and go back into the house,' he raised his hand, which appeared to be holding a handgun, and went back inside. Seconds later, he reappeared, still holding the 'gun', seemingly paying no notice to instructions to drop the weapon, then went back inside the flat. A siege situation developed. The ARV officers were joined by a police dog handler and the police traffic department provided flood lighting trained on the building allowing officers a better view of the occupant, who continued, at intervals, to point his weapon out of the kitchen window and ignore instructions to unarm himself and walk out of the flat.

At around 7 p.m. Michael's girlfriend was joined by two of his female neighbours, one of whom, Kate Bellamy, also told the police that there were only replica firearms in the flat. The three women were taken to Bedford police station for their safety.

By 8 p.m. a superintendent of Bedford police and a tactical firearms advisor were on the scene; both were satisfied with the decisions taken thus far. While waiting for negotiators to arrive, the superintendent called the landline in Michael's flat, and on the second attempt the occupant answered and said his name was Mick. He sounded drunk and, despite the officer's attempts to engage him in further conversation, he ended the call. During this time Michael's brother John and a friend had both phoned Michael at his house. Michael was crying when he answered his brother's call. John later told the inquest, 'Michael said, "I think I have done something really stupid. I am under siege. I have got all the police outside. I am surrounded." I thought it was a joke. I thought he was messing about. If I thought it was serious, I would have gone right there.' According to the friend, Michael sounded tired and said, 'I think they are going to storm the house.' The phone then went dead. Unaware of the unfolding events at Michael's flat, neither had cause to report their calls to the police.

At 8.19 p.m. the occupant appeared again. He pushed the handgun through an open window, but withdrew after shouts from officers. Within seconds he reappeared, standing in full view at the window, naked from the waist up, and again adopting, in the words of the police, a 'threatening' stance aiming what appeared to be a handgun at the officers. One unarmed officer dived to the ground, while the firearms officer observed through his gun sight that the barrel of the handgun seemed directed at him. After a further appeal of 'Armed police. Drop the gun or you will be shot' was ignored, the firearms officer squeezed the trigger of his carbine and fired a single shot, which hit the occupant in the chest. Officers and paramedics entered the premises where they found Michael Fitzgerald lying face down on a bed in the back bedroom. Following the shooting it was discovered that Mick had spent the afternoon drinking and had left his jacket with his house keys in the pub; a taxi driver reported seeing him walking towards his house at about 5.45 p.m. and described him as 'very drunk'. Indeed, the subsequent toxicology report showed that he had a blood alcohol reading of 352mg per 100ml, a level of intoxication which would have made a moderate drinker either extremely drunk or comatose.

The Police Complaints Authority (PCA) investigation into the incident leading to Mick's death sought to establish why no negotiator had arrived at the scene in time to prevent the fatal shooting. On that day five of six trained negotiators were attending a conference in Brighton; the sixth was uncontactable. Nevertheless, the investigation concluded that no wrongdoing had been committed on the part of the police. The marksman had committed no criminal offence; he had 'genuinely believed he was facing an intruder armed with a firearm and his life was in imminent danger. He did not know that the weapon was incapable of being discharged and gave the man the chance to withdraw in a pressurised situation.'

Following the Police Complaints Authority report, the inquest opened at Bedford Coroner's Court with David Morris, the HM Coroner for the District of Bedfordshire and Luton. Since Mick had no dependents, there was no civil claim. As reported in the press, the family were unhappy with the behaviour of the police during the ninety-minute incident and believed that the armed officer had been too quick to shoot. The inquest, therefore, was also the only hearing whereby a finding that their brother had been unlawfully killed could have been returned.

There were a great many reasons why, in my view, Mick's family were badly failed by the coroner at this inquest. It was, in my opinion, a litany of injustices from the outset. At a preliminary hearing, Mr Morris had ruled that the Armed Response officers should be granted anonymity in court because there was a genuine concern on the part of the officers that their safety could be at risk should they be named. In representing Mick's family, I firmly objected to this. There was absolutely no threat of abuse by the friends and family of the deceased, and it was insulting to them that this could be inferred. The officers, however, feared a threat from the criminal underworld. I argued this fear was unfounded, nebulous at best. Furthermore, and most crucially, the inquest was meant to be a forum for public scrutiny and this set a dangerous precedent at a hearing which is supposed to be open. Justice should be seen to be done in an open manner, I maintained, and this ruling raised serious questions about the function of the inquest in allaying suspicion and rumour. It was also unnecessarily harsh for the family to be prevented from seeing the officer who shot their loved one. I was overruled, however, and the officers gave their evidence from behind a screen, seen only by the coroner, legal representatives for each party and the nine members of the jury.

During the PCA investigation, 138 witnesses had given statements. During the inquest, however, neither these, nor the police radio logs and transmissions, were disclosed to the family, nor was the final PCA report and conclusions made available for public scrutiny at any time during the proceedings. The coroner had excluded all evidence relating to the planning and decision-making of the operation. Thus the scope of the inquest was restricted to the narrowest interpretation of the questions of who, where, when and how the deceased met his death. The coroner refused the family's request to call the police negotiator, stating that his evidence was irrelevant since he had played no part in the incident. He disclosed only twenty-nine of those witness statements to the family, which meant that crucial lines of questioning, such as the fact that during the phone call with the superintendent the deceased had identified himself as 'Mick', had not been pursued. This put the family at a serious disadvantage, unable to participate fully in the proceedings and unable to consider whether other witnesses should have been called.

There was more to come. At one point during the five-day hearing, Coroner David Morris asked a police officer to demonstrate how the officers had laid siege to Mr Fitzgerald's flat. When the policeman mimed pointing a gun at him, Mr Morris raised his hands in mock surrender and laughed. It was utterly outrageous and entirely inappropriate, and I can only imagine how Mick's family must have felt to witness that level of insult from the person they trusted to deliver justice for the killing of their brother. The last and, in my opinion, most damning aspect of the coroner's handling of the inquest, though, was his decision, in summing up, to instruct the jury to leave only one verdict: that of lawful killing. 'I find,' he stated, 'as a matter of law, for reasons which I do not need to explain to you, that the only verdict you can come to in this inquest – and I so direct – is a verdict that Mick James Fitzgerald was lawfully killed.' Thus he denied the nine independent jurors any possibility of drawing their own conclusions and delivering a verdict which might have been critical of the overall execution and planning of the police operation on that night.

The family had hoped to ask for a judicial review of the inquest, but their request for legal aid was refused. In seeking justice in the UK, all avenues were now closed, but they didn't give up. Mick's sister Theresa took a claim to the European Court of Human Rights. She contended that, firstly, there had been a violation of Mick's right to life contrary to Article

2 of the Convention; secondly, the defects of the inquest had breached the fair hearing guarantees under Article 6; and finally, the Police Complaints Authority investigation had not met the necessary requirements of independence and thus did not constitute an effective remedy within the meaning of Article 13. The Court found that there had been no violations under Article 2 of the Convention, but upheld by a majority Theresa's complaints that her rights to an effective remedy under Article 13 were breached. While this decision would not right the wrongs this family felt, again it was demonstrative that the European Court of Human Rights would step in and be prepared to be critical of the UK legal process where necessary. Although this can never bring Mick back, it is important to recognise this fact, as these precedents do alter the behaviour of coroners and judges in subsequent cases.

21

THE COURAGE OF A WIFE:
THE DEATH OF ONESE POWER
(1946–1997)

The death of a loved one can often bring out the best in people, and sometimes the very worst. It can tear a family apart or it can bring it together. There have been many times in my career when I have worked on inquest cases with a family who have not been in contact with each other for years, then a sudden death and the subsequent inquest process brings them closer and makes them stronger than ever before. The pity is that I don't know whether these new-found close relationships are sustained after the inquest, or if the relatives lose touch the moment the jury delivers their verdict and the hearing comes to an end. I've known people who crumble and don't want to face up to the devastating facts of a loved one's death, but I've also known many individuals, women in particular, who have fought and fought and left no stone unturned in their quest for the truth. The strength of these women is truly awe-inspiring and, often, against all the odds.

Take Ann Power. Ann is one of the bravest women I know. Dogged and determined, she does not quit. Ann's husband and father of their three sons, 51-year-old Onese Power, died during a dangerous Metropolitan Police pursuit in August 1997. Onese had been disqualified from driving, but he loved his motorbikes, and on that Sunday morning he was spotted travelling at quite a crack along Camden Road on his distinctive 'Ninja' Kawasaki. It was a powerful motorcycle with a high-volume revving noise, and hearing the growl of the engine, and surmising that Mr Power was driving over the 30mph speed limit, two officers in a police car, 'November One', decided to chase him. A high-speed pursuit ensued through the busy streets, with at least four more police vehicles joining in the chase. It ended in a narrow side street where, with the convoy of police vehicles hot on his wheels, Onese hit some bollards at a left-hand bend, came off his bike and died instantly.

The inquest took place at St Pancras Coroner's Court in north London the following year. I was not present at the inquest; I would meet Ann Power later and read the transcripts of the court hearings. Ann didn't have the right to legal aid and thus had no legal representation at the hearing. It was a complex case involving a contentious high-speed car chase, yet while the Metropolitan Police were ably represented by a skilled senior advocate, Ann had to go it alone. Furthermore, there were any number of irregularities during the inquest proceedings from the outset. For a start, while everyone else in the court was armed with a pile of witness statements, Ann Power was empty-handed: despite a request, she did not receive disclosure of witness statements prior to the inquest.

One of the key issues in the inquest was to investigate whether the first police vehicle, 'November One', had made contact with Onese's Kawasaki in the closing seconds of the pursuit. Several eyewitnesses had come forward to express concern about the decision to pursue Onese at a dangerously high speed along an extremely narrow residential street, potentially endangering passers-by. One eyewitness stated that she saw a police car coming towards her, followed by four more with flashing lights and sirens. She alleged that the leading police vehicle in the chase, driven by PC Collier, had closed in on Onese and made contact with the handlebar of his motor-bike. However, she was unable to attend the inquest due to ill health and her statement seemed to be afforded little weight during the hearing. Since Mrs Power had not seen the witness's account as part of disclosure, she was not able to request an adjournment.

Mrs Power argued that the police inquiry into the incident was patently insufficient: there were failures to test the police vehicle at the speed at which it was travelling at the time of death in order to replicate the tyre marks found at the scene; and to forensically examine the damage to the police vehicle which could have been caused by contact with the motorcycle. A long black scratch mark found on the side of the police vehicle was possibly consistent with such contact, but PC Lamb, a road traffic accident investigator assigned to the case, had ruled out such a finding. He said he'd been able to remove the marks on the side of the police car with a bottle of Jif, from which he concluded that the marks had been caused by contact with a black rubber handlebar-cover *prior* to the chase with Onese. They could not, he argued, have been caused by Onese's bike, because the handlebars on his Kawasaki were made of metal.

The irregularities in the inquiry didn't end there. Unknown to Mrs Power and the jury at the time of the inquest, both PC Collier and his passenger, PC Heatley, had made identical statements: *identical* save for a few words which made no contextual difference to the substance. They had made their copycat statements *a full five days* after Onese's death.

Owing to the failures in disclosure, Ann Power had to

cross-examine the officers blind without sight of their accounts, and therefore neither officer was interrogated about the disquieting similarities in their statements. Dr Susan Hungerford, the deputy coroner presiding on Onese's inquest, is in fact known to me. Here is one of life's rich ironies: Dr Hungerford was a former law lecturer at Kingston University and had taught me the law of evidence.

Rather than painstakingly examining these anomalies in police procedure, it seemed that the coroner was inclined to accept the police officers' account without much scrutiny. Critically, therefore, the jury were not made aware of the issue of credibility and impropriety which could be implied by such irregularities. I have no doubt that this would have been the first thing remarked upon by any skilled advocate. Meanwhile, the police officers were represented and thus shielded by senior counsel, and had a number of Traffic Investigation officers giving evidence to back up their version of events.

Nevertheless, Mrs Power did her best to question the police officers involved. Remember this is a woman who has lost her husband. She is not an expert on car chases and stopping speeds, nor did she have any legal training or the benefit of having seen any of the police witness statements or incident report notebooks, but she did one hell of a cracking job. In fact, she clearly dealt with the cross-examination of the police witnesses so rigorously that the jury were not satisfied with their version of events and returned an open verdict.

A year later, in April 1999, following recommendations in Sir William Macpherson's investigation and subsequent report on the death of Stephen Lawrence, the Home Office issued the police with new guidelines urging for prompt and full disclosure to families of documentary evidence before the opening of inquest hearings in cases of deaths while in police custody, or those resulting from the actions of a police officer. Speaking to the BBC, Home Office minister Paul Boateng MP said that police reluctance to provide relevant evidence was damaging to public confidence in the law enforcement organisation: 'It has given rise to unfounded suspicion that matters are being concealed by the police. We are therefore advising chief officers that there should be as great a degree of openness as possible.' (Unfounded suspicion?! I beg to differ.) Furthermore, the guidelines were only voluntary; it was a step forward, but only a change in law would guarantee full, fair and timely disclosure and a level playing field for bereaved families and their legal representatives in the coroner's court.

That same year, Mrs Power came to me because she wanted to pursue an action against the police. I gave her positive advice, but then heard no more of the matter. I subsequently learned that Mrs Power had been unable to get legal aid funding and her solicitors were unwilling to pursue the case on a conditional fee agreement because of the risks associated with the civil action, and so the case was withdrawn. Ostensibly that was that. Mrs Power received no compensation for her husband's death, nor had the chance to get to the bottom of what happened, nor were the officers ever properly called to account. As an advocate now well-versed in conducting successful civil actions against the police, this was a lost opportunity for me to re-examine the officers' evidence, rigorously grill them and potentially uncover the truth.

To all us lawyers this would have been the end of the road. But someone did not say this to Ann Power, because she did not stop there.

Nearly twenty years later, she contacted me again. She told me that she had been following my career over the years. She asked if we could meet because she had found new evidence.

A report had come to light, dated 21 April 1999, by Dr Searle, an expert in road accident analysis, which disagreed with the opinion of PC Lamb that the marks on the police vehicle did not represent contact with her husband's motorcycle.

For the past twenty years, Ann Power had continued stead-fastly to work alone on her case, trying to get hold of the police records and disclosure of the incident and specialist forensic road traffic accident reports. It turned out that there was a mass of documentation to which she never had access at the inquest. I agreed to help her to take an appeal to the High Court and we sought an order that the original inquest be quashed and a fresh inquest held. We were successful at appeal and the High Court judges were full of praise for Mrs Power and the strength she had shown in those long years spent fighting for justice.

Here was a widow and a mother who did not give up, and I was simply inordinately happy to have played a small part in drafting the submissions to the attorney general and paving the way for a new investigation.

A fresh inquest was held in March 2019. I was unable to work on this hearing so one of my colleagues stepped in. The jury found that the duration and intensity of the police pursuit had indeed contributed to Onese's death. They also found that, once engaged in the pursuit, the required ongoing assessment of risk by police officers was deficient, and the escalation of the risk inadequately assessed by the pursuing officers and not communicated to central command. As a result, the pursuit had continued long after it should have been terminated.

Although the jury concluded that there was 'insufficient evidence to determine if close proximity between the police car and Mr Power's bike was a contributory factor to the col-lision', the evidence heard at the hearings made it clear that if the police had terminated the pursuit sooner, Onese Power's death would have been prevented.

I learned an important lesson from Ann Power in this case: if you have faith, the truth *will* come out and it doesn't matter how long it takes. But it requires courage, persistence and a great deal of determination, qualities that my client Ann showed me in abundance. Yet, the tragedy is that when a close loved one dies, many clients don't feel particularly brave or have the wherewithal to be persistent. It makes me question whether our system of justice should be dependent upon the random character traits that a client may or may not possess.

2 2

IBRAHIMA SEY (1967–1996)

Shortly after the inquest into Wayne Douglas's death in police custody in March 1996, a six-month trial began of CS spray, a volatile solvent cyanocarbon tear gas used as an incapacitant by sixteen police forces in England. Two police forces decided not to engage in the trial because of concerns over the safety of the hand-held spray devices, which, according to police guidelines, are 'likely to cause pain and discomfort to the affected areas, streaming eyes and nose, [. . .] coughing, retching, sneezing and a stinging or burning sensation on exposed skin' – and in some cases breathing difficulties. These guidelines, issued by the Association of Chief Police Officers (ACPO) at the time, also stated that CS sprays were intended for use in 'only highly specific contexts and specific ways for the defence of members of the police and the public or in handling highly dangerous situations [. . .]' According to Dr Brian Rappert, a sociologist who researched the use of CS spray by police in the UK, 'Originally they were only to be used as an absolute last resort in cases of serious violence.'* It seemed inevitable that sooner or later there would be a CS-related death. We didn't have to wait

---

* Quoted in 'The Messy Truth of Police CS Spray Use', Bibi van der Zee,
1 February 2011: https://www.theguardian.com/commentisfree/2011/feb/01/cs-spray-police-weapon-use

long. On 16 March 1999, Ibrahima Sey, a 29-year-old asylum seeker from Gambia, died in police custody in Ilford.

Ibrahima was a sturdy, very fit young man who had briefly been a police officer in his native Gambia and played football at a professional level for the country's under-25 squad. His wife Amie was to be my client. Ibrahima suffered from mental health problems and on the evening of his death had been at home in Forest Gate with Amie, celebrating the birth of their second child, when he started acting bizarrely, locking her in a toilet and ordering her to eat frozen hamburgers. Frightened, Amie had managed to escape out of the bathroom window and called 999 from a phone box, in the hope, and assumption, that the emergency services would send an ambulance to take her husband to hospital to receive the medical help he so clearly needed. Instead, the police arrived. Amie and a close friend of the family explained his mental condition to them, and Ibrahima agreed to go voluntarily to the police station if the friend was allowed to accompany him. He was arrested and taken with his friend to Ilford police station. Ibrahima was co-operative; he did not resist arrest and was not handcuffed, but when they reached the station the friend was not allowed to go into the custody area. According to the friend, Ibrahima had then become agitated, pleading for him to stay with him. According to the police version of events, Ibrahima suddenly went crazy, 'violent, twisting and turning' to shake them off and they needed to restrain him. 'Officers were being lifted and flung. Sey seemed to be winning the battle,' the police evidence asserted. Ibrahima's friend said that Ibrahima was terrified, calling out: 'See what they are doing to me?' and reciting prayers.

Ibrahima weighed about 18 stone. Eight officers were involved in the struggle to force him to the ground and put him in handcuffs with his arms behind his back. In the course of the restraint, one of the officers sprayed Ibrahima in the face at close range with CS spray. To quote the official ACPO guidelines, CS spray is to be used 'primarily for dealing with violent subjects who cannot otherwise be restrained'. But Ibrahima was on his knees and *already* handcuffed when the spray was squirted into his face. Later, in evidence we heard that some of the officers in the room were so affected by the caustic effects of the CS spray that they had to be replaced by others. Yet the police said that it had no effect on Ibrahima and he was licking it off his face, a detail that we found difficult to believe because shortly after Ibrahima had been restrained, the police said that he appeared to be having spasms and then became limp. The police officers had held him face down on the floor for fifteen minutes, with two officers keeping him still with their feet on his legs. They then made three vain attempts to raise him to his feet, and in the end he was carried into the custody suite and laid face down on the floor. When an officer started to search him, he realised that Ibrahima was unresponsive. An ambulance crew arrived several minutes later to find Ibrahima lying in the same position, handcuffed in the prone position. He was dead by the time the ambulance reached the hospital. In a press statement, a police spokesperson stated that after his arrival at the police station, Ibrahima had become 'unwell' and was taken by ambulance to hospital where 'despite medical assistance he died'.

A post-mortem carried out in the presence of three pathologists, one representing the coroner, one representing the Police Federation and one representing the Metropolitan Police, gave a provisional finding of 'death following a period of exertion'. It also claimed that Ibrahima had been suffering from hypertensive heart disease. According to his widow and friends, Ibrahima had no history of heart trouble. Furthermore, when they were informed of his death, they were not told that they had the right to have an independent pathologist present at the post-mortem. An independent post-mortem was later arranged at which it was confirmed that there was no proof to substantiate the original diagnosis of heart disease.

It was a huge case. The circumstances of Ibrahima's death were highly controversial. What possible justification could there be for the use of CS spray on a frightened and panicking mentally ill man, who suddenly found himself in police custody, surrounded and forced to the ground by eight police officers and handcuffed? Chief police officers' guidelines for use of CS spray specify that 'prisoners should not be left [. . .] in a prone, face-down position. The suspect should be carefully monitored [. . .] until the effects of CS have worn off.' On the night that Ibrahima died, having been sprayed directly in the face with the CS spray, the officers let him lie there under a form of restraint already known to be potentially fatal.

I had been instructed to represent Ibrahima's widow, Amie, by Raju Bhatt, a partner at a renowned London firm of police law specialist solicitors. I worked on this case for six weeks pro bono. It was an important one; the client needed my assistance and I was being led by the fantastic and eminent Paddy O'Connor QC at Tooks Court Chambers. Unfortunately, two weeks into the inquest at the Walthamstow Coroner's Court, Paddy had a clash with a criminal trial and left me holding the case, which I did alongside Raju, the solicitor, who was very experienced and knowledgeable in deaths in custody work. I thought we made a good team. At the time it was one of the longest and most difficult inquests I'd ever worked on; an almighty battle. From the outset, the police – and the police surgeon – stuck to the same two stories: that Ibrahima had an underlying heart condition and/or had suffered 'a sudden death' linked to his mental condition. They subsequently with-drew their first claim, and medical experts roundly poured scorn on the second.

After almost five weeks the jury returned a verdict of unlaw-ful killing through an act of gross negligence, finding that Ibrahima had died from positional asphyxia as a result of police restraint and excited delirium. This was the first unlawful killing verdict that I had secured. I certainly count the ruling as one of the high points of my legal career. After the verdict, Ibrahima's widow Amie told reporters: 'I knew these people killed him. He needed to be taken to hospital not for them to kill him. The verdict means justice but it will never repay the loss of my husband.' In the outstanding film *Injustice*, Ibrahima's cousin tells the documentary-maker Ken Fero, 'I stuck my fist in the air . . . [Ibrahima] has gone, but not in vain.'*

The feeling of elation that goes hand in hand with the cer-tainty that justice had been done was, however, soon tempered by the fact that despite the jury's finding, the Metropolitan Police made no apology to Ibrahima's wife and family, and the officers involved met no disciplinary action.

Ibrahima Sey's case was interesting for a number of reasons. Firstly, back then there was no legal aid for inquests relating to deaths involving the police, so while I worked hard for six long weeks to represent Amie and protect her interests without earning a penny, those representing the state were paid by tax-payers' money. It begs some fundamental questions: if someone dies at the hands of the state, why should their family bear the onus of funding their investigation? Secondly, it was the first death in this country following the introduction of CS spray.

---

* This extraordinary film follows the relatives of Brian Douglas, Shiji Lapite, Ibrahima Sey, and Joy Gardner and is 'the one and only chance the dead have to speak', as one of the victims' relatives put it. I urge you to watch it.

Although the inquest found no evidence that the use of CS gas was directly responsible for the death, it undoubtedly served to open up the issue of its use by the police to public debate and scrutiny. In 1995 Michael Howard, the then Conservative government home secretary, had approved its use nationally as part of a drive to provide a non-lethal and more politically acceptable alternative to guns. In that respect, CS spray was potentially a positive innovation in policing strategy, but it was never intended for use at close range, nor to restrain a mentally ill and deeply disturbed man, as in the case of Ibrahima Sey, nor to facilitate an arrest.

The inquest findings were reported widely in the national media, with the *Guardian* concluding on the question of the safety of CS spray that 'the call from the Coroner will increase pressure on the Home Office to reconsider the issue.' Labour's home secretary, Jack Straw, nevertheless supported its continued use. Ibrahima's widow Amie didn't stop her fight, however. She set up the Ibrahima Sey Memorial Campaign to launch a 'National Campaign Against CS Spray' in partnership with the Newham Monitoring Project.

On the wider issue of the public face of an increasingly 'tooled up' and paramilitary-style police force, the case highlighted the dangers of positional/restraint asphyxia and CS spray, particularly in the context of the mentally ill, and once again raised serious concerns about police brutality and racism in its treatment in particular of Black and other ethnic minority people in custody. Ibrahima's death was the third within the space of two years in which a coroner's court reached an unlawful killing in police cases involving a death due to positional asphyxia. The others were Richard O'Brien, in Walworth police station in south London in 1994, and Shiji Lapite, a 34-year-old Nigerian asylum seeker in Hackney in December that same year. Yet again, despite the verdicts of unlawful killing and gross negligence, the officers involved remained on duty in our communities and on our streets.

Postscript

After the inquest jury's finding of the unlawful killing of Ibrahima Sey, the Crown Prosecution Service were obligated to reconsider whether they should take any action. A year later, the CPS told Ibrahima's family that there was no realistic prospect of any of the police officers involved ever being prosecuted, stating that 'there was insufficient evidence to justify proceedings.'

According to Home Office figures, an average of fifty people were dying in police custody every year since the 1980s. Until 2021, no police officer had ever been successfully prosecuted for any of these deaths, and in only one case – that of David Oluwale, who was found dead in a river in Leeds in 1969, were any officers convicted, and only on assault charges, not manslaughter, let alone murder.

In 2016, the former Aston Villa striker Dalian Atkinson died after PC Benjamin Monk, 43, discharged his Taser three times and kicked him twice in the head, leaving bootlace prints on Mr Atkinson's forehead during a standoff outside his father's home in Telford, Shropshire. In June 2021, Benjamin Monk was convicted and sentenced for manslaughter in relation to Mr Atkinson's unlawful killing.

In September 1998, the Department of Health set up an independent panel of experts to review the safety of CS spray when used by the police to deal with agitated or aggressive individuals. Concerns had been raised after Humberside Police used CS spray on a 73-year-old pensioner diagnosed with

Alzheimer's disease. Max Incera had been arrested at his residential care home in Hull, handcuffed and held in a police cell for several hours. In June that year, Home Secretary Jack Straw faced calls for an official inquiry when a Bedfordshire traffic policeman was cleared of assault after he sprayed CS gas twice into the face of a pensioner as he sat with his seatbelt on in his car, which was parked on double-yellow lines. The pensioner had been blinded in one eye and needed hospital treatment. Warning of a backlash against its use, the Police Complaints Authority urged all officers not to use CS spray simply to facilitate an arrest.

23

THE 'ARTICLE 2' INQUEST

Article 2
'Everyone's right to life shall be protected by law.
No one shall be deprived of his life intentionally save
in the execution of a sentence of a court following
his conviction of a crime for which this penalty is
provided by law.'

European Convention on Human Rights

In 1998 the Labour government under Tony Blair passed the Human Rights Act (HRA). When it came into force two years later, in October 2000, the rights set out in the European Convention on Human Rights 1950 (ECHR) were at last incorporated, with only minor amendments, into domestic UK law. It was a watershed moment for the UK, and for the legal profession it marked a fundamental shift in our day-to-day practice. In short, the Human Rights Act 1998 was a game-changer.

I'm often asked *why* the new law was so revolutionary. After all, you might argue, in the aftermath of the Second World War, the United Kingdom was a founding member of

the United Nations,* and British UN representatives played
a central role in the creation of the Universal Declaration of
Human Rights 1948.† Given that the UN Declaration states in
its preamble that 'recognition of the inherent dignity and of the
equal and inalienable rights of all members of the human family
is the foundation of freedom, justice and peace in the world',
given that from its inception the UN Declaration should apply
to 'all people, in all nations in the world', and given that the
United Kingdom is signed up to the UN Declaration, surely,
people say, the United Kingdom is a democratic, fair and free
society which adheres to and upholds the principles of human
rights laid out in that Declaration?

Furthermore, the UK is a member of the Council of Europe,
which had incorporated the Universal Declaration of Human
Rights into the European Convention on Human Rights
(ECHR) in 1950. The ECHR treaty, whereby these rights
were now secured by law for European Economic Community
(EEC) member citizens and other nationalities within their
borders, and could be relied on in a court, came into force
in the UK in 1953. In 1960, the European Court of Human
Rights was established; six years later the UK signed up to
grant what is known as 'individual petition', which meant that
UK citizens could take human rights cases directly to the court
in Strasbourg.

However, although the UK had signed up to the Universal

---

* The United Nations was established at the end of the war as an international organisation to maintain peace, and in 1947 it set up the Human Rights Commission, chaired by
Eleanor Roosevelt, First Lady of the United States. Under her guidance, a drafting committee worked together to compose the Universal Declaration of Human Rights, which
was adopted by the UN on 10 December 1948.
† The UDHR sets out a list of the thirty fundamental human rights and freedoms to
which every human being, 'without distinction of any kind, such as race, colour, sex,
language, religion, political or other opinion, national or social origin, property, birth or
other status', is entitled.

Declaration of Human Rights, and later the European Convention on Human Rights, which influenced our law, and our judges could look at it and be guided by it, the ECHR Articles were *not directly part of our UK law*. That all changed with the implementation of the Human Rights Act of 1998, when, finally, more than fifty years after the original UN Declaration, the articles of the European Convention on Human Rights became incorporated directly into UK law. Consequently, now all UK laws have to be consistent and compatible with the fundamental rights and freedoms set out in the Act. Everyone in the UK is entitled to these rights, which may not be breached by public authorities, and if there has been an infringement of those rights, a citizen no longer needs to travel to Strasbourg to pursue a case. The Human Rights Act can now be relied upon in every British court of law.

The protected rights are as follows:

- **Article 1:** Imposes an obligation on the Contracting Parties to the convention to respect Human Rights. The Contracting Parties shall secure to everyone within their jurisdiction the rights and freedoms defined in Section I of this Convention.

- **Article 2**: The right to life – protects your life, by law. The state is required to investigate suspicious deaths and deaths in custody.

- **Article 3**: Freedom from torture and inhuman or degrading treatment – treatment or punishment is considered inhuman when it causes intense physical or mental suffering; it is considered degrading if it humiliates and debases a person beyond that which is usual from punishment. Like the right to life under Article 2, Article 3 requires official, effective investigations into credible allegations of serious ill-treatment by public officials, and authorities must take action to prevent any future infringement of this right.

- **Article 4**: Freedom from slavery and forced labour — sadly while the slave trade was abolished more than a century ago, modern-day slavery persists in the UK. The state must enforce anti-trafficking legislation thereby making it an offence to subject someone to such practices.

- **Article 5**: The right to liberty and security — everyone has the right to freedom; the state cannot detain or imprison you without very good reason. If, for example, you are convicted in court of a crime, you have the right to go to court to challenge your detention if you believe it is unlawful, and receive compensation if you have been unlawfully detained. This right is particularly pertinent for people held in immigration detention, in the criminal justice system, or detained under mental health laws.

- **Article 6**: The right to a fair trial — if accused of a crime, or if a public authority is making a decision that impinges on your civil rights, you have the right to a fair and public trial or hearing by an independent and impartial judge, in a reasonable amount of time. This right applies equally in the context of cases of property law, planning law, family law, contract law and employment law. Anyone accused of a criminal offence has the right to be considered innocent until proven guilty. People must have real and effective access to a court; there must be 'equality of arms' on both sides – meaning a fair balance between the opportunities given to both parties, which may also necessitate access to legal aid.

- **Article 7**: No punishment without law – you cannot be held guilty of a criminal offence on account of any act or omission that was not a crime under the law at the time it was committed. Crimes and penalties can only be set by law, and the state must clearly define the relevant laws, so that people know which acts are criminal.

- **Article 8**: The right to respect for your private and family life, home and correspondence – very broadly, you have the right to live your life privately without government interference, unnecessary surveillance or unwarranted intrusion. This includes your sexual orientation, your lifestyle, and the way you look and dress. It also includes your right to control who sees and touches your body; public authorities cannot, for example, leave you undressed in a busy hospital ward or when in custody, or take a blood sample without your permission.

- **Article 9**: The right to freedom of thought, conscience and religion – you can believe and think what you like and also have the right to put your thoughts and beliefs into action.

- **Article 10**: The right to freedom of expression – you have the right to hold your own opinions and to express them freely, and join with others peacefully to express your views, without government interference.

- **Article 11**: The right to freedom of assembly and association – this right protects your right to protest by holding meetings and demonstrations with other people, and to form and be part of a trade union, a political party or any other association. Conversely, nobody has the right to force you to join a protest, trade union, political party or other association.

- **Article 12**: The right to marry or form a civil partnership and start a family – 'men and women of marriageable age shall have the right to marry and to found a family, according to national laws governing the exercise of this right.'

- **Article 13**: The right to an effective remedy. Everyone whose rights and freedoms as set forth in this Convention are violated shall have an effective remedy before a national authority notwithstanding that the violation has been committed by persons acting in an official capacity.

- **Article 14**: The right not to be discriminated against in respect of these rights and freedoms – under the Human Rights Act everyone's rights are equal. It is illegal to discriminate on a wide range of grounds including 'sex, race, colour, language, religion, political or other opinion, national or social origin, association with a national minority, property, birth or other status'. This right can be applied to discrimination on the basis of age or disability, sexual orientation, illegitimacy, marital status, trade union membership, and gender status and imprisonment.

- **Article 15**: The right to a nationality. No one should be arbitrarily deprived of their nationality and everyone has the right to change their nationality.

- **Article 1 of the First Protocol:** The right to peaceful enjoyment of your property – everyone is entitled to the peaceful enjoyment of their possessions, and no one shall be deprived of his possessions except in the public interest and subject to the conditions provided for by law.

- **Article 2 of the First Protocol:** The right to an education – no one can be denied the right to an effective education.

- **Article 3 of the First Protocol:** The right to participate in free elections and cultural life.

There was a complete sea change following the introduction of the 1998 Human Rights Act; lawyers were actually trained in looking out for human rights infringements. Once people are trained, they are going to spot things, there is going to be a new body of jurisprudence (meaning the philosophy of law; where our law comes from) to deal with new nuances of the law. This constituted a truly momentous shift in how the courts approached cases involving agents of the state, i.e. anyone or any state institution entrusted with the care and the rights of a citizen, such as prison staff, police officers or hospital workers. Most particularly the Human Rights Act radically transformed inquests into the death of a citizen while in the care of the state: in police custody; in prison; in immigration detention centres; and deaths in psychiatric and mental health institutions. In fact, ECHR case law has transformed the area of inquests perhaps more than any other that has been adjudicated under the Human Rights Act.

A lot of the cases I worked on then, and continue to do now, are those where we argue that the person has died directly at the hands of the state – for example, in police shootings – or where the state or state agent is complicit, or implicitly involved, in the death. As I have described, before 1998, the role of the inquest was limited. By focusing on 'by what means' the deceased came by their death, but not 'in what circumstances', the purpose of the inquest, therefore, was not to hold the state to account.

This was changed by the European Convention on Human Rights. One of the rights it protects is the right to life. Article 2, as interpreted by the European Court, is not simply a right not to be killed; it also imposes two explicit obligations on the state: a *negative obligation*, i.e. to not take or endanger a citizen's life; and a *positive obligation*, i.e. to proactively take steps to safeguard the lives of its citizens.

The positive obligations can be divided into three. The first is the 'systems duty', the duty to have an adequate system to protect life, including criminal law provisions that prohibit and punish violent offences. The second is the 'operational duty'. In some circumstances, where the state knows or ought to know that there is a 'real and immediate risk' to someone's life, it may have a duty to take reasonable measures to protect that person. This applies, for instance, when someone is at risk from the criminal acts of a third party. In some circumstances it also requires the state to take reasonable measures to prevent someone committing suicide, say, if they are in prison or detention. The third is the 'investigative duty'. This applies where a person dies at the hands of the state, or in other circumstances that engage the state's responsibility. Following the introduction of the Human Rights Act, these cases were now referred to as 'Article 2 Inquests'. Under the Act, there must be proper, effective investigations into the circumstances of all deaths *caused by* the state, or where it appears the State has *failed to protect life*. There is a state obligation for such an investigation also to be *prompt, independent and open to public scrutiny*.

In recent times, for example, there has been a rise in the number of self-inflicted deaths in prisons by hangings and self-harm. Before the Human Rights Act, in the wake of a death in custody, the inquest normally looked at the circumstances of the death in terms of negligence, neglect or failures. There was a short investigation and coroners were often reluctant to look beyond the actual twenty-four hours leading up to, or the circumstances behind, the death. An inquest back then, therefore, would usually have lasted two or three days.

With the advent of the Human Rights Act, coroners realised that to make an inquest meaningful and Human Rights Law compatible, they couldn't make do with a verdict that baldly stated that someone had died by 'Self-inflicted Death',

'Accidental Death' or 'Unlawful Death'. The textbook example is a case commonly referred to as 'Middleton'.* This was an appalling case of a young man who hanged himself in a prison. Everybody knew that he had hanged himself — there was no suggestion of any third-party involvement in his death — so the obvious verdict was going to be 'Self-inflicted Death', i.e. suicide; he took his own life. There had been a series of failures, however, on the part of the prison services to keep this vulnerable young man safe, therefore in Middleton, the House of Lords Court, the highest court in the land, ruled that under Human Rights Act law the state was in breach of the duty to protect and safeguard life, and that the inquest was insufficient in scope. In order to comply with Article 2, the role of coroners where a person had died at the hands of the state needed to change, the Lords said: compliance with the investigative obligation 'must rank among the highest priorities of a modern democratic state governed by the rule of law'.

Consequently, today in an inquest into a similar self-inflicted death in a prison, there has to be proper investigation into all the strands of care for people who are often extremely vulnerable while in custody. The deceased may have seen healthcare professionals at the prison, who therefore knew that he or she was suicidal but didn't record it; the prisoner didn't receive appropriate medication; the prison didn't have a prison cell bell system, whereby the prisoner could summon help if they were distressed; there was no effective 'cell watch' system in place — an intermittent check system to monitor the prisoner on a suicide watch — or if they had such a system it was not followed; the prisoner had bed sheets that could easily be used to hang themself; or the cell had a number of accessible ligature

---

* In R (Middleton) v HM Coroner for Western Somerset [2004] 2 AC 182.

points where somebody who is suicidal would have the opportunity to tie up a noose.

So, the positive obligation to protect life clearly applies when a person is killed by police, prison officers or other agents of the state. But it isn't limited to those cases. As Middleton makes clear, it applies to cases where a person commits suicide while in custody.

The Article 2 investigative duty can also apply to deaths for which the state bears responsibility in a broader sense. In Turkey, the European Court found a breach of Article 2 in respect of a disaster caused by a poorly maintained municipal rubbish dump, and in a case in Russia the European Court found a breach of Article 2 in respect of failure to protect people from a natural disaster. These principles are now clearly embedded in our law. Thus, in the Grenfell Tower fire disaster inquiry, for example, the Article 2 investigative obligation has been engaged. Article 2 is a constantly evolving area where lawyers such as myself have been attempting to push the boundaries and press the state to take increasing responsibility for killings which aren't directly the result of state violence but are caused directly or indirectly by state policy. That is how impactful European human rights law has been.

The principles of Article 2 are now embedded in the law: human rights are something the state has to adhere to, and so there is necessarily a greater priority and gravity afforded to inquests into certain deaths in state custody, and more to argue about. If, in investigating a death, you are looking at all the safeguarding issues, there will be any number of interested people involved in the hearing, from probation officers, prison staff, prison medical staff to family members, and also expert witnesses. Such complex cases today, therefore, are time-consuming. Whereas the hearings used to take a day,

maybe two, they now commonly last a couple of weeks at the
very least. Similarly, with death-in-custody cases involving the
police, if a restraint death is being investigated, it's not uncommon for the inquest to last a month.

The introduction of the Human Rights Act was also when
we saw the beginnings of narrative verdicts from inquest juries:
a series of written factual statements as to the wider context
of how somebody died, as in, for example: 'the deceased died
when he was put into his cell. At the time he was known to
be depressed. The prison had a cell bell system which on the
night of his death was not working and had not been checked.
The prison officers failed to comply with the prison's suicide
watch procedure,' and so on. Today, such narrative verdicts in
Article 2 cases are the norm, but back in the early 2000s, they
were rare because the Human Rights Law had only recently
come into force.

On occasion, the coroner might also deliver a series of 'recommendations' to the institution involved, in the hope that
those recommendations would be acted upon to ensure that
those failings did not reoccur – and therefore wholly preventable deaths might be avoided. But sadly, as history has shown
me, especially in the context of the restraint cases I am working
on to this day, in 2021, such recommendations are too often
seemingly made in vain.

All inquests and inquiries now have to fully involve the
next of kin. There is a requirement on behalf of the state to
guarantee the family's right to participate; there has to be
'equality of arms'. Equality of arms is a lawyer's term for an
intuitive concept that we all understand – the basic concept of
procedural fairness. Each party must have adequate time and
opportunity to prepare their case. Neither should be allowed
to ambush the other at the last minute with a different case to

the one they were expecting. Both should have access to the evidence the other is relying on, and the opportunity to think about how they are going to challenge it. At the hearing or trial, they should be able to call witnesses, and to ask questions of the other side's witnesses. They should each have the same opportunity to make arguments before the court and put forward their case. In short, neither should be put at a procedural disadvantage compared to the other.

These are basic, obvious principles that everyone understands. But how they should be applied in practice has long been debated by lawyers. For instance, does equality of arms mean that if lawyers represent one side, the other should also be represented by lawyers? In criminal cases, nowadays many countries guarantee the right to legal aid for people who are charged with a serious crime. But in civil cases all over the world, it is common for one side to be represented by a high-powered legal team and the other to be representing themselves. After all, we live in a capitalist world where legal services, like so much, are bought and sold, and some people have deeper pockets than others. Legal aid schemes, where they exist, are usually means-tested and don't necessarily cover every type of case.

A person representing themselves – a 'litigant in person', as lawyers call them – may have all the same opportunities, in theory, as the other side. But they may not be able to take advantage of those opportunities because they don't know enough about the law, the procedure, or how to present their case effectively.

After 2000, however, in order to make certain Article 2 inquests compatible with the Act, the government had to introduce a special legal aid scheme to fund these inquests.

Subsequently, the balance of my practice went from being

mainly police civil litigation cases to predominantly inquest work due to the exponential rise in Article 2 inquests. Many more Article 2 cases were now receiving the full and proper scrutiny they had not hitherto been afforded, and they took much more time to work on.

As I have said, for centuries a major issue for lawyers has been disclosure. A prosecutor's failures of disclosure can cause a criminal case to collapse, for instance. Does fairness mean that a party should be required to disclose evidence they hold that undermines their case or supports the other party's case? In England and Wales, we now have complex rules on disclosure in both criminal and civil cases. In criminal cases the prosecutor is required to disclose such evidence in their possession. Similarly, in civil cases we have the same process of disclosure – which used to be called 'discovery', as it still is in the US.

Over the past twenty years, we have witnessed huge improvements in the experience of the inquest for the bereaved. There is now a general right to disclosure. The family has a more central place in the investigation. The importance of learning lessons has become a duty under the primary legislation. But serious problems remain, particularly from the point of view of a family seeking justice, and an inquest is often still traumatic in the extreme. The cost of running an inquest is as big a factor as ever: funding for legal representation for families is increasingly limited, and therefore inequality of funding between those representing the state and those representing the families is often dramatic. The legal aid system as a whole is under attack, which means that underfunded, specialist law firms and barristers may not be able to survive in practice to represent families at inquests.

Equally, coroners are under-resourced and subject to

increasing budgetary pressure and, in addition, with any death in custody, or one involving any agent of the state, there is a mandatory requirement to have a jury – and a two-day jury hearing is a lot less expensive than a two-week jury hearing. While there are some excellent coroners, on occasion the focus can still be on avoiding controversy rather than doing justice and preventing future fatality. Difficult issues also arise in relation to deaths which fall outside the scope of Article 2 principles, but which nevertheless require thorough and effective inquiries. Thus there remains a risk that the inquest may exacerbate the grieving process rather than assist it.

These deficiencies in the system are all the more contrary given that the premise of an inquest is peculiarly and vitally constructive. As a result of civil proceedings, the best that can happen is that one party receives compensation. At an inquest, the possibility of preventing future deaths can be examined in a public and accountable fashion. Inquests *can* save lives, and the truth is that the families I work for value this more than any financial compensation.

Yes, the inquest system in England and Wales has much improved since I bumbled through my first case, but an inquest is a strange category, and the Ministry of Justice, I think, has never quite known what to do with the coronial courts. Unlike much judicial office – the magistrates' courts, the county court judges, the Crown Courts – which is funded by the central government, the coroner's office is funded by the local authority. Coroners are therefore subject to the individual local council's budget – and its budget cuts. The service offered by coroners' offices nationwide is consequently extremely patchy, and how well the coroner's office can serve its community is often somewhat of a postcode lottery. Some local authorities fund their local coroners' courts well, while others struggle in terms of resources and time. If a coroner is impoverished, there is real pressure to hold shorter inquests, and without juries.

This inequality was recognised and corrected in 2012 with the implementation of the Coroners and Justice Act 2009 and the creation of the office of the chief coroner: a senior member of the judiciary who oversees all of the coroners in England and Wales. The Act allows a coroner in one area to make a request of a coroner in an adjoining area to take over some of its cases. There was always a power to make such request, but in the past it was often refused. The chief coroner's responsibilities include providing support, leadership and guidance for coroners in England and Wales and setting national standards for all coroners.

I knew the first chief coroner, His Honour Peter Thornton QC* (a founder and former head of London's Doughty Street Chambers), well because he used to invite me to teach three times a year at training days for coroners at the Coroners' Society. As a barrister I would travel all around the country and challenge the coroners at inquests, and over the years I had developed a reputation as being somewhat 'difficult', and the coroners' pariah. Completely unfounded, of course – I was as nice as they come! – but my reputation preceded me and so I was a marked man. When Judge Thornton brought me into the fold and I took on my teaching role, I realised that the coroners were mostly decent, civilised people who were doing the best in difficult circumstances to get things right. In turn, I sensed that they realised I was not the troublesome nightmare they had been led to believe.

In short, when a person is killed by the state, their loved

---

* Judge Thornton was succeeded as chief coroner in 2016 by Mark Lucraft QC. In December 2020, Judge Lucraft was succeeded by the current chief coroner, His Honour Judge Thomas Teague QC.

ones and the wider public naturally want to know the truth. By whom were they killed? Why were they killed? Was it justified? Whose fault was it? What can be done to keep it from happening to someone else? Our inquest system should be there to answer those questions. Unfortunately, experience shows that it often fails to deliver what many families consider justice.

If deaths are not investigated, then the authorities cannot be held to account and democracy is threatened. And if deaths are not investigated, we are not a society that values human life. If we want to know what that looks like, we only need to look to the worst abuses of repressive regimes, from the 'disappearances' under Argentina's military dictatorship, investigative journalists on the streets of Europe being murdered, opposition leaders who are poisoned in Russia, to the murder and dismembering of Jamal Khashoggi in the Saudi consulate in Turkey. It should be obvious why the investigation of deaths is central to a democratic and free political system.

24

THE DEATH OF CHRISTOPHER
ALDER (1960–1998)

Soon after the Ibrahima Sey inquest, in the summer of 2000 and only months before the Human Rights Act came into force in the UK, I was instructed to take on the inquest at Hull Crown Court into the death of Christopher Alder. It was my first inquest into a death in police custody during which all the human rights arguments about the investigation and the right to life were explored. It was also the first case I had done whereupon seeing the CCTV footage in evidence, the jury wept at the inhumanity of man towards man. And while it was the biggest case of my career to date, the Christopher Alder inquest would become my nemesis. It is this case which, perhaps, has had the greatest negative impact on me, both personally and professionally.

In 1996, or thereabouts, my dad took early retirement and finally fulfilled his dream of moving back to Dominica. My mum joined him later, but she didn't take to living there; Dominica wasn't her island and she missed her friends and life in London, so she had come back and had been helping us with her grandchildren. Left alone, Dad didn't look after his health; he had been diagnosed with Type 2 diabetes in his early forties, and by the time he got to Dominica, his eyesight was failing.

I hadn't understood just how badly he had deteriorated until I went to visit him in early 2000. Dad picked me up at the airport and as he drove he kept saying, 'Leslie, it's really, really dark.' But it was in the middle of the day; we were in broad daylight. Dad was going blind. When we got to our family home on the top of the mountain overlooking the Atlantic Ocean where it met the Caribbean Sea, one of the most beautiful views you can ever imagine, I sat down with him, realising that he probably could not see what I could see. I had to have a conversation with this proud and fiercely independent man who was my father. I had to tell him that the diabetes was destroying his eyesight, and he wouldn't be able to drive any more. This was tough; he was still a relatively young man, in his early sixties, and he was almost entirely blind. After that, I decided that he couldn't stay in Dominica alone, and so I brought him home to the UK to be properly looked after and to find out if anything could be done to save his sight. There wasn't, and in the months after he returned to London his health continued to go downhill rapidly; his diabetes was out of control and he was very frail.

Meanwhile, my personal life was in a mess. Having been together for seventeen mostly happy years, Angela and I were going through an extremely bad patch. Our marriage had been faltering since the birth of our son Isaac in December 1997. The fault of the demise of my marriage is very much down to me. I neglected home life and Angela and had become a workaholic. I was working long cases, often spending week after week away from home, leaving Angela to look after our two young children alone. Looking back now I don't know how Angela suffered me. We had become distant, arguing all the time, and by the summer of 2000, when I went up to Hull to work on Christopher Alder's inquest, our marriage had effectively collapsed. To all intents and practical purposes, I had moved out of our family home. When I was in London, I was sleeping on a bed I made up on the floor at my mum's place and only went home at weekends to spend time with the kids. Dad was a shell of his former self. It was him, Mum and me in a one-bedroom flat and I was content for the first time in a long time. But one of my biggest regrets then is that while I was away, busy fighting for justice for others in cases where I really felt that I was needed, I didn't spend nearly enough time with my kids and my own family. The saving grace of this break-up was the fact that both Angela and myself tried to work together in terms of raising our children. And despite the fact they had a broken home, both Megan and Isaac have gone on to accomplish great things. We are both incredibly proud of all they've achieved.

When I talk about racism and discrimination at the Bar, for me, the Christopher Alder case epitomises these in every respect: in the mistreatment of bereaved families and also in the mistreatment of counsel I experienced in the course of the trial. It is and remains one of the most difficult inquests I have ever done.

Christopher Alder was a hero; he had served his queen and country. He was a paratrooper with the British Army, had fought in the Falklands and been commended for his service in Northern Ireland. You can imagine what a tour of duty must have been like as a Black man in the '80s in Ulster, where he would have been so conspicuous. Nevertheless, he survived that and returned home to live in Hull where he was training to be a computer programmer. One night, in April 1998, he went to a nightclub, had too much to drink and got into a fight outside the venue with another man. He was struck in the face, fell backwards and hit his head on the road. The ambulance arrived. Christopher was suffering from post-concussional syndrome and was taken to Hull Royal Infirmary. Alcohol combined with a head injury is not a good combination, and when he arrived at the emergency department he was confused and 'troublesome', refusing to be taken for an X-ray examination. The hospital staff eventually called the police, who arrested him for breach of the peace. He was restrained, put in a police van and taken to Queen's Garden police station in Hull city centre.

At some point during the short journey, Christopher collapsed, and on arrival at the station, handcuffed and unconscious, he was 'partially dragged and partially carried' from the van by officers, who then left him lying on the floor of the custody suite, his trousers round his ankles. The CCTV recording shows Christopher lying exposed, his clothing soiled with faeces and urine, and face down with his hands cuffed behind his back and his face to the side in a pool of blood and vomit. Five police officers stand by talking and laughing among themselves for a full twelve minutes, not even looking at Christopher, who can be heard groaning and gurgling in the thirty-seven desperate last breaths that it took him to die. A PC Dawson, the arresting officer, can be heard telling the custody sergeant, 'He is as right as rain. This is just a show. He has a simple haematoma, which is a laceration to his head.' Later he quips, 'They don't show you this on the joining video.' Another officer, PC Blakey, is heard explaining that their prisoner had earlier been 'playacting' at the hospital: 'He kept doing dying swan acts, falling off the trolley.' An audio tape recorded someone making monkey noises as he lay dead.

As Christopher is left lying there, in an indecent state and clearly in physical distress, not once does one of them go to check on him, put him in the recovery position, or try to rouse him. The officers don't even realise that he has died until they

finally notice that he has stopped moving. Then they panic.
And it was all captured on CCTV; Christopher is actually seen
on camera as he expels his last breath in front of these joking
police constables and the custody sergeant. I shed tears the first
time I watched the tape. I hadn't seen anything like that before.
The inhumanity of one human to another. The uncaring attitudes of the police officers. The indignity as Christopher was
left on the floor with officers stepping over him as if he wasn't
there, his buttocks exposed. His dying groans and moans not
worthy of attracting any attention. If you had a caring heart,
you had to shed tears. But I also cried because this was a man
in my image dying like that. A Black man, dying in a very
white world.

What a case. I was representing Christopher's family, his
sister Janet and his brother Richard. Christopher had two
young children at the time of his death. Janet Alder was a force
of nature, an incredibly strong and fearless woman who wanted
to call the police to account. She became a tireless human
rights activist following Christopher's death. Often, she and I
would debate whether my approach to the case was the correct
one. By contrast, Richard was reserved and gentle. Unusually
they were both instructed by different solicitors, who in turn
instructed me. Richard had a local Hull firm representing
him. Janet instructed a formidable civil liberties solicitor, Ruth
Bundey from Leeds, for whom I had a great deal of respect.
Ruth was one of the solicitors who had instructed me in my
early days and shown faith in me. Despite the difference in the
strategic approaches of Janet and Richard, both had a common
goal: justice for their dead brother. That was my job in the
court room.

At the time of Christopher's death, each of the Hull police
constables had separate representation. The police custody

sergeant was represented. The hospital ambulance crew were represented. The doctors at Hull Royal Infirmary were represented. There were some ten other interested persons represented at this inquest, and most of their representatives — no, *all* of them — were arguing against me. The hostility I felt from the other advocates went beyond what I had ever experienced before. The stakes were so high.

` The inquest was beset by controversy from the outset. The original jury of nine was cut to five men and three women after one of the jurors was heard to make a racist remark. In spite of Richard telling the court that the chain of events leading to his brother's death appeared completely out of character, barristers acting for the police made a point of calling Christopher's character into question with unsubstantiated and wholly misleading suggestions of anabolic steroid and drug use, mental illness and panic attacks.

Then there was the fact that potentially crucial evidence had been destroyed by the police: Christopher's clothes had been burned, and the clothes belonging to the police officers implicated in his death had been professionally cleaned.

Dr Nat Cary, now a Home Office pathologist, whom I had first met on the Wayne Douglas case, was instructed for the coroner and stated that the cause of Christopher's death was 'positional asphyxia due to inhalation of the stomach contents'. A significant contribution to this was the position he had been placed in, he said, adding that Christopher's life could have been saved by early treatment. The most likely and most significant cause of death, therefore, was the result of lack of care by the police officers in the custody suite that night. The family had instructed an eminent forensic pathologist, Professor Jack Crane, and he agreed with Dr Cary.

All five officers, who had been suspended, were called to give evidence, but because they had been charged for Misconduct in Public Office pending trial in the Crown Court, they refused to answer questions more than 150 times.* The inquest did hear that Sergeant Dunn had admitted in a police interview that he thought Christopher had been making 'excessive snoring noises' as part of an act to frighten officers. 'I thought the floor was the safest place for him. He was laid down with his face to one side,' he stated, adding that he thought he was 'blowing through blood [...] to try to upset us and rattle us', as if a dying man was blowing blood to upset the police officers who were there to care for him.

At the time this was the longest inquest there had ever been: today six weeks is nothing (the inquests into the deaths of ninety-six Liverpool FC fans in the 1989 Hillsborough Stadium disaster, for example, lasted two years), but then it was unprecedented. During the hearings, I was in Hull, an unfamiliar city to me, away from my children, going home at the weekend to see them for just one day. I lost a lot of weight that summer because of the strain and stress: stress from the case, stress from my opponents, stress from my clients, stress because of the problems in my marriage. I had by now moved out of the marital home and had an on-off girlfriend at the time and she and I were constantly arguing, breaking up, then making up again – and then the cycle would repeat itself. It was as if I had gone from one bad relationship straight into another and, to top it all, I had the worry of my father's increasing ill health. My world was falling apart and I was making a lot of bad decisions. I now see that I was on a path of self-destruction and it would

* Our UK law comes from two sources: firstly, laws which originate in and may be amended by an Act of Parliament: i.e. our elected MPs vote on a Bill which becomes part of UK statutory law, for example, the Road Traffic Act; the Coroners and Justice Act. Common Law, on the other hand, is a residual body of judge-made law which originates in a series of precedents or judges' interpretation of the law down the years.

have taken very little to push me over the edge. The one thing that was going well for me was my work and the cases I was involved in. Nevertheless, looking back, I do not know how I survived the Alder case. The one place where I got a lot of support was from INQUEST. Its co-directors of the time were Deb Coles and Helen Shaw. Gilly Mundy and Helen would regularly come up to Hull during the case to show support. Helen knew exactly what I was going through both in my personal life and at work. She was a pillar of support and encouraged me to keep going. But things would come to a head.

On 22 August, two days before the inquest was due to conclude with the jury retiring to consider their verdicts, my father suffered a stroke and went into a coma. My mum called, just before I had to put together my submissions as to which verdict the coroner should leave. I wanted him to leave an unlawful killing verdict for the jury to consider. In my submission, I had ten other representations to take into account, all arguing that this was *not* unlawful killing. I stood as the sole voice dealing with all these other submissions. Meanwhile my dad was in hospital in a coma. I went before Geoffrey Saul, the East Yorkshire coroner, told him about my father and was given just one day off to go to see him in London. Understandably, the coroner did not want to risk the inquest collapsing.

My dad was in St Thomas's Hospital. I sat beside him, looking out across the river at the Houses of Parliament, talking to him even though I didn't know if he could hear me, telling him about the incredible view from his window. I gave him a shave that day and wasn't sure if he could feel it. And I cried. I was not my dad's favourite and our relationship had been tense. Here was this man, in a London hospital, and I knew that he would have preferred to be in his village on his mountain on his little emerald island in the Caribbean.

The next morning, I went back to Hull to do the submissions. It was a long shot, but I put my all into it. I outlined my plea to the coroner and stated the reasons that he had to leave unlawful killing; he had no choice. In his summing up to the jury, Geoffrey Saul bravely left it. I can't remember how many hours the jury was out for, but they returned with a verdict that Christopher Alder had been unlawfully killed.

This was dynamite, a moment of victory, and after Ibrahima Sey's inquest the second unlawful killing verdict I had achieved. But while Richard and Janet Alder could be thankful for the justice of this verdict, they were nevertheless disappointed that the coroner had rejected their assertion that race had played a part in their brother's death. 'Perhaps he should now read the MacPherson report,' Janet told the press. The statistics, however, seemed to back up the suspicion of many of us, including the Alder family: while the overall number of deaths in custody had fallen in 1999 by a third since their record high of sixty-five the year before, the pattern of the disproportionately high percentage of young Black and Asian men dying remained a matter of grave concern: Home Office figures published in 2000 showed that twenty-nine, or 12 per cent, of those dying in police custody since April 1996, and fifty-two (or 10 per cent) of those dying in prisons since January 1996, were Black or Asian. While some of those deaths were either suicide or alcohol-related, many were the result of the use of excessive force or restraint.

The Christopher Alder case for me is also synonymous with one of the worst times in my life. That summer, as I worked Christopher's case, I had no idea that my client, Janet Alder, and I were being spied upon. It wasn't until fourteen years later that details of the police surveillance during the trial were uncovered. A team of about ten, perhaps twelve, officers were trailing me on most days during the inquest, reporting on my meetings with my clients and listening in to legally privileged conversations. The police have never been able to give any justification for this. Why, in particular, was I targeted? And what was Janet's crime? Asking awkward questions: 'Why did you detain my brother? Why did you restrain him?' Seeking justice for her brother's death?

Although I cannot prove it, I suspect that when I was working with Louise Christian on the Wayne Douglas inquest, we may also have been spied upon by the police. Louise and I talked about our suspicions that we were being monitored at the time; our phones had started to make strange clicking noises. Admittedly, this was a high-profile case in which we as lawyers were asserting that Wayne had been unlawfully killed, but why anyone would want to listen in on our conversations made no sense. Many years later, during the 'Spycops' scandal – the revelations of undercover police infiltration of more than 1,000 political and social justice groups in England and Wales since 1968 – we asked the Metropolitan Police to investigate, but they said that there was no evidence to suggest that we had been spied on. Knowing what I know now about the police's surveillance during the Christopher Alder inquest, I can only surmise that our hunch was right.

Shortly after the jury's verdict I left the court. I needed to see my dad. On the train back to London, I received a call from Janet Alder's number. A female voice said 'hello'. It was a jury member enjoying a drink in the pub with her fellow jurors after the case. She had bumped into Janet and was using Janet's phone to call me.

In any case involving a jury, as a lawyer you stand in front of them every day. You and your team watch them, speculating who is with you and who is against you. During the Christopher

Alder case we had thought that, on the whole, the jury didn't seem hostile to us. We often had nicknames for people in the court, and our nickname for this juror was Ally McBeal, or Red, because she had red hair. I was taken aback that she was ringing me now, and I admit I felt a little uncomfortable, but didn't think too much of it because the case was over.

I went straight to St Thomas's and sat beside Dad's bed for two hours watching his chest go up and down. The juror rang me again, this time from her own phone. We chatted about my father and she told me how her father had recently died in violent circumstances. I was shocked and offered my condolences. We spoke the next day and the next, and every evening I would go to Dad's bedside and she and I would talk until we developed an intense telephone and text relationship. My wife and I had separated and were barely speaking, and here was this woman whom I hardly knew, giving me a lot of time and comforting me. I would cry with her, talk about my dad, and all the while I didn't question whether or not this relationship was appropriate, or if the fact that she had been on the jury was problematic.

Two weeks later, on 1 September, Dad passed away. It was a desperately sad time. I still regret bringing him back from Dominica. Did I do the right thing? Would he have been better ending his days on the island that he loved?

I hadn't experienced such a bereavement in my life before and my grief was overwhelming. I was grieving too for the end of my marriage. After Dad died, Angela and I both knew we had fallen apart and we couldn't fix it. We had met and fallen in love as sixteen- and seventeen-year-old kids, and by the time I was thirty we had both changed utterly. Angela had a great career in social housing and was working for a housing association, while I was in a different universe, working every hour in the rarefied world of the Inns of Court. In our younger years, she was absolutely fantastic in terms of encouraging and supporting me throughout the early stages at the Bar. We were good at encouraging each other. I was behind her, pushing her, and she was behind me. But as time went on, we developed completely different ambitions and goals. A career can do that to you; all those experiences I had had made me the person I became. Towards the end of our marriage, I don't think we really knew each other at all.

After Dad's death, my relationship with the juror had run its course. I had met her on a couple of occasions, once in London, once in Hull. By October it had fizzled out. In November, I decided to go to the Caribbean for a couple of months. I was suffering from stress, the strain of the Alder case, the break-up of my marriage and grief for my father. I needed a break from my tattered life in London. Then, just before I left, I received a telephone call from a man telling me he was the juror's boyfriend. The juror had assured me they were living separate lives and were on the verge of breaking up, but it seemed he had taken her phone and read our text messages, some of which were quite intimate. He knew who I was, he said, and this was not the last I was going to hear of him.

I thought little of it, and when I rang her to tell her, she assured me they had split up and it was all bluster. It wasn't. The ex-boyfriend made a complaint to the coroner and the coroner had to investigate. The issue was whether there had been any tampering on my part with the jury during the inquest. This was all being done without my knowledge. My phone records were accessed and it was clear that there was no case of collusion: the first telephone call and text messages were all after the inquest. Nevertheless, in December, while I was in the Caribbean, I received a call telling me that the City of

London police wanted to speak to me. I was shocked. I came back to London and contacted Mike Fisher, Louise Christian's partner in her firm Christian Fisher, and told him everything. I felt so stupid; I thought I'd destroyed my career. Mike was down-to-earth and straight-to-the-point as ever. I should go to the police as requested and tell them exactly what happened. So I did. I went in voluntarily and was interviewed. The suggestion was that I had had contact with the juror before the verdict, which was nonsense and they knew that. And although I knew, and they knew, that I had done nothing wrong, I told them every relevant detail about how I met and started the relationship with the juror, and the investigation went no further. Nevertheless, I'd never been in a police interview room before, and it was extremely stressful and highly embarrassing. I thought that was the worst of it, but it still hadn't gone away.

Immediately after the outcome of Christopher Alder's inquest, the police had put in a judicial review to challenge the jury's unlawful killing decision. Because of the police investigation I had been involved in, I couldn't participate and defend this verdict. I was compromised, and felt like damaged goods. A friend of mine, Stephen Simblet, stepped into my shoes. My former mentor Courtenay Griffiths QC also stepped in to fight the appeal representing a different interested party. It caused me a lot of grief and anxiety in the short term, but worse was to come.

In early March 2001 a reporter from the *Mail on Sunday* rang me up one Saturday evening asking me to comment on a story they were running the next day. No comment, I said. Somebody (I can't prove it, but I assume that 'somebody' can only be a member of the City of London police investigation team) had leaked the transcripts of the telephone calls and texts between the juror and me to a reporter. The following morning the salacious, yet largely inaccurate, details of my private life were splashed all over the newspaper with the headline, 'Police probe reveals juror and lawyer's date in a hotel room: Disclosures may force new inquest into death of a man in custody.'

It may be a truism, but when you are in trouble you soon know who your real friends are. Despite the fact that I had done no wrong, many people, even colleagues in my chambers, who I thought were my friends, didn't even text or call to see if I was OK. When there was a sniff that I might have done something inappropriate, they abandoned me. I remember my mum ringing me up that Sunday morning saying that one of her friends in church had told her she had read a big story about me on the front page of a tabloid paper. I had to sit my mum down and tell her about the whole affair. Then I had to tell my soon-to-be ex-wife. Angela hadn't seen the paper and it was a terrible conversation to have to have. I was an extremely private person and it is horrific even now to remember those exchanges. When a crisis like that happens in your life, facing the people close to you, and having to reveal personal and intimate details about your life, is devastating. But that was the end of that. Or, again, so I thought.

It transpired that my phone records had been leaked to the police legal team in Hull, and they included intimate details of my dealings with the juror in their appeal against the inquest verdict. Although the police were not alleging any impropriety – rather, they were implying that this juror's mind wasn't on the hearing and because she obviously fancied me, her judgement was likely to be biased – the fact that my private life and personal communications were being pored over by a High Court judge was acutely embarrassing and professionally damaging to me. At the judicial review Courtenay conceded that while my involvement with the juror had shown 'a gross lack of judgement', he effectively argued that the relationship provided no grounds to quash the verdict. The judge agreed. He made clear that because we had only begun talking to each other after the judgment there was nothing improper on my part, and he also rejected the police's argument about the juror's lack of impartiality during the case. The police therefore lost their challenge and the verdict of unlawful killing was upheld. But my name was now eternally linked to a case in which a juror had become obsessed with me, and an inquest outcome which had been contested on the grounds of jury bias.

Postscript

In 2002, five police officers involved in the Christopher Alder case were put on trial for manslaughter and misconduct in public office, but were cleared of all charges on the orders of the judge at Teesside Crown Court. A previous investigation by IPCC ruled that four of the officers present in the police station at the time were guilty of the 'most serious neglect of duty'. It was a conclusion that was disputed by the Police Federation, the police trade union. In 2011, Humberside Police gave an apology to the family for 'our failure to treat Christopher with sufficient compassion and to the desired standard that night'.

That same year, there was another injustice and fresh insult to the Alder family. A police investigation was launched after Christopher Alder's body was 'discovered' in Hull's mortuary, eleven years after his family believed they had buried him. Following the distressing process of ordering an exhumation, Christopher's family were bewildered and upset when Hull city council could not explain why an elderly woman,

77-year-old Grace Kamara, had been mistakenly buried in Christopher's grave.

The police then admitted that they 'may have' used Christopher's body for 'training purposes'.* The Crown Prosecution Service told Janet that 'about 800' trainee Humberside Police officers had been taken into the mortuary between 1998 and 2011. Stuart Donald, assistant chief constable of Humberside Police, said the visits were to train police recruits in 'addressing matters such as identification', but an investigation failed to discover how the bodies were swapped, or who was responsible.

In an interview for the *Socialist Worker*, Janet said, 'It's disgusting – it just shows you what they do. This is the contempt they have shown us over the years.'†

Janet made a complaint to the IPCC, but it declined to investigate. Instead, 'in the circumstances', it returned the matter to Humberside Police. As Janet put it, 'This has been a vendetta against me from the start.'‡

Subsequently, the government was forced to issue an apology to Janet and Richard Alder for a series of human rights violations.

---

* https://www.yorkshirepost.co.uk/news/crime/relatives-hit-out-over-sickening-mortuary-visits-1851172
† Annette Mackin, 29 July 2014, *Socialist Worker*: https://socialistworker.co.uk/art/38671/New+injustice+in+Christopher+Alder+case+as+no+cops+will+face+inquiry+for+using+his+body+for+training
‡ Ibid.

25

CELIBACY AND LEARNING RUSSIAN

Immediately after the *Mail on Sunday* exposé broke, I couldn't face seeing anyone. It was mortifying to think that everyone who knew me had seen the story in all its salacious detail. I had parents at my son's nursery and members of my mum's church commenting on it. I lost people in chambers whom I thought were close friends of mine, colleagues I had previously invited to dinner at my house; they stopped speaking to me. I was a pariah. I felt terrible humiliation and shame.

In terms of my work, up until that point, everything I touched was turning to gold. It had been a halcyon period for me in terms of the police cases I had been doing, but now I fully believed that this incident had set back my career, irrevocably perhaps. I simply couldn't contemplate walking into a court-room, and I didn't want to do police work any longer because it was too mortifying, nor did I want a relationship with any-body ever again. I'd had my fingers burnt in that respect. My marriage was over and so while I was waiting for the divorce to come through, for about eighteen months I led a life of celi-bacy. The only relationship I invested in was with my children. Angela and I had come to an arrangement whereby we would share custody of Megan and Isaac, but I realised then how little time I had been able to spend with my children. Whenever I was in London, they stayed with me, but with my ongoing case-load it was often tough because there was a lot to juggle. Now I devoted all my time and heart to them, dropping Megan off at various extra-curricular activities and picking her up from regular social events; spending time with four-year-old Isaac, getting him ready for nursery.

In the school holidays, I decided to get away. I sought refuge with Julian, a friend from university, and his wife Marion in Donegal who had children of similar ages to mine and offered me sanctuary there with my kids. Other than Dublin, I had never been to Ireland before then and I fell in love with it. I remember walking along the beach with the children and seeing seals, being in a different world. It was a perfect haven for us. Then I went with the kids to stay with my cousin Jean and her husband Urban who had set up home on the outskirts of Stockholm and, for the next ten years or so, we spent every summer with them.

It is a period of my children's lives that holds the fondest memories for me. It allowed me to take my foot off the pedal in terms of work for a year or so, and to put more effort into being a dad. So, while the Christopher Alder case in some respects had caused such pain and tumult, indirectly it also fundamentally changed my view of life and my role as a father, and for that I have everything to be thankful for.

With time away from work, I also started to study Russian and became quite proficient. A couple of years earlier, when my marriage had started to fall apart, I decided to set myself new challenges. I was hopeless at French at school, despite the best efforts of Madame Collie, and one of my first goals was to prove to myself that I wasn't incapable of speaking another language. I started with French at my local adult education centre, sat a French A Level, and passed it. Then I took Spanish lessons at

Goldsmiths University for a year or so, before switching to the Russian class. While I was at Goldsmiths, a group of us went to Moscow for what turned out to be a crazy weekend a little reminiscent of the film *The Hangover*, and that was it: I fell in love with the country. St Petersburg is beautiful, but I love Moscow and the Russian people. They can seem a little distant at first, especially older Russians when they don't know who you are. But I think that's to be expected after seventy years of a closed, totalitarian regime, where dissent could mean ending up losing your job, any privileges, in a gulag or dead. I found that once Russian people get to know you, they are the friendliest, most generous and warm people you could hope to meet. They love sharing whatever hospitality they can offer. I have had many wonderful meals with Russian families talking about life. To be fair, the current regime has set the country back to the old days, but the current regime is not the people of Russia. This is a mistake that is generally made by the West. Russians are as diverse as you can imagine, the country having the biggest landmass on the planet. I am often asked what it's like being a Black man in Russia. My response is that I've never been stopped and searched by the police there. I've never been told to go back to my own country, or made to feel different. A few words of Russian open doors. Yes, Russia has its problems, but so has the UK. As a Black person in the UK and in particular in London, even these days I am nine times more likely to be stopped and searched by the police than my white counterparts. I am three times more likely to be arrested. And while people talk about how Russians spy on their people, that is exactly what happened to me by the British police.

Moscow is electric, edgy. After that first trip, I started spending a lot of time there. I loved the place so much that at one point I'd visit three or four times a year. Complete madness. It's a crazy place, and it has problems of its own with a clear division between rich and poor and between Moscow and the rest of the country. In fact, Russians often say in jest that Moscow is a separate country within Russia. Having been to rural Russia, I can say that there is much truth to this. Russia does not have many Black people, but, paradoxically, it was somewhere I could hide from the British establishment, media and police. I was an outsider: nobody knew anything about me or who I was, and in some ways, it gave me back my freedom and a chance to let my hair down and breathe.

When I did start to date again, I decided that I didn't want to date anyone from the UK, knowing that my partner could be vulnerable because of the work that I did. Maybe it was an irrational fear, but I knew that I had been watched by the police on at least one occasion. The furthest away I could go, in terms of my personal life, the better. It might sound contrived, but that's when my new-found linguistic skills came into their own. I went out with a girl from the St Petersburg area for about three years until the relationship fell apart.

The year after the Christopher Alder case was one of refuge and celibacy, when I retreated from the world. Eventually, though, as 2002 beckoned, I knew that I couldn't hide forever. After all, I reasoned, I hadn't done anything wrong. There was only one choice: I had to go back to work, hold my head up high and get on with it. When I stepped through the door at Garden Court, everything was much the same, but I was completely different — a Leslie reborn. The time away had shifted my priorities and now I had a whole new attitude to my life and work. The episode with the juror hadn't been forgotten, of course. People would make quips and remarks about me; I clearly now had a completely unfounded reputation as some kind of ladykiller. I let them run with it, let them make the remarks. I didn't care. And after that year and a half of celibacy, having been in a relationship with my ex-wife since I was seventeen years old and being quite shy, with zero experience of the whole dating rigmarole, I didn't have any problems finding girlfriends. Even the juror exposé didn't seem to put people off; if anything, it made me interesting or more of a catch. I couldn't hide my past because of the internet, so I decided to embrace it and tell potential partners about the incident straight away. I thought it better to get the truth out in the open rather than let them discover it at a later date on their own.

I still didn't relish returning to my old police practice, although in the end I couldn't avoid it. I resolved to carry on fighting on behalf of my clients against the police. What's more, I'd fight my police cases even harder, because now it felt personal. I knew that it had to be someone from the police who had leaked my and the juror's police interviews to the *Mail on Sunday*. I had no illusions about what or who I was up against.

I decided I was going to come back with increased vigour, and if I was involved in a police action, I was going to do everything in my power to expose their wrongdoing. Whatever was said about me, and no matter what was thrown at me, I was going to hold my head high and go for it. For the next decade that is exactly what I did: I went for it like a man on a mission. But my fears about my reputation being in ruins? It was all in my head, because the truth was that my clients didn't care a jot about my private life. Far from the whole juror fiasco scenario destroying my career, it enhanced it. On more than one occasion clients said they had picked me *because* of the 'juror story'. I remember one particular client saying in a conference, that he choose me because I had character and guts; if I could survive the 'juror scandal', he said, I was his man!

I was on fire. All my drive, passion and righteous fury simply enhanced my work, and I went on to fight a stream of big high-profile cases, one after the other, many involving serious claims against the police. My loyal group of solicitors didn't care either and a lot of the provincial firms stood by me through thick and thin. The year 2003 also saw my call to the Bar in Dominica, a first step in achieving my ambition to give something back to the people of my dad's beloved island of birth.

26

PROZAC NATION: TAKING ON
BIG PHARMA

In 2003, I was on a roll. I had a string of police action cases working with my old friend and stalwart Andre Clovis at Hallmark Atkinson Wynter, then in June I took an entirely different adversary: Big Pharma, notably the drugs giant Eli Lilly, inventors and manufacturers of fluoxetine hydrochloride, otherwise known as Prozac.

I had been doing a lot of work in the north of England for Fiona Borrill, a solicitor at a firm called Emsleys. She had a medical negligence practice in Leeds and did a lot of medical-related inquests following deaths in hospital. Fiona was a firm believer in proper access to justice and, along with a handful of women solicitors in the North, she was fighting the good fight for legally aided clients. A brilliant and well-read lawyer, Fiona tested me at times but made me understand the politics of gender and race and how they could be applied to the work I did.

I enjoyed working in the north of England. People were friendly, despite the fact that I often stood out because of my race. But this did not bother them. I felt real respect. At the time I even contemplated moving to Leeds. I was considering a fresh start after the end of my marriage and a new city or town seemed like a good idea. In the end, though, I couldn't bear to be away from Megan and Isaac. They needed to have me living close to them, especially as I was away from home so often. To permanently move away would have been a huge blow to them and removed me from their lives.

In autumn 2002, Fiona asked me to represent Professor Alastair Hay, one of the most brilliant scientific minds in the country, at the inquest into the death of his wife Wendy, who had hanged herself at their home in West Yorkshire in September that year. Fiona felt that someone needed to take on the big multinational drug manufacturers and thought I would be the right person for the job.

Alastair and Wendy had been married for over thirty-two years. 'I just adored her,' Alastair told a journalist. 'Wendy was so quick and funny. She was such a fun, supportive person to have around.'* They had brought up a child and also worked together. Alastair is Professor of Environmental Toxicology at Leeds University, and as a skilled librarian and researcher, Wendy worked alongside him, editing his papers. She was the centre of his world.

When Wendy was first diagnosed with anxiety and clinical depression by a GP in 1998, she had been prescribed Valium together with Prozac, one of a family of drugs called SSRIs (Selective Serotonin Reuptake Inhibitors), which boost levels of serotonin in the brain. Alistair had helped in her recovery by taking leave from his work and teaching himself Cognitive Behavioural Therapy techniques, and after two years Wendy weaned herself off Prozac. Four years later, however, her depression returned, and her weight had fallen to 6 stone.

---

* Interview with Sarah Boseley, *Guardian*, 4 June 2003.

Again, she was prescribed the standard daily dosage of 20 mg of Prozac, but this time the medication had no effect. Her condition rapidly deteriorated. She became extremely insecure, with feelings of helplessness and acute low self-worth, and during therapy sessions started to draw pictures of her brain buzzing and, often, exploding. She began having sleepless nights and the odd suicidal thought. In August, three weeks after she had started taking Prozac again, Wendy had made a first suicide attempt: she had tried to drown herself in the River Wharfe. Two weeks later, she hanged herself in their garage. A note left for her husband and their son said that Alastair could not look after her forever, the depression was getting worse and she could not bear to be institutionalised.

Alastair suspected that Wendy's suicidal thoughts might have been triggered by her medication. As an eminent environmental toxicologist and well-known chemical weapons expert, who had served as an expert witness in numerous courtrooms, he had a professional as well as a deeply personal interest in what had led his wife to take her own life. He started to investigate links between Prozac use and suicide. What he found was highly disturbing. Alastair had come across some literature on Prozac by Dr David Healy, then the director of the North Wales department of *Psychological Medicine*, which argued that in a small minority of people, SSRI drugs, including Prozac, can as a side effect induce akathisia, a disorder that can cause a person to experience such intense extreme agitation that they are driven to violence, self-harm and/or suicide. It can occur when stopping, starting or changing the dosage or type of certain medications.

In giving evidence at the inquest in May 2003, Alastair told David Hinchliff, the West Yorkshire coroner, that he had carried out his own study into the role that Prozac had played in his wife's death. He believed that the drug had precipitated Wendy into a suicidal state. After the opening day of the inquest, Alastair told BBC News, 'Depression is a terrible, terrible condition. I wanted something that would help her and I thought Prozac would do that, and it was just devastating to find afterwards that it might have been what killed her. There will be others going through the same experience and it is just horrendous and it is wrong. It's not that Prozac is a bad drug. I have friends who have benefited enormously from it. But there are some people who respond badly to it.'

Back in 2002, prescriptions for SSRIs like Prozac were being handed out by GPs in standard 20mg doses, but there was little or no warning about the possibility of mood changes, nor guidance offered on suddenly worsening symptoms. In epilepsy treatments, drug levels in the blood are monitored. People on warfarin to thin the blood and digoxin for the heart have their drug levels measured. People who are prescribed lithium to treat bi-polar disorder are regularly monitored to check the levels of the drug in their system. Alastair argued that further research should be undertaken into the safety of Prozac: an urgent clinical study was needed to measure blood levels of the drug alongside changes in mood. He contended that the standard dose of 20mg may have been too much in his wife's case. 'It has to be related to the drug and changing levels of the drug . . .' he said. 'Then we may have a tool for saying for the vast majority of people going on Prozac, it is going to be fine, but for this small number it is not.'

Eli Lilly, the company behind Prozac, had originally tested fluoxetine as a treatment for high blood pressure, but it proved ineffective in human trials. It was then trialled as an anti-obesity agent, but this was another dead end. The drug was then tested on psychotic patients and those in hospital with severe clinical depression with no apparent benefit, and with a number of patients getting worse. Finally, however, when Eli Lilly tested it on five patients suffering from mild symptoms of depression, all of them reported a noticeable lift in their mood. The company vigorously marketed their discovery, with the new zingy name of Prozac, as an entirely safe, easy-to-prescribe 'one pill, one dose for all' wonder drug or, as *Observer* journalist Anna Moore coined it, 'happiness in a blister pack'.* Its uptake was meteoric. By 1999, it was already providing Eli Lilly with more than a quarter of its multi-billion-dollar revenue. By the time of Wendy Hay's inquest in 2003, Prozac was one of the best-selling drugs in the world.

Despite the widely accepted view among psychiatrists that the risk of not taking medication when suffering from any severe mental illness far outweighs the risk of taking them, since its introduction Prozac had been frequently beset with claims that it could trigger suicidal thoughts or the feeling that death would be welcome as opposed to the ongoing mental pain of being alive.

The first big legal case involving Prozac was in 1989, when Joseph Wesbecker, who had been on the newly approved SSRI less than a month, walked through the Standard Gravure printing plant in Louisville, Kentucky with an AK47, killing eight employees, before turning the gun on himself. Eli Lilly settled with the families of the deceased out of court for an undisclosed sum.

In the UK in 1996, after eleven days on Prozac, Reginald Payne, a retired teacher from Cornwall, suffocated his wife then jumped off a cliff. His sons issued court proceedings against Eli Lilly.

---

* Anna Moore, 'Eternal sunshine', *Observer*, 13 May 2007.

Then in 1999, the case of Bill Forsyth came to trial in Hawaii. In 1993, also after eleven days on Prozac, Mr Forsyth, a retired car-rental business man from California, stabbed his wife of thirty-seven years fifteen times before impaling himself on a serrated kitchen knife. At the trial in Hawaii, the prosecution called David Healy as an expert witness. They had also secured Ely Lilly's research documents. On reviewing the papers, Dr Healy discovered that the drug manufacturer's own development team had reported on the drug's potentially worrying side effects as far back as August 1978. 'There have been a fairly large number of reports of adverse reactions [...] Akathisia and restlessness were reported in some patients,' the minutes from an internal team meeting noted. The family nevertheless lost the case; the jury ruled that Eli Lilly could not be held responsible for Mr Forsyth's actions.

In autumn 2002, within a fortnight of starting a course of Seroxat for anxiety, Colin Whitfield, a 56-year-old retired headmaster, slit his wrists in a garden shed. His wife said her husband had never shown any suicidal inclination before being prescribed the SSRI drug, popularly dubbed the 'shyness pill'. In March 2003, David Healy had given evidence at the inquest into the death of Mr Whitfield. He had been granted access to GlaxoSmithKline's archives in order to study the data from the original clinical trials and had found that a small number of volunteers in perfect health, who took part in early trials of the drug, had become very agitated or suicidal. 'A lot of people going into the inquest just know the person would not have committed suicide in the normal course of events. You get a sense of their utter bewilderment,' he said.

Dr Healy had recommended the creation of a central database to record all deaths of people on SSRIs and pointed out that suicide verdicts – which in cases concerning SSRI antidepressants could be debatable – deprived families of insurance payouts. Most coroners, he said, did not know about the controversy surrounding this relatively new group of drugs, and so he had written to 148 coroners in England and Wales, and also to the review of coroner services, which had been set up after the Harold Shipman case.

At the conclusion of Mr Whitfield's inquest, the then Brecon coroner, Geraint Williams, had undertaken to write to the secretary of state for the Department of Health asking for an urgent inquiry into the safety of the drug: 'I am profoundly disturbed by the effect this drug had on Colin Whitfield. [. . .] I have grave concerns that this is a dangerous drug that should be withdrawn until at least detailed national studies are undertaken,' he had told the court.

This fresh inquest into another death involving Prozac was timely. In 2002, more than 22 million prescriptions for antidepressants had been written in Britain, most of them for SSRIs including Prozac and Seroxat. In December that year, after mounting concerns about their safety, the Labour government public health minister Hazel Blears announced the establishment of a Committee on Safety of Medicines (CSM) expert working group to conduct an 'intensive review' of SSRI use, including an investigation into problems with severe withdrawal symptoms, side effects and the issue of suicide risk. In March 2003, however, two months before our Leeds inquest, the credibility of the SSRI working group was called into question after it came to light that most of the members had shareholdings or other links to the drug manufacturers.

Given the timing, the verdict of Wendy Hay's inquest could undoubtedly have a significance for the ongoing CSM inquiry. For these hugely influential, multi-billion-dollar pharmaceutical industry manufacturers, the stakes were high, and consequently media interest in the case of Wendy Hay was intense.

We knew we were in for a fight. And we knew that the drug company had hired a collection of suits to represent them at the inquest. We decided to called Dr David Healy, whose critical book on the widespread and indiscriminate prescribing of Prozac, *Let Them Eat Prozac*,* was about to be published. It was the right decision; Dr Healy was a compelling witness. When Prozac was first approved for use in the late 1980s, he had been among the psychiatrists who prescribed it, but had soon become aware that some of his patients became agitated and had even attempted suicide. He had subsequently written papers and presented lectures on his view that all SSRI anti-depressants should show warning labels, as they could 'trigger suicidal and violent behaviour'.

He told the court that having considered several clinical studies of Prozac alongside his own assessment of Wendy Hay's medical records, he could only infer that 'on the balance of probabilities the drug contributed to her suicide'. Had she discontinued, or amended, her use of Prozac, she possibly wouldn't have hanged herself. 'She wasn't taking her own life with the usual intent,' he said.

As Mr Hay's legal representative, the question in my mind when cross-examining Dr Healy and the other witnesses was one of responsibility. I felt it was my job, and in the public interest, to challenge the manufacturer Eli Lilly's categoric denial that there was any link to suicide when taking the standard dose, and so I pressed him on what measures should be taken to prevent future harm or deaths of anyone pre-scribed with Prozac. Dr Healy's answer was simple: 'I believe

---

* David Healy, *Let Them Eat Prozac: The Unhealthy Relationship Between the Pharmaceutical Industry and Depression* (NYU Press, August 2003).

the pharmaceutical company Eli Lilly, who in effect willed this drug into the world, have the primary responsibility to issue stronger warnings about the possible side effects of their product.'

This was a relatively short inquest, just two days, at the end of which David Hinchliff took the unusual step at that time of recording a narrative verdict, concluding thus: 'There was evidence during the inquest that in a minority of patients who take this drug it may have adverse side effects. This drug may or may not have contributed to Wendy Hay's action.'

After the inquest ended, Susan Pezzack, a legal director for Eli Lilly, continued to rebut Mr Hay and Mr Healy's claims, citing in her statement a meeting held by the American Food and Drugs Administration in 1991 on the subject and a review by the UK's Committee on the Safety of Medicines in 2000: 'We take reports of this type very seriously,' she said, adding that the company was, however, 'comfortable' that there was 'no credible scientific evidence that establishes a causal link between Prozac and violent and suicidal behaviour'.

No inquest verdict could ever entirely help Alastair get over the sudden death of his wife, but at least he could hope that the widespread media coverage of the case would help to alert others to the potential risk factors in taking SSRI medication. Talking to reporters outside the court, Alastair spoke with dignity and authority and was at pains to make clear that his motive in the inquest was not to call the benefits of Prozac into question, but that more careful investigations into its alleged side effects should be carried out. 'This has not been a trial about Prozac. It has been a trial about the possible adverse effects of some dosages on some people, so people should not stop taking Prozac. That is something that everybody needs to discuss with their doctor. The concern I have is of course with my wife. It has been devastating and if this inquiry has done anything, it might have indicated that some people like her may be at more risk of suicide through taking the medication.'

Postscript

The Committee on the Safety of Medicines expert working group published its findings in December 2004, concluding that the risk of suicide in depressed patients is generally greatest around the time of their initial presentation to medical professionals. The risk factors, however, may increase in the early stages of treatment and a modest increase in the risk of suicidal thoughts and self-harm for patients taking SSRIs compared with a placebo *could not be ruled out*. Further, the group found insufficient evidence of any marked difference in suicidal risk between the different brands of SSRIs, or between SSRIs and other antidepressants.

In 2004, the mental health charity MIND contributed a memorandum to the House of Commons Health Committee entitled, 'The Influence of the Pharmaceutical Industry'.

In 2008, a meta-analysis of data on antidepressants, including SSRIs, was completed by the Food and Drug Agency (FDA) in the USA. The results of this analysis were reviewed in both the UK and in Europe. The UK/EU review concluded that the risk of suicidal acts and behaviour is increased with the use of SSRIs in young people aged up to twenty-five years and should not be used in this patient group. No evidence was found that the use of SSRIs leads to an increased risk of suicide in the general population.

On the basis of the UK and European reviews, the wording below on the risk of suicidal thoughts and behaviour with antidepressants was agreed in Europe in 2008 for inclusion in product information leaflets for all antidepressants, including SSRIs such as Prozac:

Thoughts of suicide and worsening of your depression or anxiety disorder

If you are depressed and/or have anxiety disorders you can sometimes have thoughts of harming or killing yourself. These may be increased when first starting antidepressants, since these medicines all take time to work, usually about two weeks but sometimes longer. You may be more likely to think like this:

if you have previously had thoughts about killing or harming yourself

if you are a young adult; information from clinical trials has shown an increased risk of suicidal behaviour in adults aged less than 25 years with psychiatric conditions who were treated with an antidepressant

If you have thoughts of harming or killing yourself at any time, contact your doctor or go to a hospital straight away. You may find it helpful to tell a relative or close friend that you are depressed or have an anxiety disorder, and ask them to read this leaflet. You might ask them to tell you if they think your depression or anxiety is getting worse, or if they are worried about changes in your behaviour.

27

THE COURAGE OF MOTHERS:
THE DEATH OF PETAR SUTOVIC
(1979–2004)

'To lose a child is a parent's worst nightmare, but
then to be subjected to more than two years of High
Court litigation to prevent an investigation from
being conducted and to inflict mental cruelty on
his family in the public domain is shocking. I was
subjected to humiliation and trauma and accused of
making wild allegations. I just wanted what I was
entitled to: an investigation into how my son met his
death in accordance with the law, nothing more and
nothing less. There continues to be no investigation
as to how Petar lost his young life. Please, all I want
is justice, closure and peace, and that this never
happens to anyone again.'

Susan Sutovic, mother of Petar Sutovic

My inquest work has brought me into extremely close contact with families at possibly the worst moment of their lives.
Husbands who have lost a wife, wives who have lost a husband,

fathers and mothers who have lost a child, and sisters and brothers who have lost their sibling. Death and loss affect each of these people in different ways, and sometimes I don't know how my clients get through it. But I do know that there is no right or wrong way to deal with grief. I also know that often the strength and courage of a mother who has lost her child, her son, her daughter, can know no bounds.

In February 2004, Susan Sutovic, a well-known human rights immigration solicitor, approached me directly to represent her in an inquest. Susan was originally from Serbia but she had emigrated to England many years before and set up a successful law practice in west London. She had represented Serbian dissidents against the regime led by the former president Slobodan Milošević, who in 2002 was convicted of crimes against humanity and of war crimes by a tribunal at the International Criminal Tribunal for the Former Yugoslavia at The Hague. I had not come across Susan before. She told me how she had been woken in the early hours of 27 January 2004 by a phone call telling her that her eldest son Petar, a UK citizen living in Serbia, had been found dead in the flat she owned in Belgrade.

Petar, a promising former law student, was just twenty-four. Susan was close to her son. He had been diagnosed as diabetic as a student, and when he was knocked down by a lorry while on holiday in Israel, Susan had nursed him back to health. After his accident, Petar had put his studies on hold. It appeared that he had become addicted to heroin. In 2003 he had gone to live in Belgrade where he was developing a property investment business. He had also gone into a rehab clinic to deal with his addiction, and Susan was satisfied that at the time of his death he had been clean.

She was deeply suspicious about the manner of his death

and the way he had been found. His body had been flown to the UK less than forty-eight hours after his alleged death, but there were a number of anomalies around the body's arrival and how it came about that the north London coroner took over the investigation. In cases where a British subject dies overseas and the body is repatriated to the UK, the law states that there is a duty to investigate the death as though the death occurred in this country. The question that then arises is which coroner is to assume jurisdiction of the body in order to investigate the death and direct that a post-mortem be conducted. Normally, this depends on where the body arrives into the country, where the family lives, and where the deceased is to be buried. In this case, Petar's body had arrived at Heathrow, Susan and the rest of his family live in Acton, west London, and he was to be buried in Gunnersbury Cemetery, also in west London. But for reasons Susan and I could never quite understand, the north London coroner had seized jurisdiction.

The story then gets more sinister. When Petar's body was repatriated, no medical doctor had certified him as being dead and no documentation accompanied the body wherein he was certified as being dead. The Serbian authorities had, however, provided an autopsy report by the pathologist who had approved the release of the body to the UK, which stated that the cause of death was a drug overdose.

There was a problem with that. The first time that Susan became suspicious was when she went to see her son's body in the holding mortuary in north London on 29 January. She asked for the coffin to be opened and immediately noticed that Petar's nose looked as if it had taken a battering and was broken. She also saw bruising on Petar's arms and chest. Worse was to follow. Two days later Susan went to view her son's body again and a female officer working for the coroner's office told her that Petar's heart had not been returned with his corpse. 'It happens all the time when bodies come back from abroad,' the officer casually informed her.

A post-mortem examination was carried out by a retired 72-year-old pathologist, Dr Rufus Crompton, on 2 February. Bizarrely, in Susan's opinion, despite the disfigurement of Petar's nose and the other visible signs of harm she had noted on his arms and chest, Dr Crompton declared that he found no injuries whatsoever on Petar's body, 'externally or on further examination'. He also confirmed that her son's heart was missing. Petar was buried two days after the post-mortem examination, but Susan's concerns remained.

Six months later, she decided to fly to Belgrade to make her own inquiries. She got hold of a copy of the initial post-mortem report by Serbian officials at the Institute of Forensic Medicine. This noted some of Petar's injuries and also said that morphine had been found in his blood – but not the morphine associated with heroin use. Instead, it suggested that it could be traced to the painkiller Tramadol. Susan knew that Petar had been prescribed the painkillers after the accident in Israel.

During that July visit to Belgrade, she received a file of photographs, said to be contemporaneous crime-scene pictures taken by police on the night Petar died. The images showed her son's body lying on the bed where he had been discovered. Beside him, on a cluttered bedside cabinet, was what appeared to be the usual shooting-up paraphernalia of a heroin user: a burnt spoon with drops of brown liquid around it.

On her return to London, Susan showed me the photographs of this handsome young man, and I could see that his nose looked badly out of shape, as though he had been punched in the face, which looked cut and bruised. The autopsy report from Serbia made no reference to these facial injuries. There appeared to be fresh blood on the duvet cover, and a weaker, almost watered-down blood staining on the white sheet and pillow. Susan had also spoken to the housekeeper at the block of flats who described a splattering of blood across one wall in Petar's bedroom 'as if something burst on to it'. Susan later hired an investigator to inspect the flat. The inspector reported that the room in which he was found had bloodstains everywhere.

Susan was convinced that her son had been murdered. She didn't know by whom or why, but because of the way the official Serbian autopsy purported to hide these injuries, she suspected a cover-up by the Serbian authorities. I looked at the case and immediately told Susan that this was bigger than both of us – I sensed there was something extremely sinister at play. It would be difficult to unpick and get to the bottom of what had really happened, but I was prepared to represent her and do my very best at an inquest to get the answers she so desperately needed.

Everywhere that Susan turned she was stonewalled. One could understand perhaps this wall of silence if the Serbian authorities were somehow implicated in Petar's death, but the last thing we thought was that we would receive the same silent and obstructive treatment from the UK authorities. This is exactly what happened.

The inquest was held at Hornsey Coroner's Court in north London in front of Dr William Dolman. I had previously acted in several inquests in front of Dr Dolman, in the course of which he and I had clashed on a number of occasions. Our encounter was no less turbulent than on these earlier cases. From day one, we had great difficulty convincing Dr Dolman to hold a full and proper investigation and, try as we might, instead of looking at the case with an open and enquiring mind,

I felt that he approached this inquiry with a closed and stubbornly incurious, if pragmatic, mindset. He showed reluctance to accept the evidence that Susan had produced, or to follow up even the most obvious lines of enquiry. Everything seemed to be deemed too difficult because it happened in Serbia; the coroner's officers said there was nothing they could do. This in turn simply fuelled in Susan's mind the conviction that there was a conspiracy to cover up how her son had died, and now she strongly believed that the conspiracy involved the governments of both the UK and Serbia. She could not understand, given the evidence she had managed to obtain from the various investigators, why nobody wanted to look more closely and more critically at the full circumstances of her son's death.

Dr Dolman repeatedly shut me down and frustrated me in terms of the investigations I wanted to make, and he came back with an open verdict, describing the cause of death as 'morphine poisoning'.

Although the experience had left us completely disheartened, we decided to fight on. We thought there *was* sufficient evidence that Petar had died unlawfully. There were basic enquiries that could have been made, and the coroner had simply refused, so we were left with no choice but to challenge his decision and the manner in which he conducted his investigation at a judicial review.

Death can of course really take its toll on an individual, and the way the inquest proceedings had played out put my relationship with Susan under too much strain. She desperately needed to get the result she wanted and to know whether Petar had been murdered, and so at times her grief and her anger held sway over rational argument.

Susan would agree that she was not the easiest of clients, but she was *right*. Her son's heart *was* missing; they never got to the bottom of that. In all probability there *had* been a cover-up concerning Petar's death. While I may initially have been critical of Susan and the manner in which she pursued some of her seemingly more outlandish conspiracy claims, I can only conclude that the evidence certainly appears to point to third party involvement; maybe unknown individuals, possibly high up in the Serbian state or other state agents being involved in her son's death.

At the time, though, I remember leaving chambers and going home and having this case on my mind all the time. How were we going to get the British courts to carry out their own rigorous and effective investigations? One morning I was riding my motorbike into work when Susan rang me on my mobile. She was distraught. I instantly absorbed all her emotion and upset, and when I got back onto my bike, my mind was still replaying our telephone conversation, I wasn't concentrating on the road and had an accident. The stress had taken its toll. My injuries were not life-threatening, but it was a warning. Becoming ill was the one thing I had been so afraid of; as a single parent of a twelve- and seven-year-old without much support, I simply couldn't afford to. Although Mum was nearby and I could call on her in a real emergency, she was still working part-time and I was all too aware that she was suffering her own grief having lost Dad, her husband of nearly forty years. She had seen my marriage fall apart, was trying to be there for her grandchildren, for me, my sister and Trevor, and was trying to be strong for all of us, but it was too much to expect of her. No – I had no time to be sick or even to entertain the idea; it was tough enough dealing with the array of childhood mishaps, which are an inevitable part of family life. Susan and I had to part ways.

This didn't stop her. Susan battled and battled to get to the truth in relation to how her son died, and every now and again,

I'd see a case or a report showing that she was still either doing it herself, or had another barrister to represent her. In May 2006, she was successful in challenging the north London coroner William Dolman's open verdict. At a judicial review the High Court judges Lord Justice Moses and Mr Justice Beatson ordered a new inquest before a different coroner on the grounds of the new evidence which Susan had gathered. 'The evidence which has now emerged', they ruled, 'may cast a very different light upon the circumstances of Petar Sutovic's death.'

Susan's twelve-year fight for the truth about the circumstances of her son's death culminated in 2016 when I heard on the radio that the east London coroner, Elizabeth Stearns, had found that Petar Sutovic had been unlawfully killed. Susan had not given up; a new coroner had come in and looked at the matters afresh. With an open mind, she had looked at the evidence and made a finding of unlawful killing, which in my opinion was the right verdict. And that showed me that being tenacious, not accepting the official version and battling on, can at times pay dividends. As Susan puts it herself on her Facebook page dedicated to Petar's memory: 'Someone said, "I don't know how you do it." I said, "I wasn't given a choice."'

28

THE NEW CROSS FIRE: A
SECOND INQUEST

In memory of:
Andrew Gooding – 14 years old
Owen Thompson – 16 years old
Patricia Johnson – 15 years old
Patrick Cummings – 16 years old
Steve Collins – 17 years old
Lloyd Hall – 20 years old
Humphrey Geoffrey Brown – 18 years old
Rosaline Henry – 16 years old
Peter Campbell – 18 years old
Gerry Paul Francis – 17 years old
Glenton Powell – 16 years old
Paul Ruddock – 22 years old
Yvonne Ruddock – 16 years old
Anthony Berbeck – 20 years old

After 2004, my practice went from dealing with individual tragedy to tragedy on a much larger scale. My first public disaster case was to represent twelve of the victims' families at a fresh inquest into the events surrounding the New Cross Fire in which thirteen young people lost their lives and, in the aftermath some years later, caused one more to take their own.

On the night of the fire, 18 January 1981, Armza Ruddock had thrown a joint birthday party for her sixteen-year-old daughter Yvonne and Yvonne's friend, eighteen-year-old Angela Jackson, at their home at 439 New Cross Road, London SE14. To all intents and purposes, it was a fairly typical party. There was music on a sound system and dancing that continued into the early hours of the following morning. By 5.30 a.m. the party was drawing to a close. Most of the guests had already left, but some of the youngsters were upstairs on the first floor continuing to dance or listen to lovers' rock, a few more were up on the second floor, while a group of adults were gathered in the kitchen downstairs at the back where the food and drink were being served. At some point just after 5.45 a.m., one of the adults went into the empty front room and discovered that a fire had broken out.

The fire spread rapidly, ripping through the house and trapping those young people on the upper floors. Some perished in the blaze, while others (the New Cross Survivors), trapped upstairs behind a wall of smoke and flames after the stairs collapsed, escaped by jumping out of the upper windows and were badly injured. Many continue to suffer not only from the physical scars of the fire, but also the psychological trauma. Wayne Hayes, who was seventeen at the time and suffered severe burns requiring 140 skin grafts, saved his life by climbing from a second-floor window onto a drainpipe, but then fell onto the pavement outside, shattering 163 bones. In an interview for *Huffington Post* he recalled the horror of the scene inside the house as the blaze took hold. It was so hot, he said, that 'people's skin was peeling back'.*

This case held great symbolic and emotional importance

---

* *Huffington Post*, 'The Story of the 1981 New Cross Fire', March 2020.

for me. The fire that night left a deep wound of grief and had repercussions that went beyond the immediate personal losses, especially so, perhaps, for a Black working-class child like me who was growing up in inner-city south London: you couldn't be a child of London who grew up in the early '80s and *not* be aware of the tragedy of New Cross. Close friends of mine had been at the party that night. I could so easily have gone there too. We all thought that it had been brought about by a racially motivated attack. In the immediate aftermath, the press reports stated that 'the fire is believed to have been started deliberately' and 'was almost certainly started by a petrol bomb', adding that there was, however, 'no official confirmation of this last night by Scotland Yard'.* There were eyewitness reports that something had been thrown through a ground-floor window minutes before the fire started. Young people who had left the party just before the fire took hold were quoted in the press describing a white car being driven quickly away from the house.†

It wasn't simply the possible racist attack that inflamed anger and frustration. While local community activists rallied round to support the families of the dead and the survivors of the tragedy, little or no official support was forthcoming – not even messages of condolence from the Queen or Prime Minister Margaret Thatcher. Velvetina Francis lost her seventeen-year-old son, Gerry, in the fire; in a 1981 BBC interview she said, 'Had it been white kids, [Margaret Thatcher] would have been on the television, on the radio, and sent her sympathy.' Journalist Martin Bedford later wrote in a letter to

---

* 'Petrol bomb theory after blaze kills nine at all-night party', Lindsay Mackie, *Guardian*, 19 January 1981.
† Mr Carl Wright, aged twenty, of Camberwell, who had just left the party, said: 'I heard the sound of breaking glass and then there was the fire. I saw a white car being driven away.' Quoted in ibid.

the *Guardian*, 'That same weekend a number of teenagers died in a fire at a disco in Ireland, prompting an immediate letter of condolence from Buckingham Palace. No such message was sent to the families of those who died in Deptford. This only fuelled the suspicion that the establishment, the police, the media and white society in general regarded the deaths of Black people as less important. They are not "ours", we will not mourn them.'*

There was an overwhelming sense of injustice, because it seemed that the authorities didn't seem to care. We genuinely believed that this family and its partygoers had been burnt out by racist murderers, who had not been properly investigated by the police. Indeed, recent history appeared to support this theory. Let's not forget that this was the era of far-right extremism and the rise of the National Front. At that time, and throughout the '70s, the far right held considerable sway in south-east London, and made its presence felt with frequent racist attacks. In a Deptford council by-election in 1976, the National Front and the National Party achieved a combined vote of just over 44 per cent. A year later, on 13 August 1977, an organised National Front march from New Cross to Lewisham resulted in violent clashes between the National Front, anti-racist protesters and the police, events which are now remembered as the 'Battle of Lewisham'.

Furthermore, over the previous decade, there had been several racist arson attacks in the area. In 1971 a Caribbean house party in neighbouring Forest Hill had been attacked by a firebomb, leaving twenty-two injured. In December 1977, the Moonshot, a New Cross youth club popular with young Black people, was destroyed in a firebomb attack: a month

---

* Martyn Bedford, Letters, *Guardian*, 8 January 2011.

earlier, a newspaper had reported that a National Front meeting had included talk of burning it down. Then, in July 1978, three years before the fire on New Cross Road, Deptford's Albany Empire, a local community theatre and the hub of local anti-racist activity, was burned down. The next day a note was pushed through the charred door of the building saying, 'GOT YOU'.

There was, therefore, already a lack of faith among Black communities in the official response to these earlier travesties, and a general distrust of the police. David Michael, who was posted to the London borough of Lewisham in April 1973 and was the first Black police officer to serve there – and at the time one of only eleven Black police officers in a force of more than 22,000 – described the force as behaving like an 'occupying army'.* There were significant criticisms by sections of the Black community of the way the Metropolitan Police Service conducted the initial investigation into the New Cross Fire, leading to suspicions that there was either a cover-up of a 'racist hate crime' or a lack of political will to bring the 'racist' perpetrators to justice. Instead, almost immediately in the days after the fire, the victims themselves became suspects. The police quickly dismissed the initial line of inquiry into a firebombing, suggesting instead that the party had been a scene of drunken disorder, there had been trouble when a fight had broken out between a group of boys and the 'unruly' Black youths had somehow caused their own deaths.

Consequently, a number of the survivors were detained for questioning. Activists later revealed that these children were encouraged to sign false statements. Robert McKenzie, a friend of Yvonne Ruddock's brother, was one of a number of boys

---

* *The Economist*, 'Race and the Police: No Quick Fix', 20 September 2008.

called in for questioning. 'They refused to listen to me when I told them that there wasn't a fight,' he told an interviewer. 'They gave me no respect and I felt like I had been arrested – not asked to share information. They didn't want to listen to the truth. [. . .] They had their version of events and I felt I had to go along with them. In the end I caved in and told them what I thought they wanted.'* Then there is the story of Denise Gooding, which is recounted by Carol Pierre in *Black British History: New Perspectives*. At eleven years old, Denise was subjected to hours of interrogation into the early morning and pressured to admit there had been fighting at the party.

Poet Linton Kwesi Johnson, who wrote his 'New Craas Massahkah'† in response to the fire, later recalled that 'a lot of people were angry . . . not just about what happened, but about the way the whole business was handled by the police and the way it was reported in the press and the media'.‡

A week after the fire, Moonshot Club (in new premises on Fordham Park) hosted a mass meeting which was attended by over a thousand local people. A New Cross Massacre Action Committee was formed and led by civil rights campaigners John La Rose and Darcus Howe (then editor of *Race Today*, member of the British Black Panther Movement, and one of the original Mangrove Nine defendants), and weekly mass meetings were organised in New Cross. On 2 March 1981 the committee called a 'Black People's Day of Action'. Over an eight-hour period, thousands (some say 20,000) took to the streets to join in a peaceful march from New Cross to Hyde Park. The protesters processed along the route to the beat of chants such as 'Black people united will never be defeated'

* https://stillwerise.uk/2020/12/12/the-new-cross-fire-13-dead-and-nothing-said/
† Listen at https://www.youtube.com/watch?v=FUMYAqAlAXA
‡ 'Stand up and Spit' blog.

and carried an array of homemade posters and banners with slogans that read, 'Thirteen Dead and Nothing Said', 'No Police Cover-Up', 'Come what may, we are here to stay', and 'Blood Ah Go Run If Justice No Come'. David Reid, who lost his school friend Owen Thompson in the fire, was one of those who took to the streets. 'People were saying it was the National Front that started the fire,' he recalled. 'It made sense – National Front supporters would call us nigger, spit at us and throw rubbish as we walked. That was the norm in the '70s and '80s. There were no-go areas for Black people in London. The only time there was a sense of safety was when we were in church, a youth club or our parties and dances. The march was the biggest gathering of Black people we had seen besides the Notting Hill Carnival. Black people came from all over the country to ensure our voices were heard.'*

Although on the whole the march had been peaceful and largely without incident, the *Sun* newspaper's coverage of the day of action ran with the headline, 'The Day the Blacks Ran Riot in London'. Others went with 'When the Black Tide Met the Thin Blue Line' (*Daily Mail*) and 'Rampage of a mob' (*Daily Express*).

Importantly, however, the Black People's Day of Action had seen the largest single political mobilisation of Black people in the UK to date. As playwright Rex Obano, later quoted in the *Guardian*, said: 'To me, the New Cross fire, the fact that no one in authority seemed to care, forced the Black community to unify, to find its voice in a way it hadn't before. This politicised people from all over the country. They marched in protest: thousands of people on a workday. I was thirteen at the time

---

* Lorraine King, 'Inside horrors of New Cross fire tragedy which left 13 dead – and nothing said', *Daily Mirror*, 15 January 2021; https://www.mirror.co.uk/news/uk-news/inside-horrors-new-cross-fire-23328321

and I always thought the older generation was comparatively passive. New Cross shows it wasn't like that at all. They dealt with so much. There had been other uprisings. But this was a line in the sand.'* And in the words of Linton Kwesi Johnson, one of the organisers of the march, and steward on the day, 'In Dublin when they had the fire in the discotheque, they had a day of mourning and the Prime Minister made a speech, but not a single member of our parliament mentioned the massacre. That is why we demonstrated to show the country at large, the police, the government, and the fascists, that we're no longer prepared to have so many people killed and say nothing about it, but we're here to stay and if it comes to it we're prepared to fight and soon.'†

But if the number of failings in the Metropolitan Police's investigation had added another layer of distress to the grieving families and already traumatised survivors, so too did the original coroner's inquest at County Hall in London. It began four months after the fire on 21 April 1981 – before the police had time to properly investigate or come to any conclusions – and ended on 13 May. The New Cross Massacre Action Committee maintained a presence outside the building throughout.

In spite of the fact that they were more than ably represented by barristers Ian Macdonald, (our former head of Garden Court Chambers who was also was the barrister in the Mangrove Nine case‡), Mike Mansfield (Tooks Court) and Rock Tansey (25 Bedford Row), all of whom had to do battle with the coroner, Dr Arthur Gordon Davies, the bereaved families felt that the entire hearing, and the manner in which

---

* Quoted in Hugh Mur, 'Hideously diverse Britain: Memories of the New Cross tragedy never fade', *Guardian*, 11 January 2011.
† Interview with Desmond Hunt from *Other Side Magazine*, September 1981.
‡ Ian was the bespectacled barrister represented in Steve McQueen's acclaimed BBC *Small Axe* series of films.

the inquest was conducted, was biased. Dr Davies refused to take notes of evidence during the hearing and simply read from the witnesses' earlier police statements (which many had later refuted, asserting that they had been made under police pressure), even when he was summing up for the benefit of the members of the jury, which, as lawyers for the families argued, was not only biased but in contravention of Section 6 of the Coroner's Act 1887. Indeed, in the *Guardian* obituary of Ian Macdonald, Geoffrey Robertson QC recalled that during the New Cross Fire inquest, 'Ian was seen jumping on his bike to ride to the High Court for urgent orders quashing the decisions of a legally ignorant coroner.' At the end of the three-week hearing, Dr Davies spent a third of his summing up discussing the theory that a fight had broken out at the party – even though every single one of the statements supporting that idea had been retracted in the court. 'I saw no evidence that the police had applied pressure onto these young men,' he later said. 'Other outside influences had put pressure on them to say things, but not the police.'* The jury in each case returned an open verdict. In May 1982, the Attorney General granted the families application to review the verdict. However, following their review in July, while the High Court justices accepted that there had been irregularities in the manner Coroner Dr Davies had conducted the inquest, these 'did not impinge upon the fairness of the hearing' or 'offend the rules of natural justice'. The open verdict therefore remained. The grieving families were appalled. 'It was a farce,' said George Francis, Chair of the New Cross Parents' Committee, whose seventeen-year-old son Gerry had DJ'd at the party and died in the blaze. My good friend Helen Shaw of INQUEST said,

---

* https://stillwerise.uk/2020/12/12/the-new-cross-fire-13-dead-and-nothing-said/

'Everything that could go wrong for families in the criminal justice system went wrong for these families.'

The New Cross Fire was a landmark in race relations in this country, a notorious event of great significance to the Black community in south London and in London as a whole. The truth is that for too long British Black people had felt marginalised and isolated from justice. When I was doing the case, I was given VHS tapes of the original footage from the time of the New Cross Fire, and they were a haunting reminder of what was going on at the time: the police's abuse of the so-called 'sus' law, a constant thorn in the side for young Black men in particular, and for some communities a near-daily reminder that the police were racist and discriminatory. Along with all the stop-and-searches, all the inappropriate behaviour by the police, the Black community had had enough. On top of this, the perceived injustice of the handling of the New Cross Fire investigation, the way the police so quickly began to demonise the youngsters, was a central factor in the general feeling of dissatisfaction and unease then, which ultimately bubbled over into the Brixton Riots and other 'race' disturbances up and down the country that same year. It was this outpouring of anger in a year of social and civil unrest which, more than anything else, led to Lord Scarman's inquiry and consequent report, the abolition of the 'sus' law with the introduction of the 1984 Police and Criminal Evidence Act (PACE), and a reassessment of the way police worked with Black communities. All this momentous change stemmed from the 1981 riots, and in part the catalyst was the New Cross Fire. In turn, the experiences of those affected significantly influenced the MacPherson inquiry into the police's investigation into the murder in April 1993 of Stephen Lawrence, and a change in the way that policing and the investigation of race crimes were conducted.

At the time, though, in May 1981, a lot of the Black community had real scepticism about whether they would get justice. It was generally accepted that the initial inquest into the fire was defective, having been held before the police had completed their investigations, and after the open verdict. The New Cross Massacre Action Committee, which had supported the families in preparation for the hearings, began immediately to work with them to demand a new inquest. In May 1982, an application was made to the Divisional Court for a judicial review and a new inquest was sought. This application was rejected. It was only in later years that there was a thaw in the relationship between the police and the victims of the fire, and a reappraisal of the police's approach to the case, thanks in large part to individual officers like Dr David Michaels MBE, who steadfastly supported the families in terms of getting the case properly investigated.

Subsequently, in 1997, the Metropolitan Police began a new investigation into the cause of the fire. Following an exhaustive reinvestigation, and thanks to advances in forensic science and computer-aided reconstructions, the police believed that they had been able to pinpoint the exact location of the fire when it started. Moreover, it was the Metropolitan Police who secured a judicial review before the Divisional Court in 2002. The attorney general granted the application, giving the families leave to appeal against the open verdict, thus paving the way for the possibility of a new inquest. In summary, the court said that there was important new scientific evidence, but, even more crucially, the facts were such that the interests of justice demanded that there be a new inquest. The coroner therefore conceded to an application to reopen the inquest on the basis of fresh evidence.

In 2004, nearly twenty-five years after the fire, I was

instructed by Susie Labinjoh and Patrick Allen of Hodge, Jones
& Allen Solicitors to represent the families of twelve of the
young victims at a second inquest. I had to be interviewed for
this job, and I remember nervously meeting Patrick and Susie,
who quizzed me to see if I would be someone the families
would be interested in instructing. I met George Francis. He
liked me. Later Susie rang me and told me the families were
impressed with me and wanted me to represent them. I was
delighted. Since the coroner had agreed to reopen the inquest,
it had taken two years for the families to secure funding
for the families' legal representations. It was difficult to see
how thirteen different families could have represented their
own interests or how the coroner could have done so, given
the amount of evidence and its complexity in this case, and
yet various reviews and appeals had to be made to the Legal
Services Commission. Eventually funding was agreed and
granted, but only after some of the other interested persons
(the Metropolitan Police, Lewisham council and, indeed,
the coroner) supported the families' application. This was
unprecedented in my experience. I needed a leader on such a
high-profile case, and I could think of no better person alongside me than Courtenay Griffiths QC. Thus, Courtenay and I
would be teamed up once again. Armza Ruddock, mother of
Yvonne, whose sixteenth birthday was being celebrated, and
son Paul were represented by barrister Henrietta Hill from
Doughty Street Chambers, Charles Collins represented himself
on behalf of his son, while Jason Beer, a well-known police
advocate, represented the Metropolitan Police.

The second inquest into the New Cross Fire, before retired
judge His Honour Gerald Butler QC sitting as a Southwark
deputy coroner, opened on 2 February 2004. It was a highly
important case – not least because the serious omissions in the

first investigation needed to be corrected. More so, perhaps, because almost a quarter of a century had passed, and the new inquest was the last chance for the New Cross parents (many of whom were now in their late seventies or early eighties) to put this terrible event behind them and get on with what was left of the rest of their lives. Of equal significance, of course, was the fact that the New Cross Fire was an event of great serious-ness to the Black community in south London and in the city as a whole. It was hoped by all involved that the new inquest would be wider-ranging, and as far as possible no stone would be left unturned in the pursuit of the truth and what happened that fateful night. It was a huge responsibility, therefore, to ensure that justice be done so that the families, and the wider community, would be given the reassurance of finally *seeing* and *knowing* that justice had been served.

I was honoured to be given that responsibility and gladly accepted the case, thinking that it was likely to be a highly politicised inquest, a wide-ranging investigation that would look at the sins of the '80s, the endemic racism and the National Front, and the failings of the police. I was sixteen at the time of the fire and I had been subjected to stop-and-searches under the 'sus' law. But what I didn't know was that nearly twenty-five years after the fire, the families whose loved ones had died simply wanted the truth. Many of my clients told me that they didn't want politics coming into it; the first time round they had felt that there had been an over-politicisation of their case at the expense of the truth. And that was a real eye-opener for me, because it made me realise that what mattered *wasn't* the lawyers' political spin on a case, which is sometimes very easy to do, but *what was best for the clients*. And what was best was the truth about how the fire started and, in an ideal world, who or what started it, and, perhaps most importantly, *why* anyone would want to set fire to a such a party. As George Francis told a reporter, 'We will not rest. We want an answer. Every other case or tragedy has been solved. Ours seems to be at the end of the pack and this time we are determined to have an answer.'

Some of those who had been at the party, however, still refused to talk to the police, making this search for the truth even more painful for the families, and my role as their representative at the inquest more pivotal. I remember George Francis saying to me plainly, 'Leslie, we've been waiting long enough. Take the gloves off. We don't care how dirty this gets, we just want to get to the truth of how our children died.'

It was one of the longest inquests in British coronial history and, unusually for me, there was no jury. When you are doing an inquest like this one, in the coroner's court every single working day for four months, the case becomes your life. Rarely does the coroner say, 'Let's have tomorrow off', because most of the time they want to get through the hearings as quickly and efficiently as possible. The fact that a former Lewisham police officer, David Michaels, was very supportive to me throughout the case was helpful; he had retired, but we discovered that he was a fellow countryman, a Dominican, and his faith in me was a big vote of confidence in my abilities. There was also a lot of local support for the families. The legal department and the mayor of Lewisham council provided invaluable resources for the elderly parents, including buses to transport them to and from court, generous lunches, and counselling services. Troy Robinson and Kathy Newman from Lewisham Legal Department were brilliant and offered me a lot of support as well.

Nevertheless, the New Cross inquest was intense and not without drama. It was one of the most forensically detailed cases that I had worked on. Given the advances in computers,

3D scene-reconstruction graphics and forensic science methodology, the technology used at the inquest was impressive. The Metropolitan Police, for example, provided a digital reconstruction of the fire and the movements of persons in the house and video evidence was played for the consideration of the court. The court used LIVENOTE, an instantaneous court transcribing system, which meant that all the lawyers had access to the evidence on laptops as it was given from the witnesses. Two witnesses were abroad, and their evidence was heard during the inquest via a live video-conference link. We, the families' lawyers, also commissioned Digital Law to scan all forty-five lever-arch files of evidence into digital format which was searchable in a number of ways, including by witness, case theory and timings. Any search criteria could be created and timelines from which preparation of questions could be formulated.

The key questions were: how the fire was started; if possible to determine who was responsible for the fire; where the fire was started (specific location in the room); what the possible causes of the fire were; and, more particularly, the timing of it.

This was never going to be an easy task. The coroner called a large number of witnesses. One day, I arrived at the court and heard someone call my name. I turned around and it was Frank, or Franklin, one of my friends who didn't go to my school, but lived around the corner from me. It should have dawned on me earlier that he might be called as a witness, and I would have to cross-examine him. I brought it to the attention of the coroner, but Frank was a factual witness and there was no conflict.

Two likely theories were run at the second inquest: firstly, that the fire had been started accidentally, by a gas fire in the front room, perhaps. The second was that the fire had been started deliberately from the inside. What became apparent was that, contrary to the earlier opinions, and speculation, the police forensic evidence showed that in all likelihood the fire had been started by a naked flame applied to an armchair in the front room. The scientists were able to pinpoint the exact time the fire broke out – between 5.22 a.m. and 5.46 a.m., a time when only a few partygoers could have been downstairs in that room. Because it raged out of control so quickly, it was also suggested that an accelerant must have been used. It wasn't an accident; it had been started in the house deliberately. Thus, the likelihood was that the person who started the fire was known to some of the victims.

In preparation for the inquest, I had learned that, although they didn't want to make this a point of contention in the hearings, the police were asserting that some in the Black community knew all along that the fire had not been the result of racist attack. Supposedly, those individuals already suspected that it had been started by someone who had attended the party, but they had decided to suppress that truth. That was the police argument. I didn't need to go into that during the inquest, partly because I didn't necessarily trust what the police were saying. After all, they may simply have been saying it in order to cover up their own failings. But now, on hearing the new forensic evidence, I had to completely rethink my perceptions of the case. When it became clear that the cause of the fire may not have been a racist attack, certain people, indeed those who initially had been shouting the loudest, simply fell utterly silent. Their vocal support of the victims' families seemed to have immediately dwindled. While many of my clients felt that their truths were being sacrificed in terms of political expediency, for the activists, it wasn't expedient to bring to light the new truth that this wasn't, in fact, a racially motivated outside killing.

Mr Collins, the father who was representing himself, continued nevertheless to explore the possibility of a racist attack, a faulty paraffin heater, a gas leak, an electrical fire. I had the feeling that he was intent on pursuing anything and everything save for the fact that the fire could have been started internally by one of the partygoers, but that was his right. Armza Ruddock, meanwhile, was not answering questions fully, or was answering with no comment, but again that was her right and nothing can be read into that.

What I had to explore, therefore, was who among the partygoers – and when I say partygoers, it was the adults who were suspected, not the children who were upstairs dancing when the fire started – had the potential motive to light the flames. What were those adults, who were said to be in the kitchen when the fire broke out, doing in terms of not being able to protect the children upstairs? The inquest was an opportunity for me to call those adults to account for their actions, or lack of action, when the fire was discovered. Unfortunately, because this second inquiry was carried out some twenty-three years after the fire, many important witnesses could not attend due to old age, ill health or because they were dead. A number of other witnesses, adults who were known to the owner of the home, had either disappeared or refused to attend the inquest. Others now changed their statements, giving confusing or contradictory evidence, were 'shifty' and 'evasive' (in the words of the coroner) when they had no apparent reason for being so, or refused to give evidence or answer questions in cross-examination. Expressing her frustration, one of my clients, Velvetina Francis who lost her son Gerry Francis, told a TV news reporter, 'They are hiding something, shielding someone. Now some of them are standing with lawyers behind them. They are witnesses. Why?' It was, therefore, essentially a case of trying to do the best with the evidence that existed. This meant re-examining several witness statements, which had been taken over the years, and comparing and contrasting them with more recent statements of these and other witnesses.

When I examined the evidence there were a number of people in the house that night who may have been possible suspects for starting the fire, for all sorts of reasons – basic, all-too human motivations such as jealousy or being shunned.

It transpired that Mrs Ruddock's teenage daughter Dawn was apparently in a relationship with Maspin 'Danny' Higgins, who had lived with the family for three years. Just months before the night of the party, Armza Ruddock had kicked the pair out after Higgins, a former boyfriend of hers, admitted he was having sex with Dawn. The pair had subsequently moved to Haringey. Four weeks after the fire, Higgins had threatened to leave Dawn. According to Higgins there followed a violent confrontation during which Dawn had allegedly sprinkled paraffin on his packed suitcase. According to another sworn testimony, Dawn was also once implicated in setting fire to her room in a Hither Green hostel. The couple had subsequently emigrated to America and Dawn was now married to someone else. But it must be said that these sensational details which were explored at the inquest are nothing more than speculation and innuendo and do not amount to solid evidence pointing to a suspect.

Once again, there was conflicting evidence from witnesses about who was or was not present during or shortly after the outbreak of the fire. Dawn Ruddock and Danny Higgins gave each other alibis, saying that they had both been at home in north London. Danny denied being at the scene of the fire until sometime after 10 a.m. the following day. But his alibi was completely at odds with the evidence of his brother Norman Higgins, which put Danny outside the house shortly after the discovery of the fire at some time between 6.15 a.m. and 6.45 a.m. Moreover, a witness claimed that she had seen a woman fitting the description of Dawn at the rear of the premises. Dawn refused to answer questions, as was her right, in this regard. Norman Higgins claimed not to have been at the party, however, twenty-one witnesses gave evidence to the contrary. Significantly, Danny, Dawn and Norman had each left UK jurisdiction shortly after the fire and moved to America. Danny Higgins didn't come back for the inquest because he claimed not to have a passport, but his brother, Norman, was there, as was Dawn (Young, née Ruddock).

I was robust in my cross-examination of Mrs Ruddock, while her counsel Henrietta Hill did a very good job of protecting her during the hearings. I have a lot of respect for Henrietta; she is a brilliant barrister who had been brought into the case at the last minute, mastered the voluminous set of papers and was fearless in her defence of her client. She deserved much respect. I was also unrelenting in my cross-examination of Dawn Young, but this was a frustrating line of questioning, due to the necessary remit of the inquest. When I tried to raise the allegations made against Dawn in evidence during the inquest, including the issue of the other fires Dawn was allegedly involved in starting, I was halted by the deputy coroner, who reminded her that she need not answer my questions if she thought there was a risk of incriminating herself. Nevertheless, I continued: 'The suggestion is that as a result of this argument you got so upset with Danny that you poured paraffin over his suitcase as he was about to leave and threatened to set it on fire. That's right, isn't it?' No reply. I went on, 'Are you somebody who is prone to making threats with paraffin and matches, Mrs Young?' No reply. Dawn vehemently and consistently denied any involvement in starting the fire or having been near the

New Cross house until later the following morning after the party. Passions ran high in the court. As she stepped down from the stand and passed the public gallery, one of my clients rose in her seat and shouted at her, 'You murdering bitch.'

It was all highly dramatic, salacious – and sad. Fourteen kids were dead, and many more gravely injured as a result of the fire on that night.

The inquest concluded on 6 May. The deputy coroner Gerald Butler stated that he was satisfied that the fire was not started by a petrol bomb or any other incendiary device, either thrown from outside or inside the house at 493 New Cross Road. He concluded that while it was not possible to determine *beyond reasonable doubt* that the fire had been started deliberately, he stated in his closing remarks that he felt that on a balance of probabilities it had been: 'While I think it probable [. . .] that this fire was begun by deliberate application of a flame to the armchair near to the television [. . .] I cannot be sure of this. The result is this, that in the case of each and every one of the deaths, I must return an open verdict.'

If this case were to be heard today, however, following the recent decision of the Supreme Court in a case in November 2020, it is highly likely that an unlawful killing verdict would be returned since the standard of proof to return such a finding is no longer the stringent criminal threshold of 'beyond a reasonable doubt' or 'satisfied so that you are sure', but the civil standard, namely 'meeting the balance of probabilities'.*

---

* R (on the application of Maughan) v HM Senior Coroner for Oxfordshire [2020] UKSC 46.

Postscript

Shortly after the conclusion of the second inquest, I made an application on behalf of the families for a judicial review to challenge the coroner's finding of an open verdict. The grounds were as follows: the coroner's failure to take into account and/or ignoring relevant matters/evidence when coming to an open verdict; secondly, a perversity challenge to the judgment on the basis that no reasonable coroner would have come to such a conclusion in the light of the evidence that was either ignored or missed by the coroner. The families were not asking for a new inquest, but for the coroner to reconsider his decision. The judicial review application was heard in autumn 2004. The application was unsuccessful and the conclusion was upheld.

Working on this case, it was terrible to contemplate that this appalling incident that sparked a summer of discontent in 1981 was, perhaps, all about pathetic human frailties. Nevertheless, even if the fire had been started deliberately by someone inside the house that night, forty years on and despite having sat through two inquests, the families of those who died still have no final answers. The tragedy is that the second inquest failed to get to the heart of the matter because many witnesses did not tell the truth. To this day, different theories and speculations about the fire persist. Yet nobody has come forward, none of us knows who started the fire, no one has ever been charged in connection with it and the case remains unsolved. It's one of those sad stories where perhaps we will never learn the whole truth.

29

A DEATH IN PRISON: MARTIN
GREEN (1977–2002)

'If I had a dog and I let it suffer and it died, I would
be punished.'

Pamela Green, mother of Martin Green

By 2007, I was well used to working on inquests involving
deaths in police custody and prison settings. I have had to
become hardened to death, so there are not that many cases
which make me cry these days. The tragic case of Martin Green
is an exception. One of Louise Christian's protégés, a talented
clinical negligence solicitor called James Bell, asked me if I
would act for the Green family on a case which had medical
negligence overtones to it, but had occurred while in prison
custody. I agreed.

Martin Green was the father of four young children and
twenty-five years old when he died on 15 July 2002. Earlier that
year, following an altercation with a parking attendant in a car
park, Martin had received a twelve-month sentence for dangerous driving. It was his first offence. He would never see his

family as a free man again. He duly entered HMP Blakenhurst, in Worcestershire, on 4 July. Martin was a recovering heroin addict and on a methadone opioid substitution programme, but this withdrawal treatment was not available at the prison.

Martin was significantly underweight and had an ongoing digestive disorder for which he had received treatment from his GP. He told the prison medical staff about this, but no record was made nor was it considered by those responsible for his care in the prison. He was declared fit to be detained by the admissions doctor and a detoxification regime was commenced. With a sudden cessation of his methadone treatment, Martin began to suffer extreme withdrawal symptoms with almost constant vomiting for the next eleven days. When he was transferred to a cell in the medical wing, his weight had dropped from 9 stone to 6 stone 7lb.

Over the next six days he was struggling with his detoxification regime. He continued to vomit and was refusing all meals. Ten days into his prison sentence, the prison doctor examined him, and due to his rapid deterioration, booked him into an outside hospital. However, this decision was overruled by a governor on the grounds of 'staffing issues'. Instead, prison officers gave Martin paper towels for his cell floor – so that he didn't slip in his own vomit.

At 8.30 a.m. the next morning, Martin asked a nurse if he could see a doctor as he felt unwell. The doctor noted that Martin was lying motionless, covered in and surrounded by his own bodily waste. He was dead. The cause of death at post-mortem was dehydration and electrolyte imbalance, vomiting and narcotic withdrawal.

Three years after Martin Green's death, in December 2005, the Crown Prosecution Service decided that there were insufficient grounds to bring charges of manslaughter caused by gross negligence. The family challenged the decision, but were unsuccessful. Then as now, prisons enjoy Crown immunity from prosecution – this was one of the issues that Martin's mother Pamela Green wanted to call into question. Furthermore, because more than one person was involved in Martin's care, or the lack thereof, it would be hard to apportion blame.

Martin's parents were understandably struggling to accept that seemingly no one would be held accountable for their son's death. I wanted to do my utmost for them. The inquest opened in October 2007. I was prepared and determined to leave no line of questioning unexplored in order to get the answers that Martin's family deserved.

I told the court that, with a couple of exceptions, the staff who were responsible for Martin's care deserved to hang their collective heads in shame. At one point towards the end of the evidence, the coroner, Dr Geraint Williams, dramatically adjourned the inquest for forty-eight hours and asked the CPS to reconsider their decision because he was so concerned by some of the testimony. But the CPS again ruled that there was not enough evidence to bring a case against any members of the prison staff and they were not going to prosecute.

Martin Green's case was memorable for a number of reasons, but for me what stood out the most were the actions of the coroner. Geraint Williams was a family man, an excellent and robust advocate, and throughout the inquest process was caring and understanding towards this grieving family. Martin's death had left four young children without a father, and I've never seen a coroner show such compassion and humanity. Pamela was now looking after two of the younger children, and on the second day, the coroner brought them into the court. One was seven and the other six years old, and as they were guided in, the older one looked up and said to Dr Williams, 'Are you the man who is going to help find out what happened to our daddy?' Everyone in the court wept. Her father had been in prison for a motoring offence.

The jury were out for five whole days. At the time, this was the longest I had known a jury to retire and deliberate. When they returned, in a critical narrative verdict, they absolutely slammed Blakenhurst Prison. They concluded that inadequate care and a failure to monitor Martin's rapidly deteriorating physical and mental condition, coupled with poor assessment, planning and communication, had contributed significantly to his death. Afterwards, Pamela read a statement outside the court: 'My son was in for a first offence. My son should not have been there. I lost him through a prison sentence at Blakenhurst and I get angry that they let my son die. He wanted to live.'

Postscript

Immediately after the inquest, James Bell and I started to prepare the family's case in a civil claim of medical negligence, under the Fatal Accidents Act 1976, against two of the prison doctors responsible for the medical care and medical treatment given to Martin, and an action under the Human Rights Act 1998 against the Worcestershire NHS Trust. Martin was a vulnerable inmate, in a position of complete dependence vis-à-vis the prison and the NHS staff. He should have been provided with proper care. His life should have been protected. It was not. I do not know what happened to the civil claim after the inquest as I had another pressing case to begin and had little more to do with it after the inquest ended. This was a case I was sure was not going to be fought at a trial given the damming jury conclusion. I can only presume that it settled.

In January 2008, at a meeting arranged by her local MP Mark Todd, Pamela Green took her battle for justice to the Lord Chancellor, Jack Straw,* seeking assurances that action had been taken to prevent a similar tragedy. She continued to insist that there should be disciplinary action against the prison staff involved. 'I told Jack Straw that my son shouldn't have died that way. I gave him a photograph of Martin looking like a holocaust victim. It was like he was a skeleton and he had black blood over him,' she told a local news reporter. 'I asked why doctors that were talked about during the inquest were still working in the community. Nothing was set in stone but he went away with our questions and we will get answers.'†

Following the meeting, a Ministry of Justice spokesman said: 'Every death in prison is a tragedy affecting families, staff and other prisoners deeply and our sympathies are with the family of Martin Green. Ministers, the National Offender Management Service and the Prison Service are completely committed to reducing the number of such tragic incidents. We note the findings of the inquest and will continue to work hard to ensure that we offer the best possible care and help for those placed in our custody.'

---

* http://news.bbc.co.uk/1/hi/programmes/politics_show/7202286.stm
† *Redditch and Alcester Advertiser*, 6 February 2008.

3 0

WOMEN IN THE PRISON SYSTEM: PETRA BLANKSBY (1984–2003)

'Why are so many mentally ill young people sent
to prison when they really should be receiving
psychiatric care?'

Lord Giddens, House of Lords' debate, 20 October 2005

By the mid-2000s, I was dealing with a lot of cases involving
deaths in prison, where the state had let down extremely vulnerable, and often mentally ill people who had ended up in the
judicial system. Sadly, for many helpless women suffering from
acute mental and behavioural disorders, a prison is the only
place that will take them in at their time of crisis. But, as the
story of Petra Blanksby's life and death illustrates, prison was
no fit place for them.

On 25 November 2003, nineteen-year-old Petra died six days
after a suicide attempt while serving a sentence at HMP New
Hall, Wakefield. Her father and her twin sister Kirsty wanted
to know why she was allowed to be sent to New Hall prison,
where there was no resident psychiatrist, when, clearly, like

many other women in that institution, one glance at Petra's mental health history would have shown that she desperately needed proper psycho-medical care.

At the inquest before the Wakefield coroner Mr David Hinchliff, the court heard that Petra had been under the care of the mental health services for many years and had a long history of serious attempts at self-harm. Her father explained that Petra's problems had started in early childhood. After the twins' birth, their mother had suffered severe postnatal depression, struggling to form an emotional bond with her daughters. When the girls were four and their parents divorced, Petra and Kirsty suffered unbelievable abuse. 'We were forced to drink urine, slammed against the wall and once made to eat dog food,' Kirsty told the jury. Sometimes they wouldn't get fed and when they were about seven, police used to find the young girls wandering around the streets at night.

When they turned nine, social services were called in and the twins were sent to live with different foster carers. Five years later they were reunited when they found themselves on the same ward at Tameside Hospital. Kirsty had taken an overdose and Petra had cut herself. The sisters were placed together in the care of a new foster family. But that was not the happy ending that one might have hoped for the sisters. Petra was sexually abused when she was twelve, triggering the episodes of self-harm that would become such a devastating pattern in her life. At fourteen, after she was moved to a children's home, she was raped. There, at seventeen, Petra got pregnant by a teenage boy who refused to have anything to do with their child. She moved to a halfway house for young mothers, but she was severely depressed and struggled to bring up her son. Petra asked social services to help find a nursery place for her baby to give her some respite, but her request was rejected.

She continued to self-harm – cutting and burning herself, or overdosing. Again, social services failed to intervene.

Her twin sister Kirsty understood Petra's illness only too well. She too had been self-harming since her early teens, and her own body bore the scars. 'The deeper you cut, the better you feel,' she told a reporter after her sister's death. 'You are hurting so much inside you can't let it go unless you hurt yourself.' She said that the general absence of professional awareness of their mental health problems, however, hurt even more.

In December 2002, Petra suffered a breakdown and tried to commit suicide. She was sectioned under the Mental Health Act and her son was taken into temporary foster care. Three months later, Petra was discharged. She was judged to have a 'borderline personality disorder' which, according to hospital psychiatrists, was not treatable under the Mental Health Act. Instead, they decided that Petra was to be monitored as an outpatient.

In the months that followed, Petra's acts of self-harm grew increasingly desperate and ever more frequent; she swallowed razor blades, took an overdose, burnt off her hair, and also tried to throw herself off a bridge. On 7 July 2003, Petra telephoned her community psychiatric team. She had cut her wrists by smashing her hands through the window of her flat. When the mental health workers arrived, they found that Petra had tried to gas herself. Despite this, no one reassessed her mental state, nor took any action to safeguard her wellbeing. One of the psychiatric team told the jury that Petra's condition was considered untreatable, so there was 'no point': 'Nothing would be achieved by her re-admission. [...] We don't keep people in hospital to stop them killing themselves.'

As I responded in court at the time, it simply beggars belief that such a clear cry for help was ignored.

Three hours later Petra set fire to her mattress and called 999. This, we believed, was a last, desperate cry for help, but the local police and magistrate saw things differently. Instead of receiving help for her psychiatric problems, Petra was arrested, charged with arson to endanger life, convicted and transferred on remand to New Hall prison. Her son was placed for adoption.

Over the next 130 days while awaiting trial, Petra was involved in at least ninety incidents of self-harm, many requiring hospital admission. While placed on suicide watch, she was not monitored twenty-four hours a day and on 19 November Petra made another suicide attempt. She managed to make a ligature using the hems from her sheets, wound this round her neck and strangled herself in her prison cell. Petra's suicide attempt left her in a coma. Six days later, with her father and identical twin sister Kirsty by her side, doctors switched off her life support machine. She should never have been put in prison in the first place. The evidence revealed that the fire was, in fact, an act of self-harm. Petra had been trying to kill *herself*. The only life endangered was her own.

At the inquest, the jury heard that Petra's medical records had noted a consultation in which she had said that once her son was safe, she would be free to go. I called consultant forensic psychiatrist Dr Keith Rix as an expert witness, who told the jury: 'I would like to think that in a civilised society someone as severely mentally disordered as [Petra] should have been in the care of ordinary or forensic psychiatric services and not in prison. However, mental health law, as it was at the time, did not allow this and there were no appropriate NHS facilities.'

In her short life Petra had never known maternal love or received the kind of care that most of us take for granted. She was a young woman crying out for help, for someone to take responsibility and to look after her, and to help her to look after her baby. Campaigners at INQUEST and the family questioned why the magistrates in their wisdom would seek to imprison a young girl with Petra's history. I did too – but an investigation into that decision was considered outside the coroner's remit. On behalf of Petra's family, at the inquest I did query whether HMP New Hall, in particular, is a suitable place to hold vulnerable women, many of whom are on remand or serving short sentences for minor offences. And Petra's death was not unique. She was one of fourteen women who took their lives in prison in 2003.

At the end of the inquest on 1 February 2008, the jury returned a critical narrative verdict declaring that in view of Petra's diagnosis, prison for her was 'not a suitable place', noting that there 'appears to be no infrastructure in the forensic mental health service for people with her problems'. There were also concerns about the role of Derbyshire Social Services and a collective failure of various authorities to understand the impact of her son's adoption on Petra's mental health. Procedures, staff training and access to resources at HMP New Hall on the day of Petra's death invited similar censure.

HM Coroner David Hinchliff said that he had been struck by the comments of Dr Keith Rix and announced he would be using his power under Rule 43 of the Coroners' Rules to write to the Prison Service and the Department of Health to call for both to start providing adequate facilities for women with similar problems.

As I commented at the time, 'This was a needless death. If the system ever let someone down it was this case. As one prison officer said during the inquest, "Petra was a death in custody waiting to happen." I couldn't agree more.'

Postscript

After her sister's death, Kirsty Blanksby helped to lead a public campaign highlighting Petra's tragic life and death, and calling for better treatment of mentally ill women. Then, in November 2018, I heard that Kirsty had died, fifteen years and one day after her twin sister Petra. At the inquest into her death, the cause of death was found to be pneumonia and combined drug intoxication.

I'd like to be able to report that things have changed since 2008, but the problem persists. Women are particularly vulnerable while in custody, especially in the prison system. Many have suffered abuse and have acute mental health issues. Often, if they are mothers, they have the added pressure of being separated from their children. The death behind bars of women like Petra Blanksby remains one of this country's biggest tragedies.

31

THE CHANDLER'S FORD
SHOOTING: MARK NUNES (1972–
2007) AND ANDREW MARKLAND
(1971–2007)

On the morning of 13 September 2007, the quiet town of
Chandler's Ford in Hampshire was the site of a double fatal
shooting by the Metropolitan Police's CO19 firearms team.
The victims of the shooting were Mark Nunes, thirty-five,
and Andrew Markland, thirty-six, both Black British males
who had been attempting to rob a cash-laden G4S security van
outside the HSBC bank.

Nunes was believed to be the ringleader of an armed gang,
and along with seven other men, had been responsible for tar-
geting low-security routes in England's rural interior between
April 2006 and September 2007. The gang's biggest single haul
had been in May 2006 when they got away with £165,000, after
allegedly pistol-whipping a guard outside a bank in Bristol.
Consequently, an operation codenamed 'Hurlock' had been
launched to track down and arrest Nunes and his accomplices.

When they set out from London for Chandler's Ford
that morning, Nunes and Markland were being followed

by officers from the Specialist Firearms Command (CO19) who were watching – and recording on camera – their every move. When the driver of the security van got out in front of the bank, a baclava-clad Mark Nunes approached him, his 9mm handgun pointed at the guard's head. A split-second later Mark Nunes was shot by a police Flying Squad marksman. Andrew Markland saw his accomplice shot, appeared to pick up Nunes' gun lying discarded in the road, then clearly thought better of it. Once the armed officers made their presence known, Andrew raised his hands, which might be interpreted as his surrendering. The firearms officer did not agree with that interpretation and in that moment he shot at Andrew too. He fell to the ground and was shot once more. He was declared dead at the scene, while Mark Nunes died later in hospital.

Sarah McSherry from Christian Khan Solicitors asked me if I might work on behalf of Andrew Markland's family and in particular represent his mother at the inquest into the deaths of the two men. My colleague Sean Horstead, also at Garden Court, had been instructed to represent Mark Nunes' family. It was not going to be an easy case because there was little doubt that the two deceased men had been involved in wrongdoing; the question, however, was whether their deaths were avoidable. I watched the video footage of Andrew being shot and instantly agreed to take on the case. I thought Sean had the more marginally difficult task, but we could collaborate and do our best.

The inquest opened on 3 October 2011, and the timing could not have been more sensitive. Just two months earlier, on 4 August 2011, Mark Duggan was shot dead on the streets of Tottenham, north London by a Metropolitan Police firearms officer. Mark Duggan's killing had sparked rioting across the country on a level that had not been seen before nor since, with violent street clashes and looting.

The inquiry into the shooting of Mark Nunes and Andrew Markland, was therefore both high-profile and highly contentious. We were at Winchester Coroner's Court in front of Grahame Short, the Central Hampshire coroner. Both the deceased were Black men, who had been shot in a predominantly white, middle-class, suburban county. I knew in advance that the jury were unlikely to be reflective of the diversity of London. I was right.

Two issues were central to this case; firstly, whether the police should have arrested both men earlier, before they got close to holding up the security van; secondly, given the video evidence in relation to Mr Markland, whether the police were right to shoot him. Our 'case theory' was that Andrew had been unlawfully killed. Sean and I argued that there was sufficient evidence to charge Nunes and Markland with being in possession of a firearm, with intent to commit an indictable offence and/or conspiracy to rob *before* they approached the GS4 security van. At least a year before the double shooting, the Metropolitan Police Service, in co-ordination with the Avon and Somerset police and the Hampshire police, had placed Mr Nunes and other members of his gang under surveillance, following them to gather sufficient evidence to make an arrest and to secure a conviction. The inquest heard that the 'meticulously planned' covert operation that morning by the Met's Flying Squad had been set up to intercept and detain the suspected robbers. Why, then, had the police not arrested the gang members earlier, in a safer way, as opposed to allowing them to carry out an armed robbery in broad daylight, when it had become a potential life-or-death situation?

The IPCC investigation, led by Superintendent Battle of the Firearms Unit of West Yorkshire Police, had concluded that there were ample opportunities during the operation in which it could have been successfully and non-violently resolved, including over the few minutes immediately prior to the pair's deaths. Yet, the police commander on the ground that day, Detective Chief Inspector Terry Wilson, had allowed the operation to escalate to such a dangerous level that we and the inquest jury were invited to believe that firearms officers were left with no other option but to use lethal force. In evidence, DCI Wilson claimed that the officers needed to catch Nunes 'in the act' as there was not enough evidence to arrest him, thus allowing a narrow, risk-fraught window in which to enact a non-violent arrest of the suspects. When Mr Nunes had pulled out his handgun, DCI Wilson said he had taken the armed officers 'by surprise'.

The bereaved families believed that the planned Hurlock operation was heavily weighted against achieving a non-violent arrest and brought about circumstances in which the risk to life was deemed non-consequential. I certainly believed there was merit in this view. The belief that the two men had, in effect, been deliberately cornered and shot was compounded in the case of Andrew Markland by the fact that he appeared to have been shot twice in the back *after* he had dropped Nunes' gun. The shooter at the inquest disputed this and said it was at the same time. Furthermore, the police had no evidence to suggest that lethal force would be used by Nunes in this robbery or had been used in any of the gang's previous robberies. Sean and I suggested that it was therefore reasonable to assume that the only risk of harm in this specific instance came from the Flying Squad officers themselves towards the targets of the operation.

At every turn, Sean and I believe we were being hampered in our endeavour to represent the bereaved families' interests. The police withheld secret evidence relating to Operation Hurlock on the grounds of Public Interest Immunity. Other evidence including police radio communications and further CCTV footage was not disclosed and a crucial document detailing key tactical decisions made on the day of the shooting had supposedly been 'lost' during the IPCC investigation. Our appeals to Coroner Grahame Sharp for full disclosure were overruled. At the end of the hearings, the coroner instructed the jury that they could only consider an open verdict or one of lawful killing. I felt, rightly or wrongly, that the coroner was not dealing properly with the contentions we were raising. I felt we were not being listened to. And when you are not being listened to, the time comes when you have to down tools. So, before the jury retired, that's what Sean and I did; our clients withdrew their instructions, believing the hearing was now a farce, and without client instructions we had no choice but to walk out of court. For me, this inquest epitomised the failing of a society to allow for a full and open investigation involving the family in a meaningful way – and a system that does not truly value Black lives.

The jury subsequently found the killings of Mark Nunes and Andrew Markland to be lawful.

Postscript

It is undeniable that there were severe flaws in the police's handling of the Chandlers Ford operation. The coroner recommended that, in future, an independent commander should be appointed to oversee similar firearms operations, i.e. a senior officer who is not involved in the wider police investigation into the suspects. This would reduce any bias given to the need to secure prosecutable evidence and, in doing so, disregarding the potential risk to life. The police said that they had themselves implemented this recommendation as a procedure prior to the coroner's report being published.

3 2

SEAN RIGG (1968–2008)

Having worked on the restraint-related cases of Wayne Douglas and Christopher Alder among others, I thought lessons would have been learned. Articles had been written, numerous papers published, police forces up and down the country had been trained in the dangers of positional asphyxia. Officers had also learned to recognise signs of excited delirium where people are in a state of derangement as a result of a mental health condition, a head injury, drugs, or a combination of all three. I therefore naively thought these cases would become a thing of the past. How wrong I was.

On 21 August 2008, a decade after the death of Christopher Alder and thirteen years after that of Wayne Douglas, another relatively young man by the name of Sean Rigg died in police custody. In 2012, my good friend Daniel Machover, of Hickman & Rose Solicitors, instructed me on behalf of the Rigg family to get justice at Southwark Coroner's Court for Sean. It was a mammoth undertaking. The legal team would be Daniel and a young solicitor called Helen Stone, myself and a former pupil of mine, Tom Stoate.

Sean Rigg and Wayne Douglas both died at Brixton police station. Sadly, given my professional experience of Brixton police, this didn't feel like a coincidence. In terms of public perception, however, there was a big difference between the two. With the death of Wayne Douglas, because of the nature of the crime of which he had been accused, we did not have public sympathy on our side. Sean Rigg's death was different.

One of five siblings, forty-year-old Sean Nicholas Rigg came from a close-knit West Indian family. Charming, boisterous and widely popular, Sean was a talented musician and rapper who had produced artists for his own record label. A black belt in karate, he had no physical health problems. After his one and only experience of LSD, however, he had suffered his first psychotic breakdown. Thereafter, his mental illness – paranoid schizophrenia – affected the rest of his life. Sean's family were closely involved with his mental health care at the South London and Maudsley NHS Trust. Sean had a history of stopping his medication and falling into relapse and he was known by Brixton police to have mental health issues.

Prior to his arrest on 21 August, his behaviour began to give cause for concern. When psychotic, Sean became aggressive and paranoid, imagining that he was fighting who knows what demons in his mind. On the day that he died, he certainly thought he was under attack. According to staff at the high-support mental health hostel in Balham where Sean was living, he was acutely psychotic, aggressive, practising his karate moves and behaving bizarrely. Repeated 999 calls from the staff over a three-hour period went unheeded. During the final call, the operator insisted that Rigg was not a police priority, told the hostel-worker to contact her MP if she was dissatisfied, and ended the call. After causing damage and threatening the staff, Sean went unchallenged when he walked out of the hostel unaccompanied. He was naked from the waist up, wandering the streets of Balham, a potential threat to himself and to others. Eventually, a concerned member of the public called the police.

Now is not the time to look at the failings on the part of his mental health team or of the hostel staff. That tale is told elsewhere. Regardless of the sins of the many professionals who let him down, what happened to Sean on the day he died can only be described as the dishonour of Metropolitan policing. Four Metropolitan Police officers (two probationary officers and two non-probationary officers) eventually chased Sean down, cuffed his hands behind his back and restrained him in a prone position, the officers leaning on his back for eight minutes. He was arrested for assault, public disorder and the theft of a passport. It was his own. He was placed face down with his legs bent behind him in the back cage of a police van and taken to Brixton police station. During the journey Sean's condition deteriorated. And, as in the case of Christopher Alder and Wayne Douglas, within thirty minutes of his being arrested and restrained, Sean was dead. And, as in the case of Christopher Alder, the last painful minutes of Sean's life were recorded on a CCTV camera. At the inquest, the court would see one of the arresting officers claiming that Rigg was 'faking it' as he was left to die lying on the concrete floor of Brixton police station.

A subsequent eighteen-month investigation carried out by the IPCC found no evidence of neglect or wrongdoing; the Brixton police officers had acted reasonably and proportionately. Understandably, Sean's family were disturbed and disappointed by the IPCC's conclusions, and more determined than ever to find out the truth about how Sean had died.

Proper tribute must be made to Sean's sisters, Marci and Samantha, and his brother Wayne, who tirelessly pursued justice on his behalf. They had endured a painful four-year-long wait for the inquest, and an ongoing battle for legal aid funding. They were not prepared to accept non-answers or wrong answers. The family wanted the truth.

The inquest into Sean's death was scheduled for the first week of June 2012. We had problems with disclosure from Brixton police throughout our preparation, our repeated requests being met with prevarication and unhelpful delays. Initially we had been served with a DVD compilation that spliced together the various CCTV camera angles at various times in the custody suite. The video, about an hour long, purported to show Sean being brought into the police station and placed in a caged area where he collapsed. The footage showed Sean dying about twenty minutes later. There was something strange about this video, but we couldn't quite put our fingers on it. And then eagle-eyed Marci, Samantha and Wayne spotted that the footage had been edited in such a way as to omit a significant chunk of time. There was no explanation for this missing piece of time and we never got to the bottom of it. That block of time proved crucial.

Then, a matter of days before the inquest was due to open, the police barristers served us with a deluge of documents and disclosure, including tens of hours of raw CCTV footage from each of the different cameras at Brixton Police station. We didn't know how we were going to manage to scrutinise all the new evidence so late in the day, but the Rigg family said they would watch the CCTV footage and tell us what was on it. The Riggs were relentless and they crunched that footage.

When a detainee arrives at a police station, his or her welfare is the responsibility of the on-duty custody sergeant, who should satisfy him- or herself of their safety. Sean was extremely vulnerable, in the throes of a critical mental health crisis, and, as such, in great need of care and protection. And yet, the CCTV footage revealed that when Sean had arrived at Brixton police station he had been left in the back of the van for at least ten minutes before being brought into the custody suite. When he was interviewed in March 2009 by the IPCC investigators, the custody officer Sergeant White said that he had gone out of the station to check on Sean in the parked van. He claimed that Sean had looked at him, he had looked at Sean, and he had satisfied himself that Sean was alive and well. Having no concerns about the detainee's welfare, Sergeant White had returned to the custody suite.

I remember, before the inquest started, the Rigg family taking me through the video tapes. They had meticulously studied hours of footage, every frame of every tape from every angle, following Sergeant White step by step as he walked around the custody suite. They jumped from camera angle to camera angle, making sure that they could see him at all times until their brother was brought in from the van and into the holding cage. There was a problem with Sergeant White's evidence to the IPCC – it was all a lie. As was manifest from this footage, he hadn't left the police station at any point to check on Sean in the van. I had to think carefully about how I was going to deal with this evidence at the inquest.

The inquest opened on 11 June 2012, sitting before Dr Andrew Harris at Southwark Coroner's Court. It was to last for seven weeks.

I like doing cases out of Southwark, for a number of reasons. Firstly, Dr Harris is an excellent coroner. He's respectful and thorough. Secondly, his staff are accommodating and a pleasure to work with. But most importantly, Southwark is my local court. On my motorbike I could be there in less than twenty minutes, and after court I make it swiftly back home to be with my children. I could help them with their schoolwork, prepare meals for them and generally be around.

Two days into the inquest, on the evening of 13 June, along with a good number of my colleagues from Garden Court, I had ironed my shirt and donned my best suit for the annual black-tie dinner bash for the Legal Aid Lawyer Awards. I was one of three members of our chambers to be nominated that year. We all went along in hope, but with no real expectation of leaving with a gong. To the delight of our table, one of our juniors, social welfare and children's rights barrister Shu Shin Luh, was named Young Legal Aid Barrister of the Year for her work on behalf of vulnerable children and adults, particularly those with complex needs or mental health issues. To my utter astonishment, I was awarded the Legal Aid Barrister of the Year award, commended for my empathy and desire to work for the less fortunate in society, in particular representing bereaved families at inquests. The highlight of the night, however, was when Michael Mansfield QC presented Doreen Lawrence OBE with a special award for the exceptional commitment she has shown to fighting for justice over many years. The Lawrence family's solicitor, Imran Khan, also received an award for outstanding achievement, and the room rose as one in a rousing and emotional standing ovation. It was a fantastic night out, and exactly the boost that I needed, both to my confidence and my resolve to fight for justice for Sean and to keep fighting to be a potent voice for the dead and for the families they have left behind.

The following month, on 11 July, a number of police officers were giving evidence, including the Brixton police custody officer, Sergeant Paul White. Sometimes, you could say, I am one for drama. Sergeant White took the stand and gave his evidence and then it was my turn to question him: I had about ten minutes or so before a lunch break. I took Sergeant White through his evidence, underscoring the details of the account he had given earlier, circling him in and cutting off any avenue of escape, getting him to confirm what he had said earlier in evidence. Once I had him well and truly ring-fenced, I said, 'Sergeant White, you are a liar. And I'm going to demonstrate that you are a liar after lunch.'

Apart from my team, no one in court had any idea where I was going with this, and you could see the jury wondering in anticipation what we had up our sleeves. They would have to wait. Thinking back on it now, it must have been the longest hour for Sergeant White; did he have any idea what we had discovered? He had been investigated by the IPCC and they had not discovered any discrepancies in his account and the CCTV footage – someone there had dropped the ball. Also, because the CCTV footage had been served so late in the day, I suspect that the other interested persons had not studied it in the meticulous way the Rigg family had done.

When we came back in after the break, we played the CCTV video for the court. We followed Sergeant White backwards and forwards until Sean had been brought into the cage and the court saw that he did not leave the police station once. When I cross-examined Sergeant White on his evidence and the contradictory CCTV footage, I put it to him that he had not in fact ever gone to the van to check on Sean's welfare, 'Sergeant White, you will agree that you never made any assessment, partial or otherwise, of Mr Rigg's condition when he was in the van for ten minutes or so?'

'Sir, from memory, I thought I went to the van, and from memory, I still think I spoke to the officers,' he replied, some-what confusingly.

But when pressed on the evidence of the tapes, Sergeant

White conceded that he was wrong, 'The CCTV quite clearly shows that I did not go to the back of the van. [. . .] I had it in my mind that I did.'

Finally, I put it to Sergeant White that he had grossly failed in his duty of care to Sean Rigg.

'No, sir. I accept I did not go to the back of the van and, therefore, I could not have looked through the back of the van and made a risk assessment of him there.'

Again, finally he had admitted the truth.

At the conclusion of the inquest on 1 August, while the jury found that Sean died from a heart attack, their judgement also stated that the length and violence of the restraint in the prone position had 'more than minimally' contributed to his death. The jury also said that it was questionable whether the relevant police guidelines or training regarding restraint and positional asphyxia were sufficient or were followed correctly.

Outside the court, Marci Rigg, on behalf of Sean's family, read the following statement, which in its eloquence and dignity I have reproduced in full:

Sean was a wonderful, talented and caring brother and son. For years he had lived with schizophrenia. He was under the care of the South London and Maudsley NHS Trust, and known by Brixton police to have mental health issues. We have sat through a long and painful seven weeks re-living the final days and hours of Sean's precious life. This pain has been compounded by officers at best misleading the jury and at worst lying under oath. The evidence we have heard has left us in no doubt that Sean died as a result of the wilful neglect of those who were meant to care for him and keep him safe. If the South London and Maudsley Trust had done their job properly and provided the care and help that Sean urgently needed, he would be alive today. If the police had not ignored repeated 999 calls from the hostel, and taken Sean to the hospital as they should have done, he would be alive today. It was perfectly apparent to ordinary members of the public that Sean was having some kind of mental crisis on the 21 August 2008, when the police were called for help. When the police did eventually arrive they restrained him, arrested him for theft of his own passport, put him in the back of a police van, drove him with sirens, not to the hospital for urgent medical care, but to Brixton police station, left him in a Perspex cage in the van and finally brought him to the caged area at the back of the station where he died on a concrete floor, surrounded by police officers.

Sean was a fit and healthy man who died less than an hour after being picked up by the police. Nothing will bring him back but we want to know that justice will be done. We want to know that those responsible will be held to account for Sean's death.

We feel utterly let down by the Independent Police Complaints Commission investigation into Sean's death, which was inadequate and obstructive from the start. Until it is fundamentally reformed, the IPCC will remain incapable of exposing the truth when people die in police hands.

We call for the Crown Prosecution Service to look at the damning evidence that has come to light in this case and demand a prosecution of those responsible for Sean's death.

We call for an urgent public inquiry to establish why the system in this country consistently fails to deliver justice to the many families whose loved ones have died in police custody. We want to know why, last year, over half the people who died following contact with the police had mental health issues and why, like Sean, over half died in circumstances involving restraint. We want to know why there was also such a sharp rise in the number of Black men who died following police contact. We want to know why our system allows officers to continue in their jobs when someone has died in their care and why not one successful prosecution has taken place in this country since 1986. Until we have justice there will be no peace for us or the many other families we stand with.

We would like to thank all of those who have helped and supported us in our long and hard fight for the truth. We will continue to fight for justice for Sean.

Postscript

After the inquest jury's damning findings, between November 2012 and April 2013 criminologist Dr Silvia Casale led an independent review into the IPCC investigation into Sean's death. The Casale Report was published in May 2013, revealing an alarming number of disparities between the evidence and findings of the inquest and those of the IPCC's original investigation. The report made for dispiriting reading. It found that IPCC investigators had allowed Brixton police officers to confer – indeed, to collude – when writing their initial statements, there was an unquestioning acceptance of 'implausible' police versions of Sean Rigg's behaviour on the night of his death, and 'improbable' statements that he didn't appear mentally ill.

It was a conclusive indictment of the IPCC's many shortcomings and sadly, as my experience in similar inquests has repeatedly shown, this was far from an isolated case. If anything good came out of this catalogue of failings, however, it was that in future, following the review's recommendations, police officers should 'be separated and instructed not to speak or otherwise communicate with each other about the events until the IPCC was able to take detailed initial statements from each.'

In the winter of 2016, as a result of the evidence he gave at the inquest and my cross-examination, Sergeant White was subsequently charged with perjury and faced trial at Southwark Crown Court. He was acquitted on the direction of the judge on the basis of errors that the IPCC had made in their investigations, which may have misled and confused the officer back in 2009. Sergeant White has since retired.

After her brother's death Marci Rigg became an active campaigner for the rights of people suffering from mental illness in police detention. The rock and support to many families who would tread the same path that she and her family had trodden, Marci had meetings with the then Home Secretary Theresa May, and was instrumental in achieving change, including the introduction of body cameras and cameras in police vans.

I would like to believe that no police officer wakes up thinking, 'I'm going to kill someone today.' Nonetheless, despite everything that has been learned by the Metropolitan Police and police forces up and down the country since the mid-'90s, these errors in the use of excessive force and restraint-related deaths in custody were, and still are, happening.

33

A BREAK IN PROCEEDINGS

The inquest into the death of Sean Rigg concluded on 1 August 2012. I was elated, relieved and extremely proud that our work on behalf of Marcia and the rest of the Rigg family had resulted in a fair, rigorous and transparent public inquest and that the jury in their verdict had held the Brixton officers and the Metropolitan Police Service to account. I had no time to rest on my laurels, however, because within four weeks, on 3 September 2012, I was due at the commencement of the oral hearings at the public inquiry into the death of a young Black man called Azelle Rodney. I was truly shattered and in desperate need of some kind of respite. I just needed to get away, so at the last minute I decided to take a vacation with my then girlfriend Tatiana (Tanya).

I had been introduced to Tanya by a Russian friend of mine called Valika who lived in London and worked for a time at Garden Court as a security guard. She thought we would be a good match and set up a blind date between us. I had visited Belarus where she lived, so I knew a little about the country, which impressed her, and within a short period of time we were corresponding by text, email and on Skype. Now we had been long-distance dating for about a year.

Tanya spoke no English, and at first we relied on Google

Translate, but slowly my Russian improved and soon we were able to talk together about anything and everything: art, music, food, books, even quite difficult legal concepts about my work. We also discussed politics, but only British or American politics. Tanya did not want to talk openly about Russian politics or the leadership of her country over the phone or in person. She was constantly suspicious that she was being watched. Given what happened in Belarus in 2021, the indications that an election was stolen and the subsequent crackdown on anyone opposed to the regime there, I can now understand and fully appreciate her reticence, although it has to be said that at the time I thought she may have been a little paranoid. She was naturally cautious in a way that those of us who were brought up in the West cannot understand. She was amazed at what I would tell her about some of the cases I had been involved in against the police and the state. She had followed Sean Rigg's case closely and translated all the newspaper articles I had sent her.

We decided to meet up in Antalya, Turkey. So, at the beginning of August we flew out for some sunshine and relaxation. It was a great choice. I had never been to Turkey before and we found the people warm and friendly. I could relax and try to forget about life in London, police cases, and death. There would be more of that coming all too soon. We did all the stereotypical touristy things you could imagine. We got up to see the sunrise and spent balmy evenings gazing at the magnificent sunsets. We took midnight strolls on the beach. We went skinny dipping. We explored Antalya's historical old town. We went nightclubbing and danced into the early hours. We even tried white-water rafting, which was exhilarating. We ate great food, and of course we drank too much. It was the first time in a long time I had a chance to properly relax.

I didn't want to come back to London. I told Tanya that if

she wanted to spend some time travelling the world, I was game. We could pick the next flight from Turkey to wherever she wanted to discover next. But this was all a fantasy. I still had big responsibilities in London, not least my children, who were dependent on me. Megan was at university and Isaac was studying and preparing for his GCSEs. Still, it was exhilarating to escape, if only for two weeks, and dream of doing something else other than fighting the system.

At the end of our short holiday, I kissed Tanya goodbye at Antalya airport. We hugged and cried. Neither of us wanted our time together to end and to go back to long-distance romancing, but I had no choice. I was about to take on the elite specialist firearms unit of the Metropolitan Police.

34

A PARENT'S PAIN: THE KILLING OF
AZELLE RODNEY (1981–2005)

'No one should have to wait for so many years to
find out why their son or daughter died at the hands
of the police.'

Susan Alexander

On 30 April 2005, in a police operation gone badly wrong,
Azelle Rodney was shot dead by a member of the Metropolitan
Police Service Specialist Firearms Command (CO19) on Hale
Lane in Barnet, north London. He had been hit by six bullets
by the firearms officer, who was later found to have discharged
eight shots in just over one second. Eight days earlier, Azelle
had turned twenty-four. His long-term girlfriend was pregnant
with their first child, a daughter who was born after his death.

Once more, it was my old friend and esteemed solicitor
Daniel Machover of Hickman & Rose who had instructed me
to represent Azelle's mother Susan Alexander on the public
inquiry into her son's death. Daniel had first instructed me to
act at the original inquest, which was subsequently cancelled,

so in preparing for this case we had been working together almost exclusively for some considerable time. For an inquiry of this import and gravity, Daniel and I knew that we needed to enlist the help of the best legal minds to support us. As my junior counsel I appointed my exceptional former pupil Adam Straw, then at Tooks Court Chambers. I also enlisted my brilliant legal assistant Isabelle Maguire and my mentee, Allison Bailey, a talented young Black criminal barrister at Garden Court who was shadowing me to gain experience of inquests and public inquiries. Finally, there was my outstanding new pupil Ifeanyi Odogwu, known as Ife, a fellow alumnus of Kingston University. Charming and intelligent, Ife had graduated with a first-class honours' degree; he had chosen me as his supervisor and was keen to learn. The lad was impressive. I knew he would be going places. With Daniel was his junior solicitor Helen Stone. We were a formidable team.

Without a doubt, this was to be one of the biggest cases of my career to date. It proved to be historic.

Azelle, one of three brothers brought up in west London, had been a talented athlete, his promise on the football pitch cut short only by hip injuries. His potential thwarted, like so many young Black men, in order to gain approval and be seen as valued, Azelle had embarked on a precipitous path leading him headlong into petty crime and brushes with the law. He had undoubtedly made poor choices, but Azelle was no gangster. Before the incident leading to his shooting, he hadn't committed any significant criminal acts, nor were there any serious allegations against him.

In 2005, however, Azelle got involved with a couple of men called Wesley Lovell and Frank Graham. The trio concocted a foolhardy plan to carry out a high-risk heist on a known Colombian drugs cartel. They proposed to arrange a rendezvous with the Colombians on the pretext of a normal drugs transaction, then rob them at gunpoint of both their money and, they hoped, a sizable stash of Class A drugs.

Early on the evening of 30 April, they put their ill-judged plot into action. En route by car to the rendezvous point on an estate in Mill Hill, north London, Lovell, Graham and Azelle Rodney stopped to pick up three firearms, then drove towards their reckless encounter, unaware that, following intelligence, their Volkswagen Golf was being tailed and closely surveilled by the Metropolitan Police. Envisaging a potentially deadly exchange of gunfire when the two groups encountered each other, the police had mounted Operation Tayport, an armed covert manoeuvre to apprehend and arrest the three men before they carried out their planned heist.

As the suspects' vehicle neared Hale Lane in Edgware – Wesley Lovell at the wheel, Frank Graham by his side in the front, and Azelle seated in the back – deeming that the surveillance officers had gathered enough evidence to carry out an arrest, Operation Tayport entered its final and fatal phase. The senior investigating officer gave the order for firearms officers in three unmarked police vehicles to begin preparation for a 'hard stop'. When the police command was given –'Attack, attack, attack' – the first police car, Alpha, overtook the trio's Golf, while a second car, Charlie, rammed the back of the Golf, shunting it forwards into the back of Alpha. The third police car, Bravo, rammed the Golf again, this time from the side, with CO19 firearms officer 'E7', positioned alongside the rear window of the Golf, to provide 'static cover' so that, according to the agreed tactics of Operation Tayport, his fellow armed officers could safely exit their vehicles to arrest the suspects.

Things did not go according to plan, however. When E7's car came to a halt adjacent to the rear passenger window of the

Golf, no more than two metres from Azelle, simultaneously — within one-twentieth of a second — the armed officer fired into the rear passenger door of the stationery Golf. After discharging six shots in one instance, E7 paused briefly and then fired two more shots, aimed directly at Azelle in the back seat of the car. Two further firearms officers brandishing shotguns also fired at the car. At least one shot went through the VW and out the other side, narrowly missing a group of teenage girls.

When the shooting stopped, Wesley Lovell and Frank Graham were arrested, and Azelle's inert and bloodied body was taken out of the car. He was already dead. All this took place in front of a pub with people outside enjoying late afternoon pints in the spring sunshine, as parents and children were passed nearby on the pavement. But this, in the eyes of the Metropolitan Police Service at the time, was a wholly successful operation.

The police search of the bullet-riddled Golf found a total of three guns: a non-functional pistol situated next to Azelle (admittedly a fact neither the surveillance team nor the CO19 firearms officers could have known), and another two pistols stashed in a bag in the car's footwell, both of which lay loaded and cocked, and the smaller of which was the size of a key fob and contained two bullets.

Immediately after the shooting, police officers wrongly and deliberately briefed the press that Azelle Rodney was holding a gun at the time of his shooting. However, an IPCC investigation confirmed that Azelle had *not* been seen to be holding a gun when the firearms officer shot him dead. It nevertheless found nothing to criticise in officer E7's handling of the operation. The IPCC passed its findings to the Crown Prosecution Service, which announced in July 2006 that there was insufficient evidence to successfully prosecute any of the officers involved for Azelle's death.

I was originally instructed in August 2007 to represent the family at the inquest into Azelle's shooting. Azelle's mother, Susan Alexander, is a kind-hearted, loving woman who had lost her son. Nobody, not even Susan, was claiming that Azelle was an angel; she wasn't protesting his innocence. But she needed and wanted to know how and why her son had died. Why, if he was being closely monitored along with his associates for a few days before the day of the planned heist, did the police not apprehend him earlier in the operation? Azelle, she said, should have been given the chance to surrender; he should have been arrested like Mr Lovell and Mr Graham; like them, he should have been serving a sentence for conspiracy to commit an armed robbery. He certainly did not deserve to die at the hands of a firearms officer.

The inquest finally opened in front of Deputy Coroner Andrew Walker sitting at Hornsey in north London, whom I had last encountered at the inquest into the death of a young man in suspicious circumstances in 2005. I respect and admire Mr Walker, who in my experience has always treated me and my clients with utmost sensitivity and respect. We were, however, immediately faced with a seemingly insurmountable obstacle in this case. Under the Regulation of Investigatory Powers Act 2000 (RIPA), which covers legislation concerning information obtained from covert surveillance operations, a substantial number of redactions had been made in the police officers' evidence. The counsel for the Metropolitan Police wanted to rely on this and other classified or 'sensitive' evidence in order to justify the police's actions leading to Azelle's death. The problem for the coroner was that under RIPA, an ordinary coroner was not allowed to see that classified evidence, nor would the jury or the family be allowed to hear the undisclosed evidence. To be compliant with the European

Convention of Human Rights, any inquest, and especially any Article 2 inquest where the death of a citizen is caused by an agent of the state, must be an open hearing in which the family can fully participate and safeguard their legitimate interests. With the suppression of this sensitive evidence the coroner had no choice but to rule that a full and fair inquest into Azelle's death could not be held.

Susan was distraught. Daniel wrote to the Home Office and the Ministry of Justice to request changes in the law to allow the coroner to proceed with the inquest, but Parliament rejected proposed amendments twice, first in 2008 and in 2009. At such an impasse, it seemed that Susan was to be denied the opportunity to hear the truth about the circumstances of her son's death.

The only alternative left to Susan was to fight for a judge-led public inquiry, because under the Inquiries Act and RIPA, judges *can* see secret evidence where a coroner cannot. That decision now lay with the Home Secretary. Consequently, in May 2009, four years after Azelle's death, Daniel and I helped Susan to file a case against the British government in the European Court of Human Rights, claiming that her human rights had been breached by the failure to hold a 'reasonably prompt' and public investigation into her son's death. This elicited a government apology, but brought Susan no closer to the truth. She still did not give up, however, and finally, in late March 2010, Jack Straw, the then Lord Chancellor and Secretary of State for Justice, announced an inquiry into Azelle's shooting, naming the chairman as retired judge Sir Christopher Holland.

The Azelle Rodney case was the first public inquiry to investigate the circumstances surrounding a police shooting in this country and consequently there was weighty public interest in its findings. One of the functions of any public inquiry is to allay public concern. Following the unrest in the wake of the shooting of Mark Duggan, and the general level of public anxiety around the police use of firearms, it was vital, therefore, that the Azelle Rodney Inquiry be seen to be painstakingly thorough and wide-ranging. This, we argued, was an unprecedented opportunity for the police to improve their practices surrounding firearms operations. Susan could never get Azelle back, but at the very least she could feel satisfied that the long and hard-fought public inquiry into his death might bring about tangible and lasting change.

Sir Christopher was an interesting character. I had not appeared before him previously, and although pleasant and no-nonsense, I suspected he might be somewhat old-school. As a relatively young Black barrister leading a team of equally able lawyers, I suppose I must have seemed a bit of an upstart. All the other barristers leading the other teams were QCs. I was not. At times Sir Christopher would try to finish my sentences or say what he thought I was thinking. He did this with the best of intentions; he thought he was helping me, but there is nothing more annoying than not being able to make your submissions fully when the other silks are allowed to do so. I don't know if Sir Christopher thought I was being long-winded, which is possible, but each time I opened my mouth and for the chairman of the inquiry to interject before I had hardly uttered a couple of words, 'Yes, Mr Thomas. I understand what you mean' was maddening, to say the least. At one stage, I became so frustrated by Sir Christopher's constant interruptions that I stormed out of the main inquiry room. This left everyone in shock, but I had no choice. Had I remained in the inquiry room for a second longer I would have exploded and said something I know I would have regretted. I gave myself a ten-minute cooling-off period outside the courtroom and then walked back in and resumed the hearing. Sir Christopher said nothing, nor did the other counsel, and it was obviously the right thing to do, because after that incident Sir Christopher and I had an understanding. I made my submissions in a short, concise way, which he obviously liked, and he respected me by allowing me to do so when I thought appropriate. Thereafter he and I got along swimmingly – I even grew to understand his old-school style of humour.

Sir Christopher was assisted by an impressive legal team. Counsel to the Inquiry was Ashley Underwood QC. Earlier in my legal career Ashley and I had fought many cases against one another. We hadn't exactly gelled; in those days, for me you picked your side and I felt he was acting for the devil. Ashley was nevertheless a very good public lawyer, who had spent a good deal of time in the intervening years as counsel for public inquiries in Northern Ireland, so the Azelle Rodney inquiry was a completely different type of case for him. The Solicitor to the Inquiry who instructed Ashley was Judi Kemish, a kind-hearted and friendly lawyer. Judi had in fact instructed me in my early days at the Bar. Finally, Nick Scott, an extremely bright and talented young junior barrister, acted as junior counsel to the inquiry. I was so impressed with Nick that I later hired him as a legal researcher for me while he was looking for a tenancy.

On behalf of Susan, our line of questioning in the first instance was to ascertain the reasoning behind Operation Tayport, and to examine the risk assessment carried out before the officers executed the hard stop. We argued that the police had executed an unnecessarily dangerous stop for no apparent good reason. Now I suspect, but cannot prove, that for the officers a successful outcome would have been to have captured the north London gang *and* the Colombians. But therein lies the problem: the longer they left the operation to run, the more dangerous it became. As I said later in my summing up to the chairman, 'It is by sheer grace that there were not more fatalities or serious injuries. [. . .] As the independent experts say in this case, they have all agreed, no proper thought appears to have gone into this operation. Indeed, sir, we have heard evidence from an experienced expert that death was almost inevitable.'

Secondly was the question of the firearms officer E7's actions in opening fire on Azelle while he was sitting in the back of the car. For his part leading up to the inquiry, officer E7, who remained in service with the Metropolitan Police, had been consistent in his multiple retellings of his version of the events that led to his shooting of Azelle. He asserted that as he came alongside the suspects' car, he saw Azelle reach down, then come back up again with his shoulders hunched, and that he had interpreted these movements as those of a man reaching to pick up, and begin firing, a machine gun. Observing this, he had fired at Azelle six times; he had then paused briefly and, after it seemed that Azelle was unaffected by his initial onslaught, shot him twice again. Samantha Leek QC, who was counsel for E7, and I should add, whom I greatly respect, submitted in her written submissions to the inquiry that had E7 not killed Azelle Rodney, and I quote, 'The inquiry might well have been investigating the death of a police officer'. But as I responded to the chairman, there were *no* automatic weapons in the car. The police intelligence was simply wrong.

For years this had been E7's sworn account of his fatal shooting of Azelle Rodney, and were it not for analyses of the ballistics experts and pathologists our team worked with on this case, it may well have continued to be the official, widely known 'truth'. I was deeply impressed by the skill of the expert witnesses' painstaking work; the care and precision with which they recreated the events was breathtaking. Data recordings of the police cars' movements, camera and audio recordings of the event, physical evidence from the car and Azelle's wounded body itself all served to reconstruct scrupulously the material reality of the final moments of his life. While no amount of science could faithfully represent the thoughts of either Azelle or officer E7 at the time of their fateful encounter, the forensic expert evidence proved for a fact that E7's evidence was not credible. When the officer first discharged his firearm, Azelle had been upright; he began slumping to his side only as the shots were being fired. The last two of these first six bullets would have been fatal, so too would have the further two shots fired by E7 after his initial brief pause. This expert recon-struction, presented to the inquiry before E7 gave evidence, definitively proved that his previous multiple sworn accounts had been false. I told the inquiry that police actions on 30 April bore a great resemblance to an execution and no resemblance to a lawful, competent policing operation.

In terms of UK domestic law, E7 had to satisfy the inquiry that he honestly believed the force that he was using was absolutely necessary to deal with the threat he was facing. We argued that E7 did *not hold an honest belief* that the force he was using in discharging his weapon was *absolutely necessary*. That is why he feared the truth and had failed to answer 149 ques-tions from the IPCC under caution about why he shot Azelle Rodney. That is why, in the aftermath of the shooting, the press had been wrongly and deliberately briefed that Azelle Rodney was holding a gun. There was worse to come, however.

Forensic examination indicated that a gun found on the back seat of the Golf after Azelle had been shot dead had been moved. The gun contained blood inside the barrel, but not on the outside of the barrel – or of the gun – consistent with it having being placed in the blood afterwards. There were no blood splashes on the outside of the gun, which one would have expected had it been exposed at the time Azelle was being repeatedly shot. It was therefore improbable, as E7 maintained in his evidence to the inquiry, that he was satisfied that Azelle had bent down in the back seat and picked up the gun. Azelle demonstrably *did not* have a gun in his hand when E7 shot him. Finally, faced with the evidence, officer E7 acquiesced to the inquiry that there was no way he could have seen Azelle perform the motions he had previously described, and that the experts' account of events was likely to be closer to the truth than his own.

The Executive Summary of the Azelle Rodney Inquiry Report was published in September 2013. Sir Christopher Holland found that E7 had no good reason to believe that Azelle Rodney presented a sufficient threat to life such that it was proportionate to open fire on him with a lethal weapon, and that even if Azelle had picked up a machine gun there was no justification for E7 to fire the final two shots, either of which would have been fatal. Never had there been such a clear and unequivocal finding in a case of fatal wrongdoing by a state agent in the line of his duty. The case made history. That was truly a great day for Azelle's mother Susan and for all our team who had stood beside her on the tortuous path to justice through the British and European courts.

In lieu of E7's honesty, the crux of the inquiry was decided by forensic investigation of events that had transpired over a matter of seconds. Such split-second decisions, as much as we would try to deduce them, are ultimately inscrutable. In policing in general it is hard to definitively say what the right choice is, as the inquiry had done. But for policing at large, and what the inquiry's report didn't say, is that kitting officers out with guns and sending them out to chase suspects while ramping up the intensity by instructing them to 'Attack! Attack! Attack!' is undeniably the wrong course of action. In operations such as these, questioning why and how they went wrong often seems totally pointless, because the manufacturing of moments of such extreme pressure involving firearms necessarily predetermines violent outcomes. It was just by luck that nobody else was injured or died that evening.

Were it not for the findings and recommendations of the Azelle Rodney inquiry, the multiple structural and individual failings in the Metropolitan Police Service leading to the death of Azelle Rodney would have been ignored and most likely repeated. For that, I must pay tribute to the courage of Susan Alexander. Susan fought for five long years to learn the truth about her son's killing, to hold to account those who claim to protect us and seek justice for his death. She demanded answers and was finally able to hold her head high because in his findings Sir Christopher Holland effectively found that Azelle had been unlawfully killed. I am extremely thankful for Susan and people like her; people whose vigilance and unrelenting pursuit of the truth strive to *protect us all* from the reckless and violent excesses of the police.

Leaving aside the egregious details of his killing, as a member of the Bar and a Black British man, I also feel a sense of righteous anger at the failings of a British justice system that meant that it took *nearly a decade* for the full scope of these injustices to be brought to light. The killing of Azelle was in itself a direct act of state violence, but the subsequent lack of any proper investigation into his death can also be interpreted as the deliberate act of a violent state that dismisses any scrutiny into its use of force against Black people.

Postscript

Following the public inquiry findings there was an attempt by E7 to judicially review the decision of the Chairman. That legal challenge failed. The CPS decided to prosecute Officer E7 for the murder of Azelle Rodney. He was publicly named as Anthony Long and in July 2015 the officer stood trial before a judge and jury at the Old Bailey. At the end of his trial, by a majority verdict the jury found him not guilty of the murder of Azelle Rodney.

35

SPYCOPS AND MARK DUGGAN
(1981–2011)

By the summer of 2013 I felt that my life and career were finally getting back on track. I had been instructed to represent the loved ones of Mark Duggan at the inquest into his death in 2011, and I was busy with the ongoing pre-inquest hearings in preparation for the opening of the hearing proper in September. The Legal Aid Lawyer of the Year trophy was proudly on display at reception in Garden Court Chambers; in May, Silvia Casale's report of her independent review of the IPCC investigation into Sean Rigg's death in custody had roundly castigated the conduct of all those involved, giving grounds for hope that its findings might lead to lasting reforms and greater police accountability. Then, on 5 July, we learned that Sir Christopher Holland's report of the inquiry into the fatal shooting of Azelle Rodney had resulted in the unlawful killing verdict we had fought so hard to secure.

Things were going so well for me professionally that everybody was asking me why I didn't take silk, i.e. apply to become Queen's Counsel, or QC. To give its somewhat grand definition, a QC is 'one of Her Majesty's Counsel, learned in the law.' In practical terms, QCs are 'senior' barristers or solicitors who have been able to demonstrate a high level of courtroom skills to the Bar's independent appointments commission. It is an award for excellence in advocacy. It doesn't necessarily mean that junior barristers are either very young or inexperienced – I have known excellent leading juniors of all ages – it just means that they have decided not to apply for silk. Taking silk is not for everybody, in other words.

The competition for silk is a two-phase process. First, I had to submit an eighty-page application form. I had to list a required number of cases to illustrate that I was deserving of silk – those with a high profile, or high monetary value, or cases involving a certain complexity of law – and write what amounted to several lengthy essays in order to satisfy the judging panel that I met certain competencies; namely, of leadership and diversity, complex law and oral advocacy. Then I had to find referees, or 'assessors' as they were called, both judicial assessors and peer assessors. That was the first stage. If I managed to get through to the second stage, I would be called for an interview with a two-person panel.

I could, I think, have applied for silk before 2013, because I'd been working on important and high-profile cases for quite a few years, many of which were perhaps beyond the scope of what a non-silk should have been doing. Knowing that the selection panel also considers professional judgement, however, I thought that my liaison with the juror after the Christopher Alder case in 2000 might have been held against me. I still felt ashamed and I couldn't face being asked about it. The other thing that had held me back was the cost involved. Simply to put in the application was about £3,000, and if you are successful you have to pay another £4,000 on top, so to become a Queen's Counsel is an expensive undertaking. You could spend that initial £3,000 and get nowhere, and many people do. Some people apply over and over again. I wanted to make sure I had a fairly good chance of being successful the first time round.

By 2013, having just done the Azelle Rodney inquiry, the Sean Rigg inquest in 2012, and with the pending Mark Duggan inquest due to commence (which was a major case), along with the inquest into the New Cross Fire (probably the most high profile and noteworthy of my career to date), I decided that I should go for it. So, in the evenings during the Azelle Rodney inquiry, I filled out the lengthy application for the 2014 competition for silk. I sought the advice and guidance of colleagues who had taken silk before me, and they were more than generous with their time, giving tips about how they had gone about their applications. I approached Rajiv Menon QC in chambers, who gladly shared his experience with me. Steve Cragg QC, a former pupil of mine who had taken silk a year or two earlier, was also incredibly kind and told me how he had handled the form and the questions. There were countless other people I have to thank for getting me through the arduous process: Una Morris, my pupil at the time, who has an excellent eye for detail, had worked in the public sector for a while, so knew how to tackle form filling. I called in favours from my former English teacher Nick Gunning and Melanie Carter, a close friend of mine who was then vice chair and a partner in a big city law firm, with whom I had done a lot of work when I was chair of Central London Law Centre. They reviewed and proofread my application form, pointing out silly mistakes and typos, or where I had written something that simply made no sense and needed clarification. This was crucial for me, and I'm indebted to them all. I couldn't have done it without their help and support, because by the time I had applied for silk I had spent most of my adult life as a jobbing barrister – I hadn't made an application for a new position or a job in almost a quarter of a century.

You would think that, being a barrister, the task of filling out a silk application form would be an easy exercise, but it is not. Many barristers don't make it past the first post because they fail to approach the form in the manner expected by the Queen's Counsel Assessment (QCA) panel. Many are surprised at this and every year there are many disappointed applicants who have spent a significant amount of money and time and are never even interviewed. At times, more than 50 per cent of the applicants can be rejected at round one. If you assume you know what you are doing and do not get someone to spot-check everything and audit your application, it can be fatal – and by the time you find out it is too late.

Happily, I was humble enough to appreciate the reality of my situation, namely that when it comes to filling in forms and demonstrating core competencies, I needed guidance. Ironically, I discovered that my main problem was precisely that: my humility. Everyone who knew me and read my application told me that, in terms of describing my experience, the cases I had done and my level of success in achieving some of the against-the-odds outcomes for my clients, I was underselling myself. I found it so difficult to 'big myself up'. Bragging always sits uncomfortably with me.

If I am honest, I found the whole process of applying for silk stressful and see no shame in openly saying so. I *knew* I was good enough to be a silk and a leader, because I'd already been doing that for quite a few years. I am a team player and – on *all* my cases – I like to collaborate with my junior team members and solicitors and because of my considerable experience I tend to naturally take a leadership role in strategic decisions. But spelling that out on paper just seemed like hubris. Nevertheless, I made the suggested tweaks and blew my own trumpet a bit, completed the form, sent it off and hoped for the best.

Once the application form had been submitted was when I really began to feel the pressure. The nagging doubts started to creep in as to whether I had chosen the right assessors or judges to comment on me. I began to hear horror stories about peer barrister assessors doing the 'dirty' on you, sabotaging your chances when they were contacted by the QCA and asked for comment on your work. Or about horrendous judicial assessors, judges or coroners who put the knife in and, for this reason or that, tell the QCA they don't think you are ready. You would never know whether this is because they genuinely believe that, or if it's because you have crossed swords with that particular judge or coroner, and scuppering your chances of silk is their way of getting back at you. I subsequently learned that most applicants approach all their peer and judicial assessors in advance to ask whether or not that judge or barrister might be sympathetic to your application. I did not do this. I would have been much too embarrassed; it would have felt like begging. In the two years before applying for silk, the majority of my work had been in the coroner's courts and the application form at that time made it clear that only the last twenty-four months of work were relevant. In terms of the judicial figures I named as assessors, I decided that I had to include several coroners and two High Court judges. A couple of my 'usual' opponents in police actions had encouraged me to put in my application and I specifically recall Anne Studd QC and Samantha Leek QC from 5 Essex Court Chambers, both of whom were involved in the Azelle Rodney and Mark Duggan cases, urging me to apply. I put the two of them down as my peer assessors.

I had also broken another rule in that I went public with the fact that I was applying for silk. I didn't care who I told, but quite frankly I had not thought it through. Apparently, many applicants keep it under their hat in case they are unsuccessful.

But I had told myself, 'Commit to the process and just get through.' It was a kind of 'burn the bridges' approach: you simply apply and never even contemplate that failure is an option. Would I get an interview at the very least? I could only wait and hope.

So, there I was, riding high professionally, thinking life was good and feeling reasonably confident that I would soon be a QC, and then the Christopher Alder case, my nemesis, came round again. In 2013, the Spycops scandal broke: the sorry story of a number of officers from a top-secret police squad sent deep undercover to spy on certain political groups, climate change and environmental activist organisations such as Greenpeace, who had subsequently entered into relationships with the women they had been spying on. Although senior officers tried to dismiss it as the actions of a few aberrant policemen, the truth was that undercover police had routinely adopted new identities – often assuming the names and life stories of the dead – in order to insinuate themselves at the heart of over 1,000 political movements, mostly those on the left, since as far back as 1968. Furthermore, subsequent investigations revealed that the police weren't just spying on protesters and activists and so on; they were also actually spying on victims, and on the families of those victims. Among the many individual instances that came to light was that Stephen Lawrence's parents and their family solicitor Imran Khan had been spied upon by the Metropolitan Police. Consequently, Theresa May, the then home secretary, requested that police forces across the UK produce a list of all those who had been placed under surveillance.

On 25 July, Janet Alder and I both received letters from a senior commissioner from the IPCC informing us that it had found 'information to suggest' that Janet and I had been put under 'improper surveillance' in the run-up to and during the time I spent in Hull at the inquest fighting for justice for her brother Christopher. Janet had always believed that someone was surveilling her. Back in 1998 she had claimed that she was being followed when leaving Hull police station in the days after Christopher's death, but her allegations were dismissed by police. 'I was told there was no evidence. I was made out as if I were crazy or something, or making these things up, fabricating it for some unknown reason.' *

But the letter from the IPCC confirmed that her suspicions were right. 'I never in my life knew anything like this – I always believed that the system did the right thing. For that to happen to me, it was so scary. I was just a normal working-class woman looking after my kids.'†

The IPCC immediately opened an investigation into the Humberside Police force to identify whether any subject of the investigation may have committed a criminal offence, whether any subject of the investigation, in the IPCC's opinion, had 'a case to answer for misconduct or gross misconduct, or no case to answer', and whether 'the ethnicity of the persons under surveillance had any bearing to the surveillance operation'. This last matter was particularly upsetting to me. In my responses to the investigation, I made it clear that it had not escaped my attention that, despite the fact that there were several lawyers working on this case from two different firms of solicitors, I was the only lawyer to have been surveilled. For some reason

---

* Extract from transcript of a speech made by Janet Alder at a joint Centre for Crime and Justice Studies and The Monitoring Group conference on police spying and racism in February 2015; Centre for Crime and Justice Studies.
https://www.crimeandjustice.org.uk/publications/cjm/article/what%E2%80%99s-worst-could-happen-death-christopher-alder
† *Guardian*, 26 November 2015.

still unexplained, the Black lawyer, namely myself, and my Black client were singled out in this way. My team on the Christopher Alder case was entirely white. Who knows what they hoped to uncover by spying on a family member of a dead man and her lawyer, but surely, if they were going to go to such lengths, then one might have thought that the police would spy on the whole legal team? Yet, along with Janet, my outspoken and courageous Black client, the only lawyer they decided to spy upon was me.

I told the IPCC in no uncertain terms that the racial undertones surrounding this case caused me much additional distress – and they continue to do so to this day. Also, while Richard Alder was very retiring, his sister was an agitator: she was protesting vocally about her brother's death and the actions of Hull police, and indeed had been reprimanded by the coroner for disruptive behaviour during the hearings. But I wasn't doing anything *except being a lawyer*. The family were not doing anything other than being a grieving family.

When all this came to light, I wanted to deal with it behind the scenes. I had been so badly scarred by the hideous exposé in the *Mail on Sunday*, and the humiliation of having intimate details of my private life laid bare in the press, that I didn't want it stirred up again. However, quite naturally I suppose, Janet Alder wanted to deal with it in the media. I was therefore named in an article in the *Guardian* and various other publications, saying that I had been spied upon.

This was going on during that summer when I was applying for silk and I was about to start the Mark Duggan inquest. I was attending highly legally contentious and complex pre-inquest hearings and preparing for what was bound to be an intensely stressful case.

The inquest hearings started on 16 September at the Royal

Courts of Justice. We were sitting before His Honour Judge Keith Cutler CBE as assistant deputy coroner, who told the jurors that they were on a 'quest to find the truth'. After a few moments of silence as a mark of respect for Mr Duggan's family, the coroner told the jurors, 'At the centre of the hearing is the tragedy of the regrettable loss of a young life. At the heart of your deliberations it may be that you decide whether Mark Duggan was killed lawfully or unlawfully.' It was a highly controversial case, and a difficult inquest for me personally from the outset, not least because I was dealing with the CPS and the IPCC and the fallout from the revelations of having been spied on. And, on top of everything else, I wasn't getting on with my fellow counsel Mike Mansfield QC.

We had both been instructed by Marcia Willis Stewart from Birnberg Peirce Solicitors; I was representing the mothers of Mark's children, while Mike was representing Mark Duggan's mother, Pamela. I have so much respect for Mike's longevity in fighting for human rights and justice, but this was the first time I had worked alongside him on a case and we weren't seeing eye to eye as a team. I have since worked with Mike on several other cases and we understand each other and what we both bring to the table. After the Mark Duggan case we collaborated on the Hillsborough inquests, and at the time of writing this book we are working closely on Grenfell. Perhaps at the time of the Mark Duggan case, however, we were simply not used to each other's methods. On every other case, I had been used to a collaborative approach as part of a team, but Mike had his own style. He wasn't involving me in some of the decisions he was taking, nor communicating with me effectively, which I found frustrating. In approaching the inquest and deciding our objectives, we had divided up the arguments so that Mike would deal with the failures of the police in the operation and the planning surrounding Mark's death, and, given my recent success in the Azelle Rodney inquiry, I would deal with the actual shooting itself. But at times I felt that there was a straying into my area and that was difficult, especially when it affected my planned cross-examination, which I then had to re-think it on the fly.

Then, to add to the pressure, one of the barristers who was representing another interested person, I felt bullied me during the hearing, in a manner that felt deeply unpleasant, unprofessional and inappropriate. In the middle of the inquest in early November, I was named Lawyer of the Year by *Black Mental Health UK* journal and in the same week I was awarded an LLD Honorary Doctorate from Kingston University for services to civil rights. The following Monday in court, while everyone else was generally pleased for me and generously congratulatory, this barrister took it upon himself to be downright petty, making a sneering and dismissive comment about how these honorary degrees were being handed out two-a-penny. He clearly thought this was hilarious. Later, in the course of the proceedings, I made a mistake in relation to referring to a document in court, an item of disclosure that the parties had agreed not to refer to. It was a genuine error on my part. The barrister went ballistic, but not in a normal, acceptable sense. Instead, he behaved in a manner I can only describe as spiteful, condescending and abusive in court. He went crimson in the face and shouted at me. I immediately apologised, and said I would put it right, but he continued to vent in front of the coroner to the point that it felt so directed and venomous that I could only assume that he was hoping to intimidate me. At this time, I was a junior and my opponent was a silk, but I held my ground with him throughout the inquest, determined not to be cowed. If it were to happen to anyone else, I would urge them to seek the support of a sympathetic senior counsel and make a complaint to the Bar Standards Board. It embarrasses me to say this now, but I didn't feel able to do this during the Mark Duggan case because of the differential in power between my opponent and myself, and I feel ashamed and regretful that I didn't take a more defensive stance to protect my mental wellbeing.

The Mark Duggan inquest was extremely traumatic for the families and loved ones involved. For we lawyers representing them, it was a difficult case. We felt under siege by those representing the state and the police. The media was hostile and presented Mark in an unfair and degrading way. But I was working alongside a phenomenal group of supportive lawyers. The Birnberg Peirce team, in the guise of Marcia Willis Stewart and Cyrilia Knight Davies, her fairly new junior solicitor at the time, were outstanding. Marcia is very maternal with her team on cases and, unlike many solicitors, is always concerned about people's mental health and wellbeing. She was also able to smooth out the teething difficulties I had experienced with Mike in the early stages of the inquest. Cyrilia was a force to be reckoned with. She was an extremely talented young Black female solicitor and at the time I had no doubt that she was destined for great things. I would often have lengthy discussions with her and Adam Straw as to how to take on and tackle the officers and what approach we should use. Adam was our secret weapon on the inquest. He is a workhorse and he digested and analysed the mountains of papers like a supercomputer. In short, he was the best junior I could have asked for on a case like this, as he had been on the Azelle Rodney inquiry. We worked together in perfect harmony. When dealing with evidence and cross-examination of officers, to use a cricket analogy, he would bowl me a ball and I could hit it for six. There are no two ways about it: I would tease Adam and say that I was the puppet and he was the puppet master. Yes, Mr Straw is *that* good.

During the inquest I was called up for that elusive silk interview. It was to be at the end of September. I was nervous, distracted and excited at the same time, because as with the application form, I had no idea how to handle it. It was some time since I'd faced an interview process and I would need to do some serious mental preparation, or fail at what, by now, I so desperately wanted to achieve. I decided to engage the services of a professional coach-cum-mentor. Many barristers use such coaches. I hadn't used a coach for my application form. Thankfully I had still secured an interview, but I wasn't taking any chances.

At the first mock interview with my coach, I was like a rabbit in headlights. She explained to me that by the time you get to the interview stage, the QCA are clearly interested in you. You have shown that you have all the necessary qualities to become a silk, so the interview is your opportunity to shine, and to deal with any concerns that the panel may have about your application. They are not trying to catch you out, but if they have any doubts about what you may have written, you have the opportunity to explain and clarify. Once I understood this, I relaxed and my second mock interview went much better.

I still had concerns, though. My biggest worry was having to explain what had happened on the Christopher Alder inquest with the juror, should I be asked about it. I had fully disclosed the circumstances of that on my form, however, and it turned out the interviewers were not interested in that. I had made it a bigger problem in my own mind.

The day of my actual silk interview came and was scheduled for about 1.45 p.m., so I would be able to attend in my lunch break during the Mark Duggan inquest. On the day itself, however, the timing was a little off because that morning and in the afternoon I was due to cross-examine some of the key police officers. I was consequently in full battle mode. I went into the interview with my hyper-focused cross-examination mindset and felt really sharp. The whole interview lasted about half an hour and was one of the most enjoyable experiences I could imagine. Everything aligned. The panel were very encouraging; they asked me questions which enabled me to demonstrate my core competencies. At one point I learned that one of my judicial assessors had said that one of my cases wasn't silk material. I explained that this case had involved a high-ranking public official, the mayor of a major suburban town, who was accused of possessing child pornography; my role was to take the police's conduct of the case to judicial review. I pointed out that the judge had praised my advocacy in what was a difficult case. When I had finished, the members of the interview panel smiled at me reassuringly and said, 'We don't understand the comment either.' When I told them that I was in the middle of cross-examining the police officers in the Mark Duggan inquest and had to get back to court, I think that may have impressed. I left the interview with a huge smile, feeling confident that I had done my best and that is all I could ask of myself.

The Mark Duggan inquest carried on through to the second week of December when Judge Cutler sent the jury of six women and four men out to begin their deliberations. On 8 January 2014, over three weeks later, the jury returned its verdict. It found by a majority of eight to two that Mark Duggan was lawfully killed; the two dissenting jurors gave an open verdict. By the same margin, the jury also found that Mark was *not* holding a weapon when the firearms officer fatally shot him. Rather, it decided that Mark had a gun with him in the taxi he was travelling in, but, in all probability, he had thrown it from the vehicle's window before the police had fully executed the three-car 'hard stop' on the taxi.

In this, as in many of the cases I fight, one might ask why some of the police officers implicated in deaths are not charged and convicted. The short answer is that it is difficult to convince the Crown Prosecution Service to bring charges. It is difficult to convict police officers. Of course, some police officers are innocent or there is no evidence to suggest otherwise, but it also has to be said that it doesn't sit well with a jury to convict a police officer, especially if the deceased is portrayed by the defence as a bad person. The bare fact is that there is such a thing as jury justice. Despite the directions that a judge might hand down, despite what the evidence might show, if they feel that a particular defendant is deserving or undeserving they can give a certain verdict. Maybe in the instance of Mark Duggan's killing, that is how the jury felt. We will never know for certain, but I do believe that the jury would have had to be strong to ignore the message disseminated by the media that Mark was not deserving of mercy. That was the picture that was painted of him by the police which was fed to the media, and the media simply and uncritically lapped it all up. The wholesale demonisation and assassination of Mark Duggan's character was such that he was made out to be the third biggest criminal in Europe – a mastermind of criminal activity. Yet, there was no history of serious violence in Mark's past. His previous offences were relatively petty crimes. Time and time again such minor offences have been weaponised and used against Black people to criminalise and denigrate. And in Mark's case, some of the mud had effectively stuck.

Postscript

I continued to work with the Duggan family, who pursued further litigation against the police. I wasn't able, however, to see their civil action through to the end because I had a clash with cases I was involved in. I was doing the Grenfell Fire inquiry, and so I agreed to step aside before, eventually, the claim was settled out of court.

I am often asked about the Mark Duggan inquest, how I feel about it and about being involved in such a high-profile case. I suppose the answer is 'mixed'. A young Black father was shot dead on the streets of London. The police officer who shot him said Mark Duggan had pointed a gun at him, which is why he was shot. None of the forensic evidence supported that contention. The jury rejected this justification but they nevertheless found that Mark was lawfully killed. I was personally stunned by the verdict. I did not expect it. But what else can I say: the jury heard the evidence and gave their verdict. The verdict is the verdict and that's the system I've signed up to. You cannot go behind the jury's decision.

In October 2015, the IPCC published its report on the investigation into why Janet and I had been spied on, and who had authorised it. Members of the surveillance team had been interviewed under criminal caution, but had mainly chosen not to answer questions.

Among the material recovered during the investigation was the operational order for the police's management of Christopher Alder's inquest, referred to as 'Operation Yarrow', and two surveillance authority applications linked to that operation. A total of eighteen, both serving and former, Hull police officers, including four surveillance commanders and the chief superintendent were implicated in the undercover operation. Janet was told that the first order to place her under surveillance was given after 'public disorder' by supporters of the family outside the court during Christopher's inquest. On 28 July 2000, a second surveillance application 'using mobile, foot and technical surveillance' was authorised.

We learned that members of the undercover squad had followed Janet and me as we left court after part of the hearings proceedings. They had then tried to listen to a conversation we were having in a car park nearby. The Humberside Police couldn't say who had ordered officers to tail us, or why. Undercover officers, it transpired, had also been planted inside the courtroom. The Hull police initially said that they thought I was having an affair with Janet Alder, which was why we were being monitored. We also found out that undercover officers from Humberside Police had started to follow Janet as soon as she walked out of the station after Christopher died. They went through the family background and obtained records from social services about the Alder siblings' time in care. As Janet said, what possible relevance did that have to Christopher's death at the hands of the police?*

During the IPCC investigation, the Hull police had come up with a further supposed justification for my surveillance, namely my supposed relationship with the juror. *But*, as I've explained in an earlier chapter, she and I had spoken to each other for the first time *after* the inquest ended, and the evidence showed that police had spied on me *before* the start of the inquest, and so we were able to demonstrate that the post-facto explanation was entirely bogus – and libellous. But why me? There is no proper motivation for police officers to spy on a

* *Daily Mirror*, 27 July 2013: https://www.mirror.co.uk/news/uk-news/christopher-alders-family-were-spied-2094593

barrister and their client – any meeting I would have had with Janet Alder or Richard Alder would have been to discuss legally privileged issues arising out of their case. As the IPCC acknowledged, the 'confidentiality of legal communications has been afforded overriding importance in English law'. Throughout the inquest proceedings, therefore, Janet Alder was entitled to expect that discussions with me were confidential. It was also an invasion of my personal privacy, which was completely violated. I don't try to make sense of it, because you can't make sense of it. What I do know is they had no justification and, indeed, they acknowledged as much.

I had already suspected that I had been spied on during the Wayne Douglas case, and later on, I also made enquiries in relation to that. The Met denied it and I cannot prove my suspicions. As a barrister, by simply doing my job, performing my role as an advocate who just happened to be representing clients who had suffered a bereavement, and whose brother had died in police custody, I was a person of interest. I think they were hoping to disrupt our fight for justice in the Christopher Alder case and, perhaps, also in the case of Wayne Douglas. I think the undercover squads were looking, not so much for insight, but for fuel for disinformation campaigns, to throw mud at the victims who had died in police custody, at their families, and at the lawyer representing them in the coroner's court. Potentially, there was also an element of intimidation.

The IPCC report was so upsetting that at the time I couldn't bring myself to read it. It made me so angry that I sent an 'outrage' letter to the IPCC, who knew they had to do their best. They bent over backwards in a sense to deal with my complaint, and even appointed Commissioner Cindy Butts, a Black woman, to oversee my case. The Chairman of the Bar Council also got involved, offering me support by intervening with the IPCC and the Home Office because they too thought it was outrageous, not to mention completely unlawful, that a member of the profession should be spied upon. They wanted assurances that steps would be taken to prevent surveillance of lawyers acting in the course of their professional duty from ever occurring again.

It didn't stop there, though. Having had the malicious allegations that I had been involved with the juror during the Alder inquest retracted, in 2018 the case was back in the headlines, when the Independent Office of Police Conduct (IOPC)* brought disciplinary action for gross misconduct against two of the more junior officers who had spied on me. My name was linked to the same allegation in the newspapers all over again. It won't go away and, what's more, the officers, who were still serving and were granted anonymity during the hearing, got off. The surveillance was found to be not lawful or appropriate, and was unjustified, but the officers themselves had 'no case to answer'. They said they hadn't realised that the orders to spy on me and Janet were unlawful, and that the orders came from further up the chain of command. A number of former senior Humberside officers gave evidence and said they didn't know the source either. The identity of that member of Humberside who issued the orders remains a mystery to this day.

---

* In January 2018, the IOPC replaced the Independent Police Complaints Commission, appointing Michael Lockwood as director general. The reformed police watchdog was intended to strengthen the organisation, enable speedier decision-making, increase the IOPC's independence from the police by abolishing 'managed' and 'supervised' investigations, and ensure greater accountability to the public.

36

TAKING SILK AND THE
HILLSBOROUGH INQUESTS

2013 had been a long and fraught year. By the time the Mark Duggan inquest concluded I was tired, to put it mildly. I had been instructed as counsel to the inquest by my friend and former instructing solicitor Joanne Kearsley, who was now deputy coroner for Stockport, on a difficult case regarding a young British soldier who had been killed in the Middle East, shot by another soldier who'd run amok one night and shot a number of soldiers in his own regiment. I had that in the background while I also flew to Belfast for the preliminary hearings of the inquest into the murders by the Ulster loyalist Glenanne Gang* of two people in the Step Inn pub bomb in County Armagh in 1976. Meanwhile, at some point during Mark Duggan's inquest, along with a number of my colleagues at Garden Court, I had been instructed on the second Hillsborough Stadium inquest by Marcia Willis Stewart of Birnberg Peirce to represent eleven of the families whose relatives had died in the disaster. I was doing one case after

---

* The paramilitary gang, with the alleged collusion of British soldiers and serving RUC police officers, has been linked to up to 120 murders between July 1972 and June 1978 in Northern Ireland's 'murder triangle' in Counties Armagh and Tyrone.

another without any significant time off work to catch my breath. I was also awaiting the decision from the QCA on my application for silk.

Meanwhile, my personal life was going pear-shaped. In early 2013, Tanya and I had broken up. Just before the Mark Duggan inquest started, I'd met a woman and stupidly walked straight into a new relationship. Ostensibly, she was professional and independent, an executive in the travel industry, and we embarked on a whirlwind romance, which in retrospect was just mad. Within a couple of months, I introduced her to my mum and my kids, but then things began to unravel quite quickly. We were bad for each other. It was the sort of toxic relationship in which we both ended up drinking too much, too many strong spirits, and far too often.

As a consequence, while outwardly my life looked like a bed of roses, my private life was imploding. In the middle of the Mark Duggan inquest, I started to feel dizzy and suffer from crippling migraines, the type where you see stars and have to close yourself in a darkened room for a half a day. I thought it was a combination of stress and, probably, drinking too much alcohol, so I saw my GP who advised me to take strong paracetamol when I felt a migraine attack coming on. I didn't think too much about it, and supposed it would sort itself out in time once I had a bit of a breather.

Before I decamped to Manchester to start on the Hillsborough inquest, my girlfriend suggested that we go away for a long weekend to get some winter sun. We flew to a luxury hotel on the Canary Islands, a perk of her job. On the first night, she drank too much over dinner and became distressed, claiming that I didn't love her, that I was being unfaithful, that she knew I'd never been serious about her. I truthfully did not know where all this was coming from, but nothing I said could convince her that she was mistaken, and so she continued to drink. Back in our hotel room, she drank the entire contents of the mini bar. By that stage, she was insensible and, exhausted, we both went to bed early.

Something made me wake up at about 2 a.m., and I found that I couldn't rouse her. She had passed out. At first I thought she was just drunk, but when I went into the bathroom I saw that my bottle of super-strength paracetamol was empty. It was the middle of the night in a foreign country. I rang the hotel reception and someone came to the room, but she was still out cold, so they called an ambulance and then the police. I therefore had to explain to the Spanish police how it was that the woman in my room, my girlfriend, had consumed my medication along with all the alcohol in our mini bar. After the police had finished with me, I went straight to the hospital where she was having her stomach pumped, but the staff didn't want me to see her. They thought I'd had a hand in her collapse.

This was in March, just weeks before I was hoping to take silk. I had no idea how I was going to get my girlfriend home. I started to imagine that she might not even survive. Much as I was worried about her wellbeing, what was also going through my head was how I was going to explain all this to my mother, my kids and also to colleagues and the powers that be at the Bar. I didn't even want to think what would happen if it made it into the newspapers. This would be the end of my professional career as I'd imagined it. Yet again, I'd put my reputation in jeopardy through an ill-judged and hasty relationship with a woman.

I went to the hospital, made sure the bill was paid and she was eventually discharged on the Saturday night before our flight home the following day. Back in London, I helped to get her into a rehab clinic. That was the end of our short-lived relationship. We never met again.

On 14 April 2014, I made silk; I'd been successful on my first application. The representative for the Queen at the ceremony was the Justice Secretary of State the Right Hon. Chris Grayling. Because of the way his government had devastated legal aid, I took the opportunity to tell him so when I was called upon to shake his hand. 'Mr Grayling, don't destroy legal aid.' The man has a powerful hand grip and as we both looked each other in the eye, he said, 'I don't intend to.' Given the state legal aid is now in, it turned out to be a false promise. Following the ceremony, I had an amazing silk's party and celebrated with all those who had helped me on my journey. Mum was there, of course, and she gave the following speech:

In 1975 I went to Leslie's headteacher and I pleaded with the man to allow my son to take the eleven-plus at the local grammar school. He said, 'No. He won't pass it and I don't want to disappoint the boy.' I remember leaving his office completely disheartened, but I never told Leslie what had happened. In 1988, Leslie qualified and was called to the Bar and by this time I was living in a different part of London, but I made the journey and I went all the way back to Belleville junior school and asked to see the headmaster. It was Mr Jerry, who was close to retirement but he was still there. 'Who should I say it is?' asked the receptionist, and I said, 'Tell him it's Mrs Thomas, Leslie's mum.' He remembered me.

'Mrs Thomas, what can I do for you?' he asked.

'Do you remember my son Leslie?' I said. 'Do you remember when I came to you and asked you to give him the chance to go to Emmanuel?'

'I do,' he replied. 'Now, how is the boy doing?'

'Well,' I told him, 'Leslie's just qualified as a barrister.'

> And do you know what? If I knew where Mr Jerry was today, I would go back to his office and tell him, 'My son Leslie Thomas has just qualified as a silk.'

That's my mum and that's how long my mum's memory is. Let's just say, things like that make you stronger. My mother was really proud of what I had achieved.

I felt I had reached a peak. But with every peak there comes a fall, and mine was just around the corner.

The Hillsborough inquests had opened on 1 April. At the end of March I drove up to Manchester where I rented an apartment. When I was instructed, the inquests were expected to last for nine months – in fact, such was the exceptional complexity of the investigation that they ran for two years.

The Hillsborough disaster was the biggest loss of life at a sports stadium in peacetime. There had already been a previous inquest, an inquiry *and* a police investigation into the events leading to the tragic deaths. The number of interested persons was huge. The number of clients and families was huge. There were ninety-six victims – ninety-six individual Liverpool FC supporters, young and old, who were killed at the Hillsborough Stadium in Sheffield on Saturday 15 April 1989 at the semi-final FA Cup match between Liverpool and Nottingham Forest – and each death had to be separately investigated.

That Saturday afternoon, over 10,000 Liverpool ticket-holders had tried to enter the standing terraces at the smaller end of the stadium and were corralled into four 'pens' separated by high wire fences that prevented them from running onto the pitch. As well as the victims who lost their lives, trampled and suffocated in the chaos, 766 people were injured and suffered inconceivable trauma.

For years, the police had blamed the Liverpool fans, dissem-
inating false stories in the media depicting them as drunken
hooligans and alleging that they were responsible for the disaster. The vilification of the Liverpool supporters persisted,
even after a 1990 inquiry chaired by Lord Justice Taylor found
that the main reason for the disaster was the failure of police
control. In 1991, in a civil claim by a survivor of the disaster against South Yorkshire Police for psychiatric damage, a
House of Lords ruling stated that the 'chief constable of South
Yorkshire has admitted liability in negligence in respect of the
deaths and physical injuries'. Nevertheless, in 1991 the first
coroner's inquests into the disaster had found that all the deaths
were accidental. For nigh-on two-and-a-half decades, the
bereaved families and survivors had fought to overturn these
verdicts, and Article 2 of the Human Rights Act was vitally
important in that campaign. Eventually, after the publication
of the Hillsborough Independent Panel's report in 2012, the
original verdicts were quashed and fresh inquests were opened,
this time in compliance with an Article 2 inquest.

Represented as interested parties to the inquest, therefore,
were ninety-six families who had lost loved ones. Then there
were the various interested persons and parties to the events
that took place that day: South Yorkshire Police, individual
police officers, the ambulance staff, fire service staff, the
Football Association, the Hillsborough stadium match commander, the owners of the stadium, Sheffield Wednesday
football club itself. There must have been at least a hundred
lawyers instructed on the inquiry, so they needed to accommodate about 600 people in the court during the hearings.

Consequently, the coroner's office had to find premises
adequate to hold such a substantial number of participants. A
warehouse building on an industrial estate in Warrington was

renovated to turn it into a courtroom. This vast space was lined with rows upon rows of functional but ugly office seating and desks, and with absolutely no natural light, only glaring strip lighting that instantly brings on a headache. And as there were no windows, there was no fresh air. Can you imagine being on an industrial estate for month after month (for some participants it was two whole years), with no natural light throughout all the seasons, and no fresh air?

The reading and preparation before and after the hearing each day was as it always is for any Article 2 inquest. But the main difference on an inquest on the scale of Hillsborough was the size and particular focus of my team. Along with four other barristers, I was specifically tasked to examine the pathology evidence.

About five months into the Hillsborough hearings, at the end of August 2014, I opened a text message from my ex-girlfriend, she of the paracetamol overdose. It read: 'I hope your billing is up to date, because you're going to have to pay me child support.' She said she was six months pregnant with my child, and I had better get my wallet ready. This was all a nasty lie, but I did not know that at the time. Stressed already from the pressures of the Hillsborough hearings, I cracked up. My heart went into sudden rapid and irregular palpitations. Something was badly wrong and I was scared that I'd had a heart attack. I had no choice but to step down from the inquest.

I was recuperating at home, obviously concerned about the bombshell that I might soon become a father again, by a woman with whom I no longer wished to have any contact, when a mutual friend rang to tell me that he had happened to bump into her. I naturally asked how she seemed, and if she looked very pregnant, and he seemed bemused. He said no, and must have thought I'd gone crazy. There was no child and my ex-girlfriend wasn't, and never had been, pregnant.

That, clearly, was a relief, but my irregular heartbeat continued to worry me. I was referred to a cardiologist who told me
that it was just one of those annoying things that I would have
to live with – a heart condition brought on by stress. Alcohol
doesn't help matters either, and so I'm now more or less teeto-
tal, I don't drink caffeine, and I just have to manage it and adjust
my workload accordingly. The cardiologist said that I also
needed to take some time out, to rest, and look after myself.

I had, however, one case that I wanted to see through, which
was the inquest into the death by stabbing of Arsema Dawit,
which Dr Andrew Harris, the Southwark senior coroner for
London South, had originally opened in June 2008. The inquest
hearings were due to commence on 2 September, but my brilliant colleague Una Morris, another former pupil of mine, was
acting as my junior, and so while I was dealing with my hospital
appointments, I knew she could amply fill my shoes for the
opening days of the hearings.

Una was the last pupil I took on before I became Head of
Chambers and is a force to be reckoned with. A young, Black,
working-class woman, she had dropped out of school, not
because she was incapable, but because the way that the school
system ran didn't accord with her. Later, she decided to pick
up her education, graduating from the University of Leeds with
a degree in Criminal Justice and Criminology, and decided to
come to the Bar.

Arsema Dawit's death was a tragic case of 'collective and
organisational failings' by the Metropolitan Police. In June
2008, just three days after her fifteenth birthday, Arsema was
killed in a savage attack by Thomas Nugusse, her 21-year-old
ex-boyfriend, who stabbed her over sixty times.

Prior to Arsema's murder, Thomas Nugusse's behaviour
towards her had become increasingly controlling and abusive.

Just two months before her death, he had punched her in the face in a McDonald's restaurant after she had said hello to a male friend. Arsema broke up with him after that, but thereafter he had harassed, followed and made threats to kill her. On 30 April, Arsema, her mother and her cousin, distressed by Thomas Nugusse's escalating conduct, visited Kennington police station where they spent almost three hours with the station reception officer, a civilian police employee, reporting Thomas Nugusse's behaviour. However, despite the consequent Crime Reporting Information System (CRIS) report detailing the information about harassment, assault and a threat to kill, the report was classified only as Actual Bodily Harm. The CRIS report was never reclassified and relevant policies, procedures and risk assessments were never implemented.

Thomas Nugusse continued to harass and threaten Arsema, and the family, having lost all hope in the police, took her to and from the bus stop each day so that she could go to school and, fearing for her safety, they refused to let her go unaccompanied elsewhere. Nevertheless, Thomas Nugusse had told Arsema's mother, 'How many days are you going to accompany her? I'll kill her one day.' He carried out his threat on 2 June, when he brutally attacked Arsema, leaving her dead in a lift at a block of flats in Waterloo. He was charged with murder, but while in prison, pending a trial, he made a suicide attempt which left him with brain damage. He was declared unfit to attend court and, in his absence, after a short 'trial of issue', a jury at the Old Bailey found that he was responsible for Arsema's death.

Arsema's mother, Tsehainesh Medhani, believed that her daughter's life could have been saved if the police had taken action when she approached them. She wanted answers as to how the system had so badly failed them and to hold the police's failings to account. As Tsehainesh said, 'This case is not simply about a brutal and unforgivable murder, but why, despite me begging the police to save my daughter, the police failed to act.'

In 2012, following a judicial review of a previous coroner's decision not to hold an inquest into Arsema's death, Tim Owen QC and myself on behalf of Arsema's family were successful in securing a full Article 2 inquest, sitting with a jury, to examine the circumstances of the death, including the actions and inaction of the police.

The inquest closed on 26 September, with the jury unanimously finding that Arsema Dawit was unlawfully killed. In relation to the failings of the police, the jury delivered their unanimous conclusions in a highly critical narrative, demonstrating that a full inquest to explore these issues and secure the rights of the family had been essential.

This was the last case I would do for some time. I was suffering from burnout. I cancelled all my other immediate commitments and went to the Caribbean to recharge my batteries. In fact, I took almost a year off work.

Postscript

In a momentous end to the longest-running inquest in British legal history, on 26 April 2016, the nine-person jury (which had been deliberating since 6 April) found that the ninety-six victims had been unlawfully killed at Hillsborough and that the Liverpool supporters were in no way to blame.

The jury said that the authorities' response to the disaster was slow and badly co-ordinated. The police had delayed declaring a major incident, and staff at the stadium from South Yorkshire Metropolitan Ambulance Service had also failed in this respect. Fire service crews with cutting gear had difficulty getting into the ground, and although dozens of ambulances were dispatched, access to the pitch was delayed because police had reported 'crowd trouble'. Only two ambulances had actually arrived at the Liverpool end of Hillsborough stadium, so that of the ninety-six dead, only fourteen were ever admitted to hospital. The jury also found that on the day of the tragedy the match commander Chief Superintendent David Duckenfield was in breach of his duty of care to the fans in the stadium, which amounted to gross negligence.

Upon hearing the jury's findings, an emotional Margaret Aspinall, chair of Hillsborough Family Support Group, whose eighteen-year-old son James was killed in the disaster, said: 'Let's be honest about this – people were against us. We had the media against us, as well as the establishment. Everything was against us. The only people that weren't against us was our own city. That's why I am so grateful to my city and so proud of my city. They always believed in us.'

I am sad that my illness cut short my service to the families in their long and unstinting quest for justice, but I am extremely proud that a total of seventeen of my fellow barristers from Garden Court Chambers had played their part in the inquests since they opened in 2014, representing seventy-seven families of those who died at Hillsborough.

37

BARBUDA:
A CONSTITUTIONAL CRISIS

I have mixed emotions about the Caribbean. Although I hadn't been completely won over by my very first trip to Antigua and Dominica to meet my grandparents as a seven-year-old, on my second visit when I was fourteen, I was able to appreciate the landscape and the people in a way that I hadn't when I was younger. From about the age of eighteen, flush from my labours at Jean Jeanie, I'd started taking holidays in Antigua with Angela every year, sometimes twice a year, and I'd decided that this place was me — it was a part of me.

When I was there, I felt at ease. Nobody was judging me because of the colour of my skin — that is, until once, when Angela and I would have been about twenty, on perhaps our third or fourth trip to Antigua, we went to a beach adjoining a big resort hotel. In Antigua, all the beaches are public — the adjoining land might be privately owned, but not the beach. Generally speaking, even if a beach hotel has some sort of security staff manning the hotel access to the beach, the hotel owners don't mind tourists going through the grounds and using the beach. On this occasion, Angela had gone ahead, but when I was making my way down to the sand, a member

348

of staff stopped and questioned me. It was only when I opened my mouth and they heard that I was English that their attitude changed. I had gone to Antigua thinking that I was free from prejudice, yet, as a Black man in the Caribbean, I could be met with a whole other type of discrimination. In this case, I could be stopped and potentially barred from the resort beach by hotel workers because they assumed I was local. They treated white and foreign tourists differently to the native population. It struck me then that even in their own country, Antiguans don't feel free. I'd begun to see this island as my own home, too, and it was a disturbing realisation.

Over the years, although vestiges of that old colonial attitude towards Black Caribbean people persist, especially in upmarket tourist settings, and one can still be made to feel like a second-class citizen, happily I've seen things slowly begin to change. After I took silk and then had my heart problem, I spent several months recuperating in Antigua. I had previously been called to the Bar in both Dominica in 2003 and Antigua in 2008, and now I started to mull over how I could do some useful human rights and constitutional work and thereby give something back to the community, and to the Caribbean islands in general.

In August 2016 I was approached by a Dominican gentleman called Cabral Douglas who wanted to bring a constitutional claim against the government of the Commonwealth of Dominica.

In late 2013, Mr Douglas, son of former Prime Minister of Dominica Rosie Douglas and a lawyer by profession, had contracted with a prominent Jamaican artist management firm for the international recording artist Leroy Russell, aka Tommy Lee Sparta, to headline at his privately owned entertainment venue in Dominica to mark the opening of Portsmouth Carnival in February 2014.

On the day of the concert, however, when Tommy Lee Sparta along with his entourage – his manager Junior Fraser, his DJ Mario Wallace, and his personal assistant Oralie Russell, all four Jamaican nationals – arrived at Dominica's Douglas–Charles airport, they were denied entry by immigration officials. The four were arrested, denied access to the lawyer provided to them at the airport, taken to the police station in Marigot, detained for twenty-four hours in allegedly unsanitary and inhumane conditions and then deported back to Jamaica without due process. Each of their passports was stamped 'denied entry' and 'repatriated' by immigration officials prior to their repatriation. Furthermore, the government of Dominica had failed to provide any reasons for their arrest, detention and subsequent deportation. The much-hyped and greatly anticipated concert was cancelled and Cabral suffered substantial financial loss. He subsequently discovered that the decision to refuse entry to the musician and his colleagues had been taken six days before the scheduled concert.

At first I wasn't at all sure whether this was something I wanted to take on, but then I decided, as a recently qualified silk, that it was definitely worthwhile investigating. I met with Cabral via Skype call and had several additional calls with him. He was living in Canada, and was insistent that his business had been destroyed by the government's action in cancelling his promoted show. He believed it was political and wanted me to represent him. He had heard about my reputation in the UK and believed I was the sort of fearless advocate who was not afraid of taking on the Dominican state. I agreed. This was a case that would be litigated in the Caribbean Court of Justice (CCJ), which was the equivalent of the UK Supreme Court. I had never argued a case before any supreme court in my own right, so I was honoured to be asked.

I assembled a team of lawyers to assist me in this endeavour, including Thalia Maragh, an experienced Jamaican attorney who was dual qualified in the Bar of England and Wales with whom I had worked closely with on the Hillsborough inquests. Thalia knew a lot about how Caribbean constitutional law worked and I learned a lot from her. I also recruited Tihomir Mak, one of my young pupils from Garden Court. Tihomir had a great deal of experience in bringing international cases. Between us we set about taking on the Dominican state.

The CARICOM* group of nations' Revised Treaty of Chaguaramas stipulates that one of its overriding objectives is the free movement of CARICOM nationals among the Member States. It places an obligation on Member States to accord media workers, sportspersons, artistes and musicians the freedom to provide services in their jurisdictions.† Thus Tommy Lee Sparta and the other Jamaican nationals were entitled to enter Dominica unhindered, and to perform as contracted at the concert. Our argument was that under the RTC, the only grounds for denying entry to a national of any member state is on the basis of them being undesirable or a potential burden on the public funds, and there was no reliable evidence in this case to suggest that this was justifiable. Accordingly, we believed that Cabral had a strong case on the basis of freedom

---

* The Caribbean Community (CARICOM) is a grouping of twenty countries: fifteen Member States – Antigua and Barbuda, Bahamas, Barbados, Belize, Dominica, Grenada, Guyana, Haiti, Jamaica, Montserrat (a British overseas territory in the Leeward Islands), Saint Kitts and Nevis, Saint Lucia, Saint Vincent and the Grenadines, Suriname, and Trinidad and Tobago; and five Associate Members – Anguilla, Bermuda, the British Virgin Islands, the Cayman Islands, and Turks and Caicos. CARICOM came into being in July 1973 with the signing of the Treaty of Chaguaramas, which was later revised in 2002 to allow for the eventual establishment of a single market and a single economy, and then known as the Revised Treaty of Chaguaramas (RTC). The main purposes of the CARICOM alliance of states are to promote economic integration and co-operation among its members, to ensure that the benefits of integration are equitably shared, and to co-ordinate foreign policy.
† Article 35 of the Revised Treaty of Chaguaramas.

of movement and the freedom to provide services, and a fair prospect of establishing that Dominica had breached its duty under the treaty.

In October 2016, we therefore filed proceedings against the government of Dominica at the Caribbean Court of Justice on behalf of Cabral. We charged that the decision by the government of the Commonwealth of Dominica to deny entry, arrest, detain and deport Leroy Russell, Junior Fraser, Mario Wallace and Oralie Russell had been taken at a cabinet meeting prior to their scheduled arrival in Dominica. It had been taken negligently in breach of the defendant's duty of care owed to all passengers landing in Dominica including but not limited to CARICOM nationals, and with the malicious intention of discriminating against them in violation of the Revised Treaty of Chaguaramas. The public hearing was held by video conference in December that year.

In January 2017, we received the judgement from the judges in the Caribbean Court of Justice – Cabral's application was denied. The reasons for this ruling were complicated, but in broad stroke, individuals such as Cabral do not have an automatic right to appear before the Caribbean Court of Justice. Four conditions must be satisfied, one of which is that the right that has been breached must 'belong or be available to the benefit of *such persons directly*'. Cabral's claim was deemed to be inadmissible on the grounds that he himself was not the service provider who had been denied his right under Article 35 of the treaty. Rather, as a Jamaican national seeking to perform in Dominica, it was Tommy Lee Sparta whose rights had been breached. Nor was Cabral the 'service recipient' – they, the judges said, were the planned audience members at the planned Portsmouth Carnival concert. Meanwhile, in December 2016, Tommy Lee Sparta's management said that the government of Dominica had made him an undisclosed offer of financial compensation, and negotiations were ongoing.

We were naturally disappointed that our application had been denied. With the court ruling, my involvement and retainer in the case came to an end. There was no other possibility of an appeal. That road was exhausted. But Cabral was furious. Citing a number of irregularities in the proceedings, he personally launched into a tour of the regional media to denounce the court ruling, arguing that there was evidence of corruption at the highest level involving the Caribbean Court of Justice president Sir Dennis Byron and Prime Minister Skerrit of Dominica, and filed a formal complaint with the Regional and Judicial Legal Services Commission. Unaware of these goings-on, I was contacted by another lawyer who sent me the articles of Cabral's complaints. Cabral was no longer my client, however, and not under my control.

In the event, the Caribbean Court of Justice issued a media statement denying allegations of corruption while the OECS bar weighed in with their own statement of outrage in which they 'strongly condemn[ed]' Cabral's comments, which they said were 'strident, contemptuous, inflammatory and even defamatory'. As far as I am aware, Cabral's crusade for a satisfactory outcome to his claim against the government of Dominica continues. I have not heard from him since.

Less than a year later, I was again approached to work on a big case in the Caribbean. This time it would be to protect the rights of a small island nation with fewer than 2,000 inhabitants.

The opportunity to play a part came about as a result of one of the biggest natural disasters to ever strike the area. On the night of 6 September 2017, category-five Hurricane Irma hit the island of Barbuda at about 185mph, leaving it in ruins.

It damaged about 90 per cent of the island's buildings, literally flattening many of them. Two days later, meteorological reports issued a warning about a second hurricane, this one named Hurricane Jose, and, fearing that Barbuda would once again be hit, Gaston Browne, the prime minister of Antigua and Barbuda, ordered a mass evacuation of all the island's residents to Antigua, which had weathered the hurricane with only minor damage.

Hurricane Irma was to prove catastrophic for the islanders in more ways than one.

When Antigua and Barbuda gained their independence from the UK in 1981, administratively they became sister islands with a joint government in Antigua. From the outset the union was uneasy. The Barbudans didn't want to have independence with Antigua, and one of the main reasons is that Barbuda has a completely different legal system of land ownership. Whereas the Antiguan system is based on the British model of tenure, with freehold and leasehold buildings, in Barbuda, conversely, there is communal land ownership. This structure had its roots in the colonial history of the island. Barbuda was never a plantation island, rather it was governed solely by the Codringtons, a British slave-owning family who had leased Barbuda from the Crown. When the Slavery Abolition Act of 1833 came into effect in August 1834, the Codringtons gave their emancipated slaves the right to occupy the island's land.

This meant that Barbuda was, in effect, communally owned by *all* Barbudans, making it the only island in the world with a communal land system. The islanders could control their environment, and the economic development of the country, to the extent that Barbuda has no big resort hotels, nor the kind of big-bucks tourism which inevitably destroys the natural landscape. It has a tiny population of about 1,800 people; there is no crime; nobody locks their doors at night; there is no tangible inequality, no homelessness, and no poverty. The Barbudans live comfortably off the fruits of the land: they hunt wild deer and wild pigs in the forests on the island, and there are ample fresh fish in the sea. There is a glorious, unmarred lagoon with translucent turquoise waters, and unblemished pink and white sand beaches. It is also, however, a small, flat island, covering just 62 square miles, which is why Hurricane Irma wreaked such havoc on the land.

As a result, the Antiguans always had one eye to what could be gained from Barbuda. The Barbudans told me that the Antiguans were jealous and wanted to seize control of their island; the Antiguans I spoke to retorted that Barbudans are all lazy spongers who make use of the historic land system to thwart well-meaning Antiguans who want to start businesses there.

With the island's entire infrastructure razed to the ground, it remained largely uninhabited. Rather than pour money into redevelopment and helping the island's displaced families to return home to rebuild their lives, the government saw an opportunity to push through legislation to repeal and replace the Barbuda Land Act, which would dismantle the centuries-old system of communal land ownership and constitutionally guaranteed rights of Barbudans. The island would thus be fair game for a 'land grab' by big-bank and foreign investors with plans for unsustainable and speculative developments. What this monumental Bill proposed was that the Barbudan people would effectively be stripped of rights to the land as they and their ancestors before them had always known them. At the same time, the process the government had undertaken had effectively silenced the Barbudan people from speaking up against the changes. John Mussington, co-founder of the Barbuda

Silent No More movement, told me: 'This land is our birthright as Barbudans and our own government is trying to silence us during a very vulnerable time in our history as we recover from a devastating hurricane. This attack on the democratic process reflects a complete lack of basic human decency during a period when we should be coming together as a nation to recover our homeland and protect our heritage.'

The fate of a whole island was at stake, and this was somewhere I felt I could do a lot of good for a group of vulnerable and dispossessed people. The law in Antigua and Barbuda specifically states that the Barbuda Land Act and the communal land rights it protects cannot be changed without the consent of the Barbudan people, and so I acted for the Barbudan People's Movement, a group of Barbudans on behalf of those who were opposed to the Bill. We filed a court action. On 20 December 2017, the Antigua and Barbuda High Court of Justice heard an application for an emergency interim court injunction to seek permission for judicial review to challenge the proposed legislative and constitutional reforms. The decision of the Hon. Mrs Justice Henry was delivered in early January 2018. We lost. The court refused our application, arguing that our application was premature.

Simultaneously, one of the government's first moves was to start building an international commercial airport on Barbuda, which before the hurricane had only a small domestic airstrip. The creation of the airport was part of the deal for the Paradise Found resort funded by Robert De Niro and James Packer, and work on the excavations resumed almost immediately after Hurricane Irma. As Kendra Beazer, a councillor on Barbuda and a member of the Barbudan People's Movement, said, 'When you hear that they're already clearing land to build the new airport, yet you haven't put up the fence at the old airport to allow for regular travel, it makes you question the government's motives.'

In addition to the fact that the new airport was an eyesore and that it would bring massive changes to the previously unmarred island, the Antiguan government didn't follow its own planning permission regulations or carry out an adequate Environmental Impact Assessment, and so failed to properly assess archaeology, biodiversity and geology aspects of the construction works. The site was in the wrong part of the island, and building had started on cavernous limestone land. In effect, the geological structure is such that there is an ancient system of natural caves under the runway, and thus potential sinkholes, which is naturally extremely hazardous to any air traffic. More importantly, the proposed commercial airport would necessarily cause the destruction of pristine forest, native wildlife, sensitive ecosystems and the agricultural livelihoods of the Barbudan people. Alongside this I had to ask: What are the standards to which we hold ourselves and our governments? How does a government get to the point of complete disregard for the laws and processes of good governance for the country? The government of Antigua and Barbuda had to be held to account.

Despite losing the injunction in relation to the repeal of the Barbuda Land Act, it was becoming clear that there had been violations of planning in relation to the airport, so we decided to concentrate our efforts in challenging the lawfulness of its construction.

At around the same time, in April 2018, an opportunity arose. A law firm in Antigua was closing down and I was offered the chance to take on some of the firm's clients and rent the building space. It was not exactly what I had planned, but I decided then and there that the time was right. I started the process of setting up my own law firm in Antigua and took on a young lawyer called Michelle Sterling who had been at the previous firm and was reliable, keen and hungry. 'Justice Chambers' was up and running and the Barbudan people were going to be our first main clients.

Shortly after the airport construction builders moved in, so did I. With the help of other members of Garden Court's International and Civil Liberties teams, I made an application for an emergency injunction on behalf of the Barbudan people to prevent the airport construction. This was heard on 2 August 2018 at the High Court of Justice of Antigua and Barbuda. Since then, the Barbudans whom I represent and the Antiguan government have been locked in an almighty David and Goliath battle. The Antiguan government has seemingly limitless resources to throw at the case and the Barbudans have very little, so I have been dealing with a lot of the work on a pro bono basis, and gladly so. In fact, I feel honoured to represent the people of Barbuda. It has been both a privilege and an uplifting experience that has brought me closer to my Caribbean roots. I've also been able to witness first-hand how some of the old colonial hierarchies are slowly being chipped away.

One of the best feelings I've experienced regarding my ambivalent relationship with the islands was on the first injunction hearing on the Barbuda case. I walked into the High Court in Antigua to find that all the attorneys representing the various interested persons were women, and they were all Black. These excellent female briefs were flanked by equally impressive junior attorneys. It was an amazing and inspiring sight. I took my place in the courtroom, and even though we were all fighting different causes and there was a degree of rivalry between us, when I made my opening remarks, I actually commented that it was so refreshing to walk into a court and to see all these sisters, each arguing a very important constitutional case.

Postscript

For Barbuda, the catastrophe is still unfolding.

In August 2018, an application for an injunction to an immediate halt to construction work was upheld. The government of Antigua and Barbuda subsequently successfully challenged the injunction, which was lifted in the following months allowing construction on a new site to resume. This was because the High Court judge was said to have breached the rules of natural justice by not hearing the arguments of the respondents. We appealed to the Eastern Caribbean Court of Appeal as to whether or not the injunction should be reinstated to stop any further airport works. Unfortunately, our Court of Appeal case regarding the Barbuda International Airport construction was dismissed, and we are now renewing our appeal to the Privy Council in London. That hearing is due to be heard, if permission is granted, sometime in 2022.

The Barbuda case was a hugely significant landmark, and since then my work in the Caribbean continues to be an important part of my life. I have done many constitutional claims. But that in itself is another story for another day.

38

THE DEATHS OF CHRISTI (1999– 2006) AND BOBBY SHEPHERD (2000–2006)

When I came back to chambers in London in early 2015, I wanted to take it easy. Then I got a call from Fiona Borrill in Leeds who wanted to instruct me on a case. The case, she explained, was to represent the parents at the inquest into the deaths of two children. They had died while they were on a half-term holiday in October 2006 with their father Neil Shepherd and his partner (now his wife) Ruth at the Louis Corcyra Beach Hotel in Corfu. I remembered it, the tragic death from carbon monoxide poisoning of seven-year-old Christianne (Christi) Shepherd and her brother Robert (Bobby), who was six.

The facts of Christi and Bobby Shepherd's deaths are well known. The holiday bungalow in which the family were staying had an adjoining out-building which housed a gas hot-water boiler. This had been poorly installed and maintained with what the coroner called 'bodged and botched' work and inadequate ventilation, making an accident almost inevitable. Three days into the holiday, Christi and Bobby started to feel unwell. On the night of their deaths, Bobby was unsteady on his feet and both children were complaining of headaches and were vomiting. Their father and his partner went to comfort them. The next morning, a chambermaid entered the bungalow to do the cleaning. She found the bodies of Christi and Bobby; Mr Shepherd and Ruth were lying nearby in a comatose state. They were admitted to hospital where four days later they regained consciousness and learned that the two children were dead. Christi and Bobby's mother, Sharon Wood, heard about her children's deaths from a news report on the radio. A Greek court found three members of the hotel staff, including the manager, guilty of manslaughter; two holiday reps employed by Thomas Cook were cleared. West Yorkshire Police had also investigated the case, but the Crown Prosecution Service decided that there was insufficient evidence to bring charges against anyone in the company.

At first I hesitated, because this did not seem to be a typical type of inquest for me. It wasn't a death in custody or a police shooting, and secondly, it involved the death of two young children. Also, I was anxious not to put myself under too much stress and I knew this case would be demanding, emotionally and professionally. However, the parents, Fiona said, needed someone like me to take on the huge corporate entity that was Thomas Cook. She also explained that this would probably be the last time that she and I would work together as she was thinking of becoming a coroner. We had worked on many big cases together and she had always been extremely supportive of me and my career. I owed Fiona a huge debt. So, I agreed, and it wasn't a difficult decision. I said that I would happily be a voice for the family at the hearings, to fight for a rigorous, fair and transparent investigation that would uncover the full facts of the tragedy, and hold all those responsible properly to account. What a case. Talk about a small person taking on the corporate giant. It was a legal rollercoaster. I was in for the ride of my life.

At that time, Thomas Cook was the biggest holiday tour operator in Europe with an annual turnover in the billions, but in the eight years since the children had died in bungalow 211 at one of their third-party hotels, the company treated this bereaved family abominably. They claimed to have offered them practical and financial support. This was simply untrue. When the children died on holiday and their bodies had to be flown back to the UK, for example, did Thomas Cook assist the family and provide a private plane for the distraught mother and her partner? No. The tiny bodies of the children came back on the holiday package charter plane that the couple flew home in along with the rest of the holidaymakers, the last of the season at the end of October. Sharon Wood saw her children's coffins being shunted into the cargo hold.

It had taken the family a long time to get to this inquest; they had gone through the Greek system and received a modest compensation settlement from the hotel. Then there had been the Yorkshire Police investigation and the subsequent decision by the CPS not to prosecute any individuals who worked for Thomas Cook nor the company itself. Lastly, in the UK they'd had to go through the complex workings of the coronial system, which had taken its time. There was a struggle to obtain funding. The coroner had ruled that this was not an Article 2 case – Thomas Cook was not an arm of the state. It was difficult to argue against this legal reasoning, which made it problematic to secure legal aid. We didn't know if we would have funding for the inquest, which was likely to last at least three weeks. Having met Sharon and Neil, I would have done their case pro bono, but I did not want to make a public statement to this effect for fear of influencing the Legal Aid Agency's decision. In the end we did manage to secure funding for the family, though at junior rates, which meant that despite the fact that I was a QC, I would be paid as if I was a junior barrister.

To be honest, I did not care; I was just pleased to have any funding at all. Herein lies the problem with the mentality of the legal aid system and the hardworking lawyers who keep it going. We become so downtrodden with one negative decision after the other knocking us back, that when we eventually get it we are so grateful for even the modest crumbs of funding we are handed. There is no doubt that the legal aid system is broken. I know for a fact that the other two QCs who were instructed on this inquest – one for the company itself and the other QC who was representing the individual employees – were paid handsomely and properly, an hourly rate deserving of a high-profile case such as this. There are no two ways about it: we do not have a fair system of remuneration for lawyers for these complex cases. Money talks, and if you are a legal aid lawyer, well, tough. You take what you are given and you don't complain.

The inquest was held at Wakefield Coroner's Court, sitting before David Hinchliff, the senior coroner for West Yorkshire. Mr Hinchliff had accepted an application from me that the case should be heard with a jury. He didn't *have* to call a jury, and many coroners would not have done so, because this inevitably added to the length and cost of the case. But in giving a ruling on this issue, Mr Hinchliff said in strong terms that if Christi and Bobby had died on British soil they would have been entitled to a jury as of right, because of the Coroners' Rules and the fact that their death was a suspected carbon monoxide poisoning. Because they died abroad, however, that automatic entitlement did not apply. Mr Hinchliff did not want justice to be a lottery, dependent on where these British children in the care of a British company had died. It was a strong ruling and clearly sent a message to all the interested persons that this would be a searching and in-depth inquiry. And it was.

The jury were sworn in. Eleven good Yorkshire people. A mix of ages and gender. The one thing that struck me about the jury hearing this case was that they looked as though Christi or Bobbi could have been their daughter or son, their grandchild, nephew or niece. Or indeed the children of your neighbours. The people sitting on the jury could easily have been on that fatal Thomas Cook holiday themselves. This was so different to the death-in-custody cases I was used to, where at times you feel there is a disconnect between the jury and the bereaved family. If the deceased person was engaged in criminal activity at the time of their death, for the counsel for the family it is a harder challenge to get a jury on side. On Christi and Bobby Shepherd's inquest, I realised I would have no problems in this regard.

It has to be said that Thomas Cook did not make matters easy on themselves in defending their decisions and actions at this inquest. Firstly, they did not call key witnesses; they used the excuse that the witnesses were abroad. If a witness is outside the jurisdiction, the coroner cannot compel them to give evidence. However, with the advent of video conferencing facilities, a witness doesn't need to be in court *physically*. The jury would have been aware of this. We suspected it was a strategic decision not to call some key witnesses. Furthermore, those witnesses in the UK who were compelled to give evidence decided to exercise their right not to incriminate themselves when giving evidence and relied on their right to silence. Any experienced advocate knows that when an explanation for a witness to rely on his or her right to silence is called, it simply looks bad. However many directions a coroner gives to a jury, explaining that it is a witness's right not to incriminate themselves and this should not be held against them, one can only imagine what the jury is thinking. It appears as if the witness is hiding something. Certainly, this jury was not happy with Thomas Cook or its employees. They looked with disdain at witness after witness who was either silent or said they were not to blame for the glaring failures and mistakes which led the third-party hotel to have dodgy boilers and inadequate ventilation. In short, a heating system which, had anyone competent stopped and inspected it, they would have condemned it at the first opportunity.

By the time the inquest opened, a new chief executive, a Swiss gentleman called Peter Fankhauser, had taken over at Thomas Cook. Although Mr Fankhauser hadn't been the CEO at the time the incident had occurred, he was called as a witness at the hearings. When I was questioning him about the failures of his company, I looked him in the eye and said, 'I'm a father, I know how these parents feel. Mr Fankhauser, given what has happened to Christi and Bobby's mother and father, would you like to apologise to my clients for the failures of your company?' He replied, 'I feel incredibly sorry for the family – incredibly sorry. But I don't have to apologise.' Pressed again to take this opportunity to offer some form of public apology to the family, all Mr Fankhauser had to say to Christi and Bobby's parents was, 'I feel so thoroughly, from the deepest of my heart, sorry, but there's no need to apologise because there was no wrongdoing by Thomas Cook.' End of story. He refused to apologise to my clients. He refused to take an opportunity to put right what was so obviously wrong. An apology would have cost him and Thomas Cook nothing. This is a corporate mindset – deny, deny, deny. I don't know whether the bottom line was money; they were worried perhaps, that to give any apology would have been an implied admission of liability. In fact, that was not the case, since the family had already settled their case in Greece. But Thomas Cook did not handle the deaths of two young children while on one of their package holidays fittingly, or with even the barest glimmer of human decency. When Mr Fankhauser said he had nothing to apologise for, the jury looked at him with daggers. Although you can't have a victory in an inquest because it can't be won or lost, I knew we had, in that moment, won. I believe at that moment the jury hated him for what he had just said and they hated Thomas Cook for what had happened to these two innocent children. At the end of the inquest on 13 May 2015, the jury came back with an unlawful killing verdict and said that Thomas Cook had been negligent and had failed in their duty of care to Christi and Bobby and to their grieving parents. It should be noted that negligence denotes civil responsibility. This is a verdict that normally simply is not permissible in an inquest and in fairness to Mr Hinchcliff he had properly directed the jury. But this jury were going to have their say. The coroner did not amend the jury's conclusion and allowed it to stand. Thomas Cook could have tried to judicially review the jury decision and get parts of it struck out, but that would have involved even further litigation and even more publicity, none of which was good for the company. There comes a time when you know not to litigate further. Thomas Cook realised that time was after the inquest verdict.

At the end of the inquest, I made a statement to the national media and reporters outside the court who had been following the story diligently. At that moment, I felt so angry with the way the company had conducted itself and I said, 'Thomas Cook should hang its head in shame as a result of these deaths. The families of Christi and Bobby have waited nearly nine years for an apology – they are still waiting.'

Yet further insult to the family was to follow, however. Four days later, on 17 May 2015, Neil Shepherd and Sharon Wood were to learn that after the Greek criminal case, Thomas Cook had received £3.5 million in compensation from the Corfu hotel; this was ten times more than the amount that they had been offered as reparation for the deaths of the children.

The following day Thomas Cook announced it would be donating £1.5 million to charity. Peter Fankhauser claimed that this amount was the remainder left after the company's legal costs had been taken by its insurers, and that 'Thomas Cook has not in any way profited from our claim against the hotel owner.' Regarding the donation to UNICEF, he said, 'I believe this is the right thing to do and I apologise to the family for all they have gone through.'

However, Thomas Cook still had not bothered to write to the children's family to offer their apology or condolences.* Nor had they consulted them about their charitable gesture. Other relatives and friends had helped to raise money for another charity in Bobby and Christi's memory, and once again, they felt that the company's actions were not about them, but all about Thomas Cook. Once again, Thomas Cook had got it all badly wrong. Their share price plummeted. There was a campaign across social and traditional media to boycott the company and it lost millions as a consequence. Fankhauser kept his job in spite of his disastrous and short-sighted response at the inquest. Clearly whoever had advised him about avoiding any admission of liability and whoever was advising him on public relations had, in my opinion, got it badly wrong. These are strategic decisions, of course. But I believe this one was shortsighted. What a good chief executive should do is not only focus on the legal advice but also

---

* A letter had purportedly been sent by the company; the family never received any written apology.

on the advisors in other areas – public affairs, the brand, what is good for the consumer – and, more importantly, that little guide that is in all of us which is known as the moral compass. Sometimes what might seem to be the right road to go down legally could be a complete disaster in terms of your reputation and corporate and public image; sometimes apologising is the right thing to do. Thomas Cook's management of the tragedy has become a case study in how not to handle a crisis, and I found myself right in the middle of the media storm.

Eventually, Thomas Cook did the right thing. They apologised. On 20 May, Mr Fankhauser told the BBC that he was 'deeply sorry' for the deaths of Christi and Bobby. He said that he personally took responsibility for the way the company had communicated with Christi and Bobby's parents, and that he regretted his answer to my questions at the inquest that Thomas Cook had done 'nothing wrong'. The next day, Mr Fankhauser had a three-hour meeting with the children's parents. They saw the family right, so in the end Thomas Cook went some way to make amends for their callous and unfeeling actions. But only *in the end*. I suppose, though, it was better than never at all.

Postscript

Following the inquest, the senior coroner David Hinchliff's report called for the immediate implementation of a publicly accessible register where holiday tour operators would be legally required to keep up-to-date information on all gas and heating appliances at all hotels and holiday homes. He recommended that the relevant UK government department should consult, draft, instigate and implement EU legislation on gas installations and carbon monoxide safety, and introduce common minimal standards for all hotels, apartments and other holiday premises.

The coroner also recommended that more clear and accessible public information was needed to educate the public about the dangers of carbon monoxide poisoning and said that there should be publicity campaigns to encourage tourists to take portable carbon monoxide detectors on holiday. In addition, 'The industry should endeavour to regulate itself by introducing improvements in the health and safety of holidaymakers', and that Thomas Cook 'should be at the forefront of such initiatives to create industry-wide protocols and initiatives on the lines that legislation would introduce, should that ever occur.'

A Thomas Cook spokeswoman said:

> Everyone at Thomas Cook was shocked and deeply saddened by the tragic loss of Robert and Christianne Shepherd in 2006. Thomas Cook recognises that the pain caused by this terrible accident will never go away and must be still very hard for friends and family to bear.
>
> The systems which were in place in 2006, which were intended to prevent such a tragedy, have since been thoroughly revised and address the criticisms made by the jury. Thomas Cook works with dedicated specialist external health and safety experts to audit holiday properties. The health and safety of our customers is of paramount importance and we continuously review and strive to improve all our procedures.

The Thomas Cook Group entered compulsory liquidation in September 2019, having made losses of £1.5 billion in that year. In November 2019, Fosun International announced that it had acquired the Thomas Cook brand and a number of its hotel properties for £11 million. Thomas Cook UK relaunched in 2020.

39

THE BIRMINGHAM PUB BOMBINGS

'Someone has to fight for them; someone has to
speak on their behalf, because they're not here to do
it themselves . . . It doesn't matter how much time
has passed.'

Julie Hambleton, sister of Maxine Hambleton, who died in
the Birmingham bombings aged eighteen

'Nobody ever apologised to us. [. . .] What
happened thirty years ago was a disaster. People
say twenty-one people lost their lives that day.
What about the six men who went to prison? We
lost our lives also. I felt sorry for what happened in
Birmingham that night, but people must remember
I done sixteen-and-a-half years in prison for
something I did not do.'

John Walker of the Birmingham Six, reflecting on the
Birmingham pub bombings, 2004

Five years after the start of the Troubles in Northern Ireland,
in 1973, the Provisional IRA extended its murderous campaign
to mainland Britain. A year later in 1974, the mainland suffered

an average of one terrorist attack – whether 'successful' or not – every three days.

Prior to a bombing of any civilian targets, the Provisional IRA's MO was the delivery of an anonymous telephone warning issued to the media or the police, which included a confidential code word, known only to the Provisional IRA and to the emergency services, that verified that the threat was real. At 8.11 p.m. on 21 November 1974, an unidentified man with a pronounced Irish accent called the *Birmingham Post*. He said explosive devices had been planted in the iconic Rotunda building, a 25-storey office block with the Mulberry Bush pub on its lower two floors, and at a tax office, both in the busy city-centre New Street.

Six minutes later, at 8.17 p.m., the first bombs went off in the Mulberry Bush pub. In the nearby Tavern in the Town, a pub in the basement below the New Street Tax Office, people enjoying a night out heard the sound as only a 'muffled thump' and carried on drinking, unperturbed.* Ten minutes later, at 8.27 p.m., just as police arrived and started trying to clear the premises, a second explosion blasted through the pub. At 9.15 p.m., a third bomb, concealed inside two plastic bags, was found in the doorway of a Barclays Bank on Hagley Road. It was set to detonate at 11.00 p.m. but failed to go off.

That night, twenty-one people lost their lives and almost two hundred others suffered grave injury, including many casualties who lost limbs. The blasts were so violent that several of the dead were blown through a brick wall. A number had been impaled by sections of wooden furniture, some ravaged by shrapnel, others had their clothes and skin burned off their bodies. The majority of the dead and injured were young

---

* Dominic Sandbrook, *Seasons in the Sun: The Battle for Britain, 1974–1979* (London: Allen Lane, April 2012), p.166.

people, aged between seventeen and thirty years old. For the people of Birmingham, it was to be remembered as the 'darkest day' in their city's history.

An inquest into the Birmingham pub bombing deaths was opened in the week following the attack, but was adjourned while the criminal investigation was ongoing. The police immediately blamed the IRA for the atrocity, although there had been no formal acknowledgement of responsibility from the terrorist organisation, and within hours of the explosions, five Irishmen were arrested at Heysham port while they waited to board the ferry for Northern Ireland. A sixth Irish man was shortly arrested in Birmingham. In spite of the lack of any reliable forensic evidence to link the six men to the explosives used in the attack, they were charged with twenty-one counts of murder and conspiring with another IRA member to plant bombs across the Midlands between August and November of that year. At the end of their 45-day trial at Lancaster Crown Court in 1975, all six were found guilty and sentenced to life imprisonment for the bombings.

On 27 November, the Labour home secretary Roy Jenkins introduced the Prevention of Terrorism Act 1974, which he described as 'draconian measures unprecedented in peacetime'. It became law two days later. The Act 'to proscribe organisations concerned in terrorism, and to give power to exclude certain persons from Great Britain or the United Kingdom in order to prevent acts of terrorism, and for connected purposes'* banned any member of the IRA from residing or travelling to mainland Britain, and granted the police there the right to arrest, detain and question people for up to seven days if they were suspected of the 'commission, preparation or instigation

* Prevention of Terrorism (Temporary Provisions) Act 1974.

of an act of terrorism' on British soil.* If guilt was proven, the Act allowed for their immediate deportation to either Northern Ireland or Eire. The 1974 Act remained in force until it was superseded by the Terrorism Act in July 2000.

The 'Birmingham Six' continued vehemently to protest their innocence, reiterating that they had never been members of the IRA. They asserted that they had been coerced into making false confessions after being subjected to severe physical and psychological abuse – which amounted to torture – at the hands of the West Midlands Police. By the mid-'80s serious doubts were being placed on the reliability of their confessions and thus their convictions. The civil rights lawyer Gareth Peirce, along with QCs Mike Mansfield and Tony Gifford, worked tirelessly to prove their innocence, supported by politicians including Sir John Farr and Chris Mullin, the investigative journalist and Labour MP. In 1985 Chris Mullin joined the investigative documentary team on ITV's *World in Action* as a researcher. Several editions of the programme were devoted to the Birmingham Six case, dismantling the evidence on which they had been convicted and thereby casting serious doubt on the men's guilt. A *World in Action* programme also named four suspects; the production team backed their decision to air those names stating that it was '100 per cent sure' they were the true perpetrators, and also said they knew the identity of a fifth bomber. In 1986, in his book *Error of Judgement: The Truth About the Birmingham Bombings*, Chris Mullin claimed to have made contact with the Provisional IRA who gave him access to the higher echelons of the IRA army council and had managed to trace and speak to the actual bombers responsible for the atrocity. It was undoubtedly an excellent piece of journalism in

---

* Ibid., 3:3.

which he painstakingly demonstrated that the West Midlands Police had put six innocent men behind bars for life. Pressure mounted on the government to review the conviction and, in 1990, the prolonged Birmingham Six campaign succeeded, finally, in bringing their case to appeal.

After sixteen years in prison – during which an appeal to have their sentences overturned had been dismissed, many more books written, documentary and Hollywood blockbuster films made, and newspaper articles published – fresh forensic and other evidence had come to light. Eventually, in March 1991, the six men's convictions were declared 'unsafe and unsatisfactory' and quashed by the Court of Appeal. I was in my first year of practice at Garden Court Chambers, having just left Wellington Street the previous summer. I remember the jubilation at this result. The establishment had been taken on and the underdog had been delivered justice; six innocent men who had been badly beaten and maltreated, and had spent years in prison for offences they had not committed, were free at last. This was national news. Indeed, it even made international headlines.

With the Birmingham Six proven innocent, the criminal investigation was reopened, led by Ron Hadfield, the then chief constable for the West Midlands, and the director of public prosecutions (DPP), Barbara Mills.

In 1993, five West Midlands Police officers were charged with perverting the course of justice in connection with their role in the investigation into the Birmingham Six. Yet after a judge ruled that it would be impossible for them to obtain a fair trial, no officer ever faced a criminal prosecution.

By April 1994, Ron Hadfield and Barbara Mills' reinvestigation had concluded. A team of at least forty officers had generated a mountain of paperwork, compiling over 5,000 documents, statements and reports, and yet they decided that there was insufficient evidence to bring proceedings against any individual, adding that the Crown Prosecution Service couldn't submit any additional reasonable lines of inquiry that should have been, or yet could, be 'usefully pursued'.

At the time of the DPP's announcement, Julie Hambleton and the other bereaved family members found themselves frustrated once more. Julie expressed her anger, telling BBC News, 'Isn't it the job of the police to go out and find new evidence? They just seem to be waiting for it to drop on their desks.'

It is odd to reflect how these events were happening in my lifetime. I was just nine years old at the time of the bombings, but I remember the fear they generated. In 1981, sixteen years old and working at Jean Jeanie in Oxford Street, I remember the IRA's Christmas bombing campaign, how the shop would be closed after reported warnings of an attack and how fearful we all were about travelling into central London, particularly during the holiday season. When Chris Mullin first wrote his book in the mid-'80s, I was at law school in Kingston. In the early '90s, by the time the campaign to acquit the Birmingham Six led by Gareth Peirce, Chris Mullin, Mike Mansfield and Tony Gifford was in full stream, I had just joined Wellington Street, where Tony, my head of chambers, was leading this case in the Court of Appeal.

This was right at the beginning of my career at the Bar and I didn't dream then that, almost thirty years later, we would be examining the Birmingham bombings case afresh – nor could I have imagined that, in a sense, I would be taking up the fight for justice where my esteemed colleague and mentor Tony Gifford QC had left off.

In early 2018, along with Tom Stoate, another fantastic former pupil of mine from Garden Court, Kevin Morgan and Malachy McGowan of the Bar of Northern Ireland, I was instructed by KRW Law LLP in Belfast to represent ten of the families whose loved ones had died in the bombings at the reopened inquest. It was a huge case and a monumental responsibility for me and my team.

Malachy McGowan and Kevin Morgan were from Belfast, where they were in independent practice at the Bar of Northern Ireland, but they did a significant amount of work for Kevin Winters/KRW Law, a firm specialising in criminal law and human rights practice that does a lot of work relating to and arising out of the Troubles. These two young Irish barristers were simply brilliant advocates and I learned so much from them, not least about Irish and British history, of which I was particularly ignorant. Malachy and Kevin lived through the Troubles and would bring the 1980s alive for me. Both were schoolboys at the time and remembered clearly the conflict before the Good Friday Agreement was signed. During the course of this case, patiently and with good humour, they educated me about the politics of their homeland and I am hugely appreciative of those lessons.

As history had shown, the Birmingham Six were not responsible for planting the bombs in the Mulberry Bush and the Tavern in the Town. At the time of the reopening of the inquest on 11 February 2019, no one had been found responsible for the attack, no one had been arrested, and no one had admitted planting the bombs that took twenty-one lives. The families of the victims and the survivors wanted answers.

My clients, the families of the twenty-one victims, said that these men were scapegoats. They had spent sixteen years after the tragedy thinking that justice had been done; there had been a murder trial and the six, they believed, had been rightfully convicted. When they were acquitted, the families asked the obvious question: *So who did it?* And, given that the names of the true perpetrators as revealed on *World in Action* had been circulating since the mid-'80s, why had the West Midlands Police not pursued any arrests? The families' grief was now compounded by anger at the fact that the real murderers had simply walked away from the carnage scot-free. The families had never seen justice for the loss of their loved ones – it was my job to see that the inquest delivered some measure of closure.

A lot of the parents of the victims are now dead, but their siblings are still alive. My client Julie Hambleton and her brother Brian lost their eighteen-year-old sister Maxine in the Tavern in the Town explosion. She had only called into the pub to hand out invitations to friends for her housewarming party, and was killed seconds later. It was thought that she had been standing directly beside the bomb when it exploded. Her friend, Jane Davis, was also killed in the blast. Jane had gone to the basement pub to look at her holiday snaps, which she had picked up from the chemist earlier that afternoon. She was just seventeen.

Julie Hambleton is simply amazing. An attractive blond woman with a warm smile and dulcet Brummie accent who worked in Higher Education, Julie was as sharp as a tack and strategic with it. She had become hardened by years of prevarication and nonsense and was determined to get justice for Maxine and the other families. An obvious leader and seen as a leading light by the other families of the victims, Julie is simply one of the most dauntless clients I've ever had. When she got angry, she told it as she saw it, with raw honesty. In 2011, she and Brian had set up a campaign called 'Justice for the 21' to protest the fact that in the absence of significant new leads about the 1974 terrorist attack the West Midlands police were making no effort to actively establish the true perpetrators of the horrific bombings. 'Someone has to fight for them,' Julie said. 'Someone has to speak on their behalf, because they're not here to do it themselves . . . It doesn't matter how much time has passed.'

One has to wonder at the competence of the West Midlands Police to lead any effective or meaningful historical investigation into the bombings. However, in a meeting in 2014, the chief constable of the West Midlands had told the 'Justice for the 21' campaigners that thirty-five pieces of evidence from the original 1974 inquiry were now missing, including the bomb which had been discovered at Hagley Road and was subsequently safely destroyed in a controlled explosion.

Although the IRA had never formally admitted responsibility for the bombings, in 2014 a former senior member of the organisation had confessed to its involvement.* After forty-five years of mourning, campaigning, fundraising, legal applications and argument, the families of the victims were adamant that the reopened inquest should investigate the identity of the true perpetrators of the bombing. In July 2018, however, Sir Peter Thornton QC, the former chief coroner for England and Wales, ruled that establishing the names of the alleged perpetrators did not fall within the scope and structure of his inquiry. On behalf of the families, we appealed the decision, but were not successful in broadening the scope of the inquest: in September 2018, the Lord Chief Justice upheld the coroner's decision and ruled that the question of identifying precisely who the bombers were would not form part of proceedings. Even though I did not agree with all the decisions he made on the Birmingham case, I found Sir Peter fair.

The inquest lasted six weeks and was heard before a jury at

---

* In 2017, one of the alleged perpetrators, Michael Hayes, claimed that the objective of the bombings had not been to harm civilians; he said the twenty-one deaths had been caused by an unintended delay (due to a telephone box being out of order) in delivering the IRA's customary advance warning to security services.

the Birmingham Civil Justice Centre, just a minute's walk away from where the two bombs exploded. This was the first time I had spent any significant time in Birmingham. The legal team at KRW solicitors booked self-service apartments for Kevin, Malachy, Tom and me. For the next six weeks we would work closely with each other. Every evening, we would have a team meeting and review the day's evidence and what was to come on the following day. We worked effectively, dividing up tasks as to who would be questioning or leading the attack on witnesses we considered to be hostile. We all worked incredibly hard, because each of the clients meant so much to us. They had waited so long for justice and saw this as their last real attempt to secure it. Mindful of the coroner's ruling on the scope of the inquests, we decided to hold nothing back in going for broke to try to ascertain the truth. In my questions to some of the key witnesses, I sailed as close to the wind as I thought I could and managed this feat without intervention from the coroner.

Our task was mammoth. Over 28,000 pieces of evidence were disclosed. Witnesses included survivors of the bombings and civilian eyewitnesses, police officers, the emergency response crew and former members of the IRA. Sir Peter Thornton QC called for a minute's silence at the opening of the hearings, then pen portraits of each of the twenty-one dead were read to the court. Later, during the first week of the inquest, we and the jury made the short walk to the sight of the bombings and in court we were shown film footage and photographs of the wreckage in the aftermath of the explosions.

Giving evidence, one of the survivors, David Grafton, who was twenty years old in 1974, told the court that on the night of the attack he had gone to the Tavern in the Town a few minutes after 8 o'clock. He chatted briefly to Maxine Hambleton, then went to the bar to buy a drink:

'I picked the glass up and then there was a flashing light and a boom and next thing I know I'm lying on the floor, not knowing where I was. Total blackness, quiet, not a sound. Then screaming and pandemonium,' he said. David was one of the lucky ones; he escaped with just two perforated eardrums.

The inquest heard that the IRA attack on the two pubs was carried out at the same time as the remains of James McDade, an IRA bomber who had died a week earlier as he planted a bomb at the Coventry telephone exchange, were being transported from Coventry mortuary to Elmdon airport to be flown back to Ireland. Fearing unrest along the route, 135 city centre police officers had been deployed to follow the cortege; in total, West Midlands Police had gathered 1,680 uniformed officers from across the force for the operation. On the night of the bombings, therefore, only fifteen police officers remained in Birmingham city centre. The former counter-terrorism chief, Anthony Mole, read from an official police report on the bombings written by a force superintendent to the court: it said that the first police officers to be pulled back from the McDade funeral procession had left only after the Aer Lingus flight carrying McDade's body took off at 8.30 p.m. The extra officers arrived at the scene at 9.10 p.m. – a full fifty-nine minutes after the warning call was received. The diminished police presence, however, had 'in no way affected the organisation and efficiency of the police at the scenes,' the report said.

I challenged that assessment.

Earlier, I had asked Mr Mole if he agreed that the 1974 IRA bombing campaign in mainland Britain had focused on 'soft targets', which were largely counting upon the police and security services to protect them. He agreed, but added that it was also the responsibility of the wider public and businesses to protect themselves, although he could not speak for the standards of 1974.

'I am not going to have that, Mr Mole,' I said. 'It doesn't matter if it was 1974 or 2019, we would expect professionals to deal with that situation. The highest priority of any police officer is to protect life and limb. [. . .] The threat was high. The threat was serious. The threats were obvious. The night of the pub bombings was both a late shopping night and payday.'

Mr Mole agreed.

We heard testimony from Kieron Conway, another witness with links to the IRA. He attended the inquest via video link from Dublin. A former IRA 'Director of Intelligence', Mr Conway is now a criminal and human rights solicitor in Dublin, and is said to have left the IRA twice: first in 1975 – before he re-joined in 1981 – and then finally in 1993. This man was an admitted terrorist, an apologist for the IRA who had spent time in jail for committing a number of armed robberies to fund their paramilitary activities. He didn't think he or his comrades had done anything wrong. My line of questioning was therefore to force some kind of admission of remorse from him, and perhaps even an admission of guilt and an apology to the families on behalf of the IRA. I put to him that the bombings represented a moral depravity. Mr Conway refused to accept this, answering, 'You want me to say it's murder and I won't say that.'

I pressed Mr Conway about the identity of the bombers, but he only admitted to knowing two of the IRA men involved, Mick Murray and James Gavin, both of whom had died in the years since the attack. 'Beyond that, I have no personal knowledge of who carried out these bombings,' Mr Conway claimed.

'You have blood on your hands,' I replied. 'You have never come forward with the names of the killers.'

In one of the most dramatic turns in this highly charged inquest, on 22 March, an individual known only as 'Witness

O', who also claimed to know the names of the bombers, gave his testimony via video link from Ireland, his face obscured to protect his anonymity so we could only hear his voice. In answering questions from the counsel for the coroner, Mr Peter Skelton QC, Witness O said that the intended aim of the mainland bombing campaign was to 'put pressure on the British government'. When asked if the aim of the IRA bombs was to injure civilians, Witness O said that they 'were warned about that'. The IRA, he said, didn't 'go planting a bomb in a petrol station' or a housing estate, because if 'you injure civilians, it is bad publicity'. Witness O insisted that the IRA had given adequate warnings to MI5 at least an hour before the high-explosive devices detonated. In other words, he would have the jury believe that it wasn't the IRA's fault that twenty-one people lost their lives and over 200 were injured when they had planted two bombs of high magnitude in two busy pubs in the heart of Birmingham's city centre at peak time on a payday night. Instead, he held, the carnage was the fault of the UK security forces, because the IRA had supposedly given ample notice.

Earlier, Witness O had told the court that about six months earlier, he had been approached by a senior IRA member who gave him permission to give evidence at the inquest and to also name the people responsible for the pub bombings. In my cross-examination, therefore, I tried to establish the name of the IRA member he had met with. However, Witness O said he wouldn't give the name because it was the present head of the IRA. 'He's in charge of me,' he told the jury. '[. . .] I could be shot dead if it got out.'

After some prompting, Witness O confirmed the names of three of the men involved in the bombings in 1974: Seamus McLoughlin, the IRA commanding officer who had selected the targets, Mick Murray and James Gavin. But he refused to confirm the identity of a fourth man. I suggested that Witness O was protecting a man he knew to be responsible for planting the bombs, claiming that he was 'harmless now'.

I urged Witness O to acknowledge that what happened in Birmingham was an atrocity. I then pressed him to acknowledge that those IRA bombers were guilty of causing the loss of twenty-one lives in November 1974. The families of the dead deserved to hear the truth from this former IRA member.

'In this courtroom there are several members of the twenty-one families,' I said. 'These people are all in pain, suffering, and they have been in pain for the last forty-four years. Let me ask you, can you understand their pain?'

'Yes, I can.'

'Can you also understand that the passage of time does not dull that pain, that pain still burns brightly. Can you understand that?'

'Yes.'

'Can you also understand this next proposition: justice must be seen to be done. Can you understand that principle?'

'I understand it, yes.'

Finally, after further prolonged and tortuous questioning, Witness O confirmed the fourth IRA bomber's name: Michael Hayes. 'Hayes. Hayes, I will give that to you now. Hayes. But he can't be arrested. There is nobody going to be charged with this atrocity because the British government have signed an agreement with the IRA to get the . . . to get the ceasefire,' Witness O asserted. (He was, of course, mistaken in his understanding of the terms of Good Friday Agreement. There is no immunity from prosecution for past crimes relating to the Troubles that *have not been tried*.)

This testimony was extraordinary on several accounts.

Firstly, when Witness O stated he had been approached by a senior IRA member who had granted him permission to give evidence at the inquest, he wasn't talking about the *Real IRA* or some other more recent splinter terrorist organisation. He was talking about the Provisional IRA. But under the Good Friday Agreement there shouldn't be *any* terrorists. Both the loyalist Ulster Volunteer Force and the Provisional IRA were disbanded under the Good Friday Agreement – and here Witness O was, claiming in an open court that six months earlier he'd been speaking to *the head* of that same now-outlawed and supposedly 'former' republican paramilitary organisation. And secondly, he might have chosen to prevaricate and obfuscate as best he could, but Witness O knew *all* of the bombers, and eventually, giving evidence under oath as a witness in a British court, he had actually spoken the name of the fourth perpetrator. You could have heard a pin drop.

Later, when Chris Mullin MP gave evidence, I was merciless and unrelenting in my cross-examination. The last chapters of his *Error of Judgement* were based on a series of interviews that he had conducted between 1985 and 1986 with members of the IRA and others. He had also met with Gerry Adams and Danny Morrison, the press officer of Sinn Féin, the political wing of the Provisional IRA. Mr Mullin therefore knew who the bombers were and he refused to name them in court. He had promised the IRA men who carried out the bombings not to reveal their identities while they were alive – but these were *IRA murderers* and it meant that they had walked free. It was out of some kind of journalistic code of honour, I suppose, but to the ears of the families of the victims who had spent forty-four years waiting to hear the truth about the murders of their loved ones, those were pretty hollow words. And bearing in mind that the six innocent men he'd campaigned for had been released, why protect the guilty? 'The families are getting older and some have passed away. More may pass away before long,' I told him. 'You understand that they are angry and astonished that you will not pass on all the information on the murderers you have.' Some journalists do reveal their sources, though in spite of my passionate pleading on behalf of the families, Chris Mullin decided not to.

After six weeks of intense and sometimes traumatic evidence, on 5 April, the jury of eleven found that a botched advance IRA telephone warning contributed to, or caused, the twenty-one deaths. There had been no error or omission in the police response to the given warning call which might have limited the loss of life.

Postscript

In an interview with ITV News on 5 April, 2019, Michael Hayes strongly denied any involvement with the attacks in Birmingham, which he described as a 'commercial bombing campaign'. Questioned about his comrades' role in the attack, Mr Hayes replied he did not 'have the right' to comment because 'these men had families'.

Following the inquest, members of the 'Justice for the 21' campaign called for an independent judge-led statutory inquiry under the Inquiries Act 2005, arguing that this was now the only remaining mechanism by which to conduct an Article 2 compliant investigation into the 1974 Birmingham bombings.

This view was endorsed by Andy Street, the Conservative mayor of the Combined West Midlands Authority, who said: 'I've come to the conclusion that the time is now right for a panel-led, open public inquiry into what happened here that night [. . .] because, just as with the Hillsborough tragedy, my view now is that only a public inquiry can provide the answers that the families deserve.'

Christopher Stanley for KRW LAW LLP, who continued to support the victims' families, said:

The recent inquest was limited in its scope. The current West Midlands Police investigation is undermined by its appearance of lack of independence and previous failings. A statutory inquiry has long been seen by us and those we represent as a mechanism to investigate all the surrounding circumstances of the night of 21 November 1974 in Birmingham. A public inquiry has been endorsed by senior politicians in Ireland and no matter which political party assumes office after 12th December it should be incumbent on them to establish this inquiry into the worst peacetime atrocity in Britain.

To date, despite a meeting with Home Secretary Priti Patel, the families have had no success in securing a public inquiry.

40

A CASE OF POLITICS: THE DEATH OF CARL SARGEANT (1968–2017)

In my thirty-years at the Bar as a civil rights advocate, the very nature of my job is to act for the small person in cases against the state. For the most part, that means taking on the police force, Her Majesty's prison service, or the NHS institutions charged with the care of the mentally ill at their most vulnerable. And while, yes, individual police officers, prison wardens or NHS services' employees may be implicated as *agents* of the state, for the most part the state is felt as a nebulous entity, all-present yet disembodied. In the case of the death of Carl Sargeant, however, I was to engage in an almighty battle involving one of the state's representatives at the highest level of power: the first minister of the devolved government of Wales.

On Tuesday 7 November 2017, Carl Sargeant, a long-serving and much-loved Labour MP and member of the Welsh assembly, was found dead at his home on a council estate in Connah's Quay, Flintshire. Carl, who was forty-nine, hanged himself four days after being sacked after unspecified allegations about his inappropriate conduct with a number of women in the Labour Party were passed to the Welsh first minister Carwyn Jones.

The dismissal – at the same time as the #MeToo scandal was

exploding in many areas of public life, including Westminster – was sudden. Mr Sargeant was called into the first minister's office in Cardiff on Friday 3 November and in a ten-minute meeting was told of his sacking pending an investigation. Two hours later Carl was also suspended by the Labour Party. He was never given any details of the supposed incidents of inappropriate behaviour towards women, but he strongly denied any wrongdoing and had told his wife that he was determined to clear his name.

Carl had served as a Welsh assembly member for more than fourteen years. He was first elected as Labour assembly member for Alyn and Deeside in 2003 and after the 2007 election had been appointed chief whip and deputy minister for assembly business for the Labour administration. Following the 2016 national assembly election until the time of his dismissal, he had worked as cabinet secretary for communities and children.

An affable and extremely popular politician, Carl had ambitions of one day becoming first minister. He led the Welsh government's response to the Grenfell Tower disaster in 2017. He also campaigned tirelessly against domestic violence.

Carl and his wife Bernie Sargeant had met in the Labour club in Connah's Quay and they had two children, Lucy and Jack. Carl's family and friends strongly believed that the way his dismissal was handled had left him in despair. Bernie said that he was 'shell shocked, destroyed', and she was angry at the lack of human decency and care provided to him immediately afterwards.

At the news that Carl had taken his own life, the Senedd was in shock. Tributes praising his stalwart contribution to Welsh politics were paid across the political divide. Friends, to whom he was known as 'Sarge', hailed him as a unique and authentic politician who never forgot his working-class roots, remembering how this 'gentle giant' had taken up crochet to pass the time on long train journeys, attracting curious stares as he worked on 'dainty pink baby bonnets'. At the time of his death he was in the middle of a new project – making a dress for his wife Bernie.

There was also, however, growing anger and concern among some assembly members at the manner of Carl's dismissal. Some senior Labour politicians shared Bernie's outrage that neither the Welsh government nor the Labour Party appeared to have exercised their duty of care over Carl after he was faced with accusations about his behaviour. On the morning of his death, he had told a number of his colleagues that he still did not know what the allegations were.

Meanwhile, there was speculation of a leak from the 'fifth floor', the Ministerial Floor in Tŷ Hywel, the Welsh Parliament's office building. It was alleged that in a potential breach of codes of conduct covering ministers, civil servants and/or special advisors, a number of people outside the government – including members of the media – had known about Carl's sacking before he had even been informed. In a blog post, one former minister wrote of a culture of 'toxic bullying, intimidation and exclusion' in the Welsh government.[*] The author claimed that Mr Sargeant had earlier been subjected to bullying and disinformation in the Assembly, and that this had placed 'a strain on his and others' mental health'. In Assembly Questions at the Senedd after Carl's death, the first minister denied all knowledge of any bullying allegations having been made.

According to the former Plaid Cymru Assembly Member Rhodri Glyn Thomas, Carl 'clearly felt he had been found

---

[*] Leighton Andrews, *Wales Online*, 4 December 2017.

guilty before he had a chance to defend himself'. The then Labour leader Jeremy Corbyn also voiced his concern about how Carwyn Jones had handled the misconduct allegations and Mr Sargeant's subsequent sacking. The implications of a potential leak from the fifth floor were equally disquieting.

In a statement, Carwyn Jones defended his actions, stating that, once he had received insinuations of inappropriate touching or groping by one of his ministers, he had had no alternative but to dismiss him. But such was the sense of outrage over Carl's suicide that many felt that the first minister's future could be on the line.

Bernie called for a public inquiry into the suspected leak and the way her husband had been treated. The following day, the first minister announced that an independent investigation into his actions would take place, led by Permanent Secretary Dame Shan Morgan, the Welsh government's top civil servant.

In 2018, Neil Hudgell of Hudgell Solicitors instructed me to represent Carl's family at the inquest. Neil also instructed me to represent Bernie and their son Jack on the inquiry which had been opened at the same time. Neil trusted me to get the right team together and asked who I would recommend as a good junior. As there were serious employment-type issues to be considered in the handling of Mr Sargeant's dismissal and treatment, I decided to bring on board some outside chambers help, namely a talented young barrister called Sheryn Omeri from Cloisters Chambers. Despite the fact she had little inquest or inquiry experience, Sheryn is a gifted, hardworking advocate who is also extremely tenacious. I knew she would be the perfect junior to work alongside me on this case. And from the moment I brought her on board, Sheryn impressed with her workload and output. What she lacked in specific knowledge, she more than made up for with her legal research skills and extraordinary acumen. As an Australian living and practising in the UK and a fierce defender of equality and human rights issues, Sheryn also brought a different perspective to the table. It was a pleasure to work with her and, if I am honest, it was great to be working alongside another person of colour.

The inquest opened on 28 November before Coroner John Gittins at Ruthin Coroner's Court in North Wales. During the first week of the hearings, the coroner heard evidence from a number of witnesses including the then first minister of Wales, and former barrister, Carwyn Jones.

Mr Jones told the inquest that he believed it would have been wrong for him to give any male cabinet member details of allegations made by women about his behaviour before he sacked him because it risked exposing the identities of the women who had made the complaints. When questioned about his duty of care toward Carl, Mr Jones said that although he had known Carl for sixteen years and considered him a friend, he had not been aware that Carl had suffered mental health difficulties. He had not contacted Carl over the weekend after his dismissal because he thought it would be inappropriate to do so. Instead, he said that Ann Jones, a veteran Labour politician and assembly member, had been assigned a formal pastoral role for Carl and had been asked to stay in touch with Carl in the wake of his sacking. The first minister said that he had spoken to Ann Jones at some point over that weekend. This turned out not to be true: a statement from Ann Jones that contradicted Mr Jones's testimony was read to the court: there was no formal support system of duty of care for sacked ministers.

Carwyn Jones gave evidence that he had told Carl to be careful about his behaviour in 2014, three years before his death, after receiving an anonymous letter in which the author claimed he was not 'fit to be around women'. In May

2016, Mr Jones claimed, another woman had come forward to make complaints about Mr Sargeant. Further alleged incidents involving 'unwelcome attention' were said to have taken place in the summer of 2017. Neither Mr Jones nor his advisors had spoken to Carl Sargeant to hear his side of the story, but when one of the women lodged a written statement in early November 2017, the first minister had decided he had no option but to sack Carl. In response, the coroner told Carwyn Jones that he was struggling to understand why he had not spoken directly to Carl as a friend.

Then, in a twist at the end of Carwyn Jones's evidence, there was what the Sargeant family believe was an attempt to smear Carl's name, when tragically he could no longer defend himself. This is a tactic that I have seen so often in inquests when evidence or witnesses are called upon in order to destroy the character of the deceased. If, for instance, credibility is at the heart of a case, such tactics are sometimes justified. I personally was not convinced in this instance. As advocates for the court, we also have to be careful about making allegations which might damage families and loved ones. In this case, in my opinion, the allegations seemed so peripheral that I struggled to see the relevance of what was being sought to be introduced in the hearings. The information was particularly hurtful to Carl's family, and the timing was, if I am being generous, most unfortunate. We had been in hearings for nearly a week. On the last day, when we were coming close to the end of the evidence, the first minister's legal team told the court about texts purportedly sent by a prominent North Wales councillor containing allegations about Carl.

Arguing that the texts could provide an insight into Carl's state of mind at the time of his death, Carwyn Jones's legal team asked for the author of these texts and other witnesses to be called, but the coroner – in my opinion quite correctly – refused. The coroner described the text evidence as 'rumour, multiple hearsay and speculation' and ruled that it was not required.

The first minister, unhappy with the coroner's decision not to admit the evidence, decided to take the matter to judicial review. The inquest was subsequently adjourned to allow a legal challenge to be made and the family had to endure months of uncertainty until the matter was heard.

At a High Court hearing in Cardiff in May 2019, Carwyn Jones's lawyers claimed that the failure to hear evidence relating to the text messages meant that the inquest was not a 'full, fair and fearless investigation'. The judge Lord Justice Haddon-Cave dismissed the first minister's appeal.

On 8 July, the inquest resumed. The now-former first minister – Carwyn Jones had stepped down in December 2018, saying that he had been through the 'darkest of times' since Carl Sargeant's death – was recalled, along with Ann Jones, who was the first to give evidence. She told the court that she had not been given a formal role to care for Carl. She said that on the night after his sacking, she had received a text message from Matt Greenough, the first minister's special advisor, asking her to give Carl 'a bell' over the weekend. Ms Jones said that she had rung and messaged Carl but hadn't heard from him until Monday 6 November, the evening before his death, when he had sent her several texts. In one message read to the court, Carl had written, 'I still have no idea of the allegation detail, all we know is off the BBC what the first minister briefed. Bastards. I'm telling no one again I'm thinking of running for first minister.'

Carwyn Jones had telephoned her only on the day after Carl's death. She told the inquest, 'He said that he was going to say to the press that he had asked me to provide a caring role to Carl. I remember saying to him: "Don't do that, that's not what my understanding was."'

The former first minister Carwyn Jones was next to give evidence. In a fiery exchange, I put it to him that he had not been truthful about the care measures he had put in place after Carl was sacked. Contrary to the evidence he had previously given at the first hearing, I suggested that he had *not* spoken to Ann Jones over the weekend prior to Carl's death at all. Mr Jones pivoted in his evidence, but insisted that his previous evidence had been a 'mistake' rather than a lie.

Carl's brother Andy, questioning Mr Jones on behalf of other family members, told him, 'For me, Mr Jones, [. . .] your statement isn't a mistake, it's a damage-limitation exercise.'

The coroner said he would make a judgment on Carwyn Jones's credibility, telling him, 'Either you were mistaken in what you said to me or I was misled, and perhaps deliberately so, with a view to some type of PR that made your position somewhat more tenable.' In the end the coroner concluded that Jones had 'erred' rather than lied. Mr Gittins said that while it may have been appropriate for Jones not to give Carl details of the allegations against him, there was nothing, however, to prevent the first minister or anyone from his office contacting him over the weekend following his sacking. Nobody had. The first minister admitted that no measures had been put in place formally since Carl Sargeant's death, adding that politics was a 'brutal business' and asking rhetorically whether police officers had a duty of care to someone who had been arrested and named, commenting, 'Where does it end?'

Coroner Gittins replied: 'It shouldn't end, we're talking about people's lives.'

The following day, Carl's widow Bernie told an inquest that her husband felt 'destroyed'. He had been left guessing at the detail of the allegations, could not defend himself and he had been left high and dry, without support from any one of his former colleagues. 'He was quiet. Carl's not a quiet person. You could feel this had come as a terrible shock to him. [. . .] He was desperate for information. No support was offered to him. He was shell-shocked.' She criticised Carwyn Jones over a television interview the day before Carl died in which he had referred to the claims of inappropriate behaviour as 'incidents' rather than allegations. Bernie said that this implicit acceptance by the first minister of her husband's guilt had only fuelled his despair; Carl had turned a 'strange colour', she said. 'He saw that as very significant.'

She said that his suspension from the Labour Party had exacerbated his feeling of hopelessness. Over the weekend after his sacking, on 'numerous occasions' Carl had tried to talk to someone at the party headquarters without success. Subsequently, Carl had spent those next couple of days in bed, 'hiding beneath the covers'. Describing how she had found her husband dead, Bernie told the inquest, 'My children have lost their dad. Lessons have got to be learned. I believe we should have had some support. We were out of our league here. [. . .] I wish we could have helped him.'

On 11 July 2019, seven-and-a-half months after its opening, the inquest concluded. The coroner John Gittins recorded a conclusion of suicide. He told the court, 'The twists and turns of the journey at times along the murkiest paths into the world of politics has been a challenge. Anyone hoping for a glowing vindication of Carl Sargeant or a damning vilification of Carwyn Jones, or indeed vice versa, will be sorely disappointed.'

Mr Gittins said the truth of the allegations against Carl had not formed any part of his investigation. An inquest is not a trial. But he stated, 'The absence [. . .] of those allegations at this inquest should in no way be seen as a diminution of the seriousness of these matters.'

The coroner criticised the first minister and his office for the way in which Carl's sacking had been handled, concluding that he did not feel that he had received adequate 'pastoral' care: 'No official arrangements were put into place by way of seeking to provide support to Carl Sargeant despite the probability that the first minister knew of Mr Sargeant's vulnerability in relation to his mental health, and that it is likely that the removal and particularly the reason for the removal would generate significant media interest.'

He told the court that he would write to the Welsh government with his recommendations that better support be provided for high-profile figures when they were sacked. Unless such safeguarding systems were put in place, he warned, there could be further deaths.

Outside court, the family accused the former first minister Carwyn Jones of gravely failing his friend and colleague – and failing to show any contrition. Carl and Bernie's son, Jack, who had since succeeded his father as assembly member for Alyn and Deeside in North Wales, told reporters:

We recognise the 'murkiness' the coroner referred to in his summing up. It's been a thoroughly distressing and dehumanising process that has added to our heartbreak. We are deeply offended by the lack of any remorse or regret from the former first minister. We very much hope that the former first minister will now come forward with a genuine apology. [. . .] Dad was let down by Carwyn Jones. Carwyn Jones said on the stand he was a friend. I can't see myself letting down a friend the way he let down his.

At times it seems to have been forgotten that this was an inquest into the death of a dearly beloved husband, father, son and brother. Instead it has felt more like a criminal trial. All too often politics have been at play with the sole aim of blackening a dead man's name to protect another. Where has been the humanity in that? We sincerely hope that no political family will go through what we have been through these past nineteen months. It's too late for Dad but it may save someone else. We hope that political parties and governments across the union take note and make it policy for safeguarding measures to be in place for all public servants.

Carl's family also expressed dissatisfaction that the first minister's legal costs were funded by the public purse while they were forced to eat into savings in order to fight their corner on Carl's behalf. Neil Hudgell told the collected media reporters, 'We have seen a puppet master that has used the public purse to pursue his own ends without any regard for wider mental health considerations.'

Carwyn Jones issued a statement in which he said: 'The nature of these proceedings has meant that there appeared to be two sides in this matter, and whilst it is right that arguments are tested, the process has driven an unnatural wedge between people who remain united at the very least in their ongoing shock, trauma and grief. Nobody wanted this, and nobody could have foreseen it. Suicide is a shattering experience, and I hope some healing can now begin.'

Postscript

In response to the Coroner's Regulation 28 report to the Welsh government regarding the prevention of future deaths, the new

Welsh first minister, Mark Drakeford, said it would 'consider this carefully and respond in full'. When he announced his first reshuffle, all ministers were reminded of the support services available as assembly members.

The Labour Party said it had made 'very significant' changes to improve safeguarding measures to make sure people who are suspended have access to help. A working group had been charged with examining how allegations and suspensions were approached.

4 1

GRENFELL

'As long as poverty, injustice and gross inequality persist in our world, none of us can truly rest.'

Nelson Mandela

The inquest into Christi and Bobby Shepherd's deaths involving Thomas Cook was a turning point for me as a QC. In an ideal world, there would never be cases like theirs, but it was a landmark case in that it showed how one family's courageous and untiring demand for justice *can* effect lasting change so that similar tragedies might never happen again. For me, this case led to a shift in direction in the type of work I would begin to take on. From concentrating almost exclusively on cases involving the police, police shootings and deaths in custody, I now began to widen my scope to concentrate on representing the small person in cases involving public organisations and the state, as well as the corporate behemoths. The Grenfell Tower Inquiry is very much in that vein.

The tower block near Latimer Road in North Kensington was completed in 1974, as part of the first phase of the new

DO RIGHT AND FEAR NO ONE

Lancaster West Estate. After its most recent refurbishment in 2015–16, carried out by Kensington and Chelsea council and the Tenant Management Organisation (TMO), the building had received new plastic-framed windows and new external cladding with thermal insulation. Just before 1 a.m. on the night of 14 June 2017, a fire broke out in the kitchen of one of the fourth-storey apartments and spread inexorably across the 24-storey structure, causing the deaths of seventy-two of the 293 people who were believed to be in Grenfell Tower that night.

The following morning, television news footage showed how the flames spread up the exterior cladding on one side of the building as firefighters on the ground stood helpless to control the blaze. That day Prime Minister Theresa May announced a public inquiry into the fire, promising that the judge-led investigation would leave no stone unturned. I think she made the right call on that occasion: individual inquests into the deaths of the victims of the fire would be delayed by a criminal investigation, and while the interests of the bereaved families and survivors may often be sidelined in a public inquiry, the scope of a public inquiry is wider than is possible in the inquest setting. Furthermore, a timely and high-profile inquiry can ensure that the government implements its findings immediately. My role as representative of many of the victims' families is to do all I can to make sure that every possible line of inquiry is fairly and rigorously examined, and as I said in my opening statement, 'to pursue doggedly, fearlessly and determinedly the truth, the whole truth and nothing less than the truth as to what happened that night'.

When I discovered that my name hadn't been automatically considered on the initial list of potential briefs for the inquiry, of course I felt a sense of pique at being overlooked, again.

Perhaps it is because of my family's history with the area, and the fact that, were it not for my mother's fear of heights, the Thomas family might well have become residents of Grenfell Tower, that I took the oversight so keenly to heart. The tragedy resonated with me on a very personal level and I feel a strong connection with my clients on this case. The lack of safe, decent and secure social housing and the plight of poor, working-class, and often immigrant, families who through no fault of their own find themselves at the bottom of the property ladder is an issue that has always been close to my heart. The story of many of the residents in Grenfell is the story of my family. After my sister Janet left university, in the 1980s and early '90s while her children were tiny, she worked for a decade in the housing department for the Royal Borough of Kensington and Chelsea and saw first-hand the problems with the housing policy of the Conservative-led council. After finishing university, at the same time as I entered the Bar, my first wife Angela had started her career in social housing, working for a women's housing association in west London near Grenfell.

I was instructed to represent twenty-three clients, including survivors, bereaved family members and loved ones, by Cyrilia Davies Knight of Hudgell Solicitors, Robert Berg of Janes Solicitors, Gary Bromelow of Saunders Solicitors, and Elizabeth Rebello and Rubin Italia of Duncan Lewis Solicitors. At the outset of the Grenfell Inquiry I was assisted by junior counsels Thalia Maragh of Garden Court Chambers and Jamie Burton of Doughty Street Chambers. In total I had a team of at least seven barristers working alongside me, and many, many more solicitors, because each of the individual affected families has their own representation. In my group we now have fourteen solicitors, but there were initially eleven solicitors, so, for that reason, we were called Group Eleven, G11. The inquiry, chaired by Sir Martin Moore-Bick, a retired judge with a background in commercial law, has since been divided into two phases: Phase 1, which addressed the events on the night of the fire, and Phase 2, which is ongoing at the time of writing, and is investigating the wider situation.

At this point in my career, one of the things I am now able and determined to do is to use my public profile and my position as a Queen's Counsel to try to do more good. In the weeks prior to the opening of the Phase 1 hearings, some of the bereaved families and survivors had expressed misgivings about the makeup of the expert witnesses to the inquiry. They had launched a petition calling on Theresa May to install an expert panel from a more diverse range of backgrounds to sit alongside Sir Martin, whom they had also criticised as being out of touch. At the outset of the Grenfell Inquiry at the pre- liminary procedural hearings in December 2017, I delivered an opening statement on behalf of survivors and bereaved families, and used that opportunity to make a point about the lack of diversity in the court:

> I make no apologies for what I'm about to say. One of the things that will not be lost on you, or anybody else that sits on this inquiry . . . you can see most of the victim core par- ticipants . . . because they're sitting right at the back. You couldn't get a more diverse group of people. Now look at the lawyers. Look at the lawyers who represent predominately the corporate core participants. And even to an extent, look at those of us that represent the victim core participants. A fairly homogeneous group, wouldn't you agree, apart from the odd exception here and there? What must [the victim core participants] be thinking in terms of 'are we going to get justice? Do they understand us?'

I then turned to the inquiry team and handed out a list of twenty-five experts from the BAME community as potential panel members. I said, 'This isn't just lip service. This isn't just saying, "I want someone who looks like me, for the sake of someone looking like me." No, it's much more than that.'

> Does this inquiry pass the smell test? What is the smell test on an inquiry such as this? I've already said, 'Look at the suits.' I've already said, 'Look at the victim core participants.' I've asked you to take a long hard look at your panel, your assessors, your team. Ask yourself: does it pass the smell test? Because that relates to perception: do they understand us, do they speak our language? Do they know anything about social housing? How many have lived in a tower block, or a council estate, or in social housing? That affects confidence. Confidence, or lack of it, affects participation. And a lack of participation from the people that matter will affect justice. And a lack of justice is injustice.

That speech touched a nerve; it struck a chord with a lot of people and the video clip went viral.

The purpose of the Grenfell Tower Inquiry is to identify the failures that caused the loss of life and terrible harm to many others. Equally important is that all those responsible for those failures *must* be held to account. The primary focus of investigation was the recent refurbishment to and cladding of the building; the inadequacy of fire safety measures; the alleged gross mismanagement of the building by the Kensington and Chelsea Tenant Management Organisation (the KCTMO, which was funded by the local authority) and others; and the treatment of ordinary citizens by the 'corporates' and public bodies alike.

One of our team's clients told us that the refurbishment had changed the building from being an 'ugly and safe council block' to a 'death trap that looked like a pretty private block'.

As a result of this 'prettification' of the undoubtedly unsightly and unglamourous landmark within a stone's throw of the gentrified environs of Holland Park and Ladbroke Grove, the fire safety of several hundred people had been compromised and yet the London Fire Brigade had simply never been told, still less consulted, about the new cladding on the tower block.

The inquiry proper, which opened in May 2018, is believed to have the largest number of core participants to date, with some 533 survivors, including twenty-one children, bereaved families and friends, and members of the North Kensington community, along with twenty-nine separate organisations. Consequently, as with the Hillsborough inquests, no existing courtroom in London would be able to accommodate the large number of core participants to the inquiry, so Phase 1 was held in an old Gothic building called Holborn Bars just past Chancery Lane. It was a squeeze, to say the least.

Phase 1 dealt with the events on the night of the fire: how, why and where the fire started in the tower block and its subsequent development, the loss of life incurred, how the people in the building that night got out, or failed to get out, and the response of the London Fire Brigade and other emergency services. Before the beginning of evidence, however, over the first two weeks, moving and often heart-breaking pen portraits of the dead were delivered by their bereaved families. Lawyers representing corporate or state bodies tend to be sceptical of such commemorations because they see them as seeking empathy and of little evidential value. But what these arguments fail to appreciate is that the family ought to be at the centre of the investigation. These pen portraits humanise the dead, so they are not seen just as a statistic. As lawyers for the families and survivors, we had therefore fought hard to make sure that this happened, and that proper time was allowed for this important process. We wanted to fix fast in people's minds that no matter how technical and how forensic some of the evidence at the inquiry may become, we are dealing with real people who had real lives, who have suffered real loss and who are in real pain, so that the hearing never lost sight of who they were, where they lived, their connection to the tower, their contribution to the local community. It was nothing less than a powerful testimonial to the dead, but it also provided a vivid sense of the loss of the community which Grenfell Tower represents. We wanted to make sure that when the chair and the inquiry comes to hear the evidence, it can be put in its proper context, that they know the people who are being referred to are not just another statistic, not just another number, not just another dead person.

On Wednesday 6 June, my Garden Court colleague and joint head of chambers Rajiv Menon QC, counsel for Behailu Kebede, in whose flat the fire broke out, made his opening statement on his client's behalf. In the immediate aftermath of the fire, Mr Kebede had found himself mercilessly scapegoated by the media and falsely accused of failing to raise the alarm. Some had even suggested that he was somehow responsible for the fire. But, as my colleague reiterated, Behailu Kebede is 'a good man'. And he did nothing wrong.

My opening statement on behalf of my clients followed thereafter. I won't reproduce the entire speech in full, as anyone interested can refer to it elsewhere, but some elements are worthy of citing here, as in essence, they sum up my involvement, and my emotions regarding the fire that devastated so many lives. I said:

Too many tears have been shed since the tragedy of this fire on 14 June 2017. Many tears were shed last week during the pen portraits. No doubt by the end of this inquiry enough will have been shed for a mighty river of sorrow to flow. Lost lives, lost loves, lost opportunities. We do not want one tear to have been shed in vain. We do not want one life to have been wasted without proper recourse for justice. We do not want one soul lost to this world to be without any meaning.

On behalf of the families, the survivors, the dead we will not permit or stand idly by, and allow the wretched souls lost on that fateful night, to have passed without a proper accounting for their lives which were prematurely extinguished by toxic smoke, fumes, and fire. [. . .] Sir, have no doubt, dangerous practices will be exposed in this inquiry and we hope that you and your team will have the courage to stand alongside us to expose wrongdoing where wrongdoing exists.

I told the story of my parents' arrival in London, and of their early married life and my birth in the borough of Kensington and Chelsea; their Rachman apartment on Talbot Road, and the vital importance of social housing outside the private rented sector to people like my mum and dad and my aunts and uncles. I told how my parents were married in the local Notting Hill Methodist church that now stands in the shadows of Grenfell, and that it was in the same church that at the tender age of three months I was baptised.

It was important for me to stress that the inquiry should not contribute to the stigmatisation of council housing or council tenants. 'In 1975, more than a third of the population was housed in council housing. This was a major achievement of post-war reconstruction and improvement of pre-war housing conditions. It benefited the lives of many people,' I said.

> Of course, the inquiry will know that the stereotype does not match the reality of Grenfell Tower. The inquiry knows that the occupants of Grenfell Tower and the estate of which it was part were mixed and as varied as the population of the great city in which they lived. A significant number of people owned their own homes. But the perception was there: council housing is for those who have failed in life. People who need to be managed, not embraced or admired. Desperate people without the agency to improve their lives: the destitute, disenfranchised, vulnerable and voiceless. Descriptions not of the people themselves, but of what society has done to them. [. . .] They were not helpless; they just were not helped.

Ahmed – the son of Elsah Elgwahry, aged sixty-four, and brother of Mariem Elgwahry, aged twenty-seven, who lived on Grenfell Tower's twenty-third floor, both of whom died in the fire – told me this: 'There is a misconception that those living in social housing are simply a group of uneducated and second-class citizens that should be thankful for living in the Royal Borough of Kensington and Chelsea.'

In this inquiry and in our society in general, it is important to remember that the people who live in a tower block are *not* members of a homogenous group: rather, they are representative of the wider society and hardworking people who make a valuable contribution to our society. Among the people who lost their lives in Grenfell Tower that night, Gloria Trevisan (26) was an architect who completed her master's degree at the University of Venice; Mohamed Amied Saber Neda

(57) had his own chauffeur business for the last ten to fifteen years of his life; his son Farhad Neda (25), who escaped the twenty-third floor along with his mother Flora, graduated from Kingston University with a BSc in engineering; Mary Mendy (54) was a carer and worked in the community; her daughter Khadija Saye (24) was a talented artist whose work was exhibited at the Venice Biennale at the start of a promising career; Pily Burton (74) worked as a contract manager for several years for several hospitals in and around the area, including St Charles Hospital; Debbie Lamprell (45) worked at Holland Park Opera House; Hamid Kani (60) was a talented chef; and Ahmed's sister Mariem Elgwahry was a successful graduate from Roehampton University, a primary carer for her mother, and a young marketing manager making positive strides in her early career.

Among the seventy-two victims of the fire, twenty-three countries or more were represented. These people, along with all the other residents of Grenfell Tower from many different lands and cultures, each of them with their own unique lives, personalities and disparate experiences, may have had the crumbs from the table of the richest borough in the country, but they had come together to form one diverse and vibrant community. Grenfell and the residents, in many ways, captured the essence of community life, the loss of which is not just personal to many, but to society as a whole. Grenfell Tower was a mirror of our society – particularly in our great capital city. It is not about one particular ethnic group or class group – the Grenfell Tower fire is a tragedy that has affected a wide range of ordinary people. However, stereotyping, I said, is what allowed the cost-cutting and the use of deadly materials in social housing to become normalised. It had also led to some appalling and false media reporting after the event which exemplified the prejudice against those people who were living in council housing and tower blocks.

'Sir, there is no inherent problem with tower blocks – they are the foundation of many strong neighbourhoods and communities. People enjoy living in them. Grenfell Tower was part of a strong and vibrant community in Lancaster West Estate and North Kensington. The problem is poorly maintained tower blocks.'

More than anything, people living at Grenfell Tower were entitled to feel, and to be, safe there. The disaster was a profound breach of the universal human right to an 'adequate home' – one that is not only in a state of repair, but also where the physical safety of occupants is guaranteed. Unfortunately, while in international law it has long since been recognised as a human right, successive UK governments have refused to incorporate the right into domestic law and allow our courts to uphold it. And had the residents of Grenfell Tower been able to enforce their rights to adequate housing, then at least some of the fire risks that we know were present would have been identified and rectified before the disaster. 'The Grenfell Tower Inquiry's legacy can and should go beyond a focus on fire safety in tower blocks, essential as that is: it stands in a unique and unprecedented position to recommend that the right to adequate housing is enshrined in our domestic law,' I said.

At the inquiry we were told that prior to the refurbishment, Grenfell Tower was constructed of virtually incombustible material, which was mainly concrete. The latest refurbishment, however, had seen the building's facade coated in polyethylene cladding, which according to Stephanie Barwise QC, another of the lawyers representing the victims and survivors, was 'now openly described by some within the industry as petrol'. In short, the refurbishment had been commissioned and carried out in such a way as to render it a death trap. This begged the question, was that refurbishment necessary or was it simply about beautifying the tower?

It was clear that, in its previous form, the building may have been considered an eyesore to some of the wealthier residents in the borough of Kensington and Chelsea. I suggested that it is a legitimate question to ask whether the money spent on the tower was not for the actual residents, but rather for those living nearby – to make it more aesthetically pleasing to them. This is not to say that poor people should live in ugly blocks – everyone deserves to live in a nice home – but the point I'm making is: *beautifying at what cost?* Were the materials used second rate? Yes. The slipshod *way* that the building was overhauled shows that it was *not* done with the welfare of the residents in mind. A culture of corporate impunity in social housing had taken root. Furthermore, despite their public words of sympathy to the Grenfell families and community, there was a reticence on the part of the companies involved in the building work to engage openly with the inquiry.

There was also the question of the government's role in the tragedy, in the sense of the wider context of successive Conservative governments' housing policy: the dismantling of the social housing infrastructure in the country following Margaret Thatcher's right-to-buy policy of the 1980s; the failure to rebuild or provide adequate social housing for the large section of society that will *never* earn enough to exercise that right to buy; the lack of affordable private rental properties; and the socio-economic fallout of the Tory government's programme of austerity. This, however, was not within the terms of reference nor the stated scope of the inquiry. Nevertheless, lawyers representing the Grenfell residents and community raised these central issues in our opening statements.

Then, there is the all-important question of the great, glaring elephant in the room throughout this inquiry: the role of institutional racism at the heart of this disaster. In May 2018, after months of campaigning and a petition backed by Stormzy and more than 150,000 supporters, our clients' calls for a more diverse panel to sit alongside Sir Martin had finally been granted by the then prime minister Theresa May. The day before I made my opening statements, on Tuesday 5 June, the eminent civil rights solicitor Imran Khan QC had delivered his statement to the inquiry. From the outset, Imran had called for the terms of reference of the inquiry to be broadened to consider the role of institutional racism in the wider context of the Grenfell fire. In this respect, he said that the inquiry should aspire to emulate the MacPherson inquiry into Stephen Lawrence's death by confronting the issue of race head on. The inquiry should examine whether Kensington and Chelsea council and its tenant management association of Grenfell Tower were guilty of institutional racism, likewise issues of religion and class should also be taken into account. In his opening remarks, Imran said:

Does the colour of a person's skin matter in this country? Does it affect your education? Does it affect whether you get stopped by the police? In short, does it affect your life chances? For most people from Black and minority ethnic communities, Britain is still either a land of denied opportunities or one in which opportunities are begrudgingly extended and extremely limited. There is grave foreboding among our clients that the race, religion or social class of residents may have determined their destiny. Our clients believe this is a proper issue to explore.

While this had previously been ruled out by the government and by chairman Sir Martin Moore-Bick, I, along with all my fellow lawyers representing the victims and survivors of the fire, wholeheartedly endorsed Imran's challenge to the inquiry. And while it may, or may not, have been fully embraced by the inquiry, by each of us continuously raising and referring to the issue of institutional racism, it kept it at the forefront of people's minds and, albeit unofficially, at the heart of the inquiry. It is now also at the forefront of the media's commentary on the Grenfell Inquiry as it unfolds.

Phase 1 of the inquiry was an emotionally charged experience for all involved. For those of us on the legal teams, it meant early starts and long, intense days. My day starts early. Normally, my team would start working in Garden Court Chambers from about 8 a.m., getting key documents together, having conferences with clients and finalising questions before rushing over to Holborn Bars to begin the day's hearings. Most lunchtimes there would be taken up with concerned survivors, victims, the bereaved – we might get twenty minutes to ourselves, but more often than not any spare time was consumed by further conferences. Likewise, at the end of the sitting, at around 4.30 p.m., we would meet again with our clients, deal with questions and issues raised, then it was back into chambers to prepare for the sitting the next day. It would not be unusual to be working until 10 p.m. depending on how much work is needed.

Sir Martin Moore-Bick's 856-page report of the findings of Phase 1 was published on 30 October 2019. (One could be cynical as to why it was released the night before Brexit was supposed to happen.) It said that Grenfell's facade was 'not compliant with building regulations. [. . .] It is clear that the walls [of the tower] didn't resist the spread of fire. On the contrary, they promoted it.'

Phase 2 of the inquiry opened the following January 2020. Many of the families and survivors had not been happy with the central London location because, if they had kids who needed to be dropped at school, or if they were old, unwell and still traumatised by the tragedy, then not only could the journey into Holborn be stressful and distressing, it could also be expensive, difficult and time-consuming. And so, following complaints from the core participants, this second phase is taking place in a new, specifically designed space on Bishop's Road, just behind Paddington Station.

Six weeks into the hearings, however, as the global Covid-19 pandemic unfolded, the country shut down and, like everything else, after 16 March the inquiry came to a standstill. The hearings resumed in April 2020 and are still ongoing, for the most part remotely. Now, since June 2021, with the easing of restrictions, some are attending the sessions in person, namely key witnesses, a handful of bereaved families, the counsel to the inquiry and the panel – with stringent social distancing measures, of course. Along with the rest of my team, therefore, I attend the hearings remotely as they are broadcast on YouTube.

This second phase is being conducted in a series of eight modules according to key themes and encompassing the extensive range of broader questions raised by the tragedy: Module 1 is an overview of the primary refurbishment, the procurement of design and build contractor, planning, the decision-making behind the choice of cladding; Module 2 is an in-depth analysis of the cladding products, including why certain materials were used as opposed to others; Module 3 is an in-depth analysis of active and passive fire safety measures in Grenfell Tower; Module 4 examines the aftermath of the disaster, the response of the Tenant Management Organisation, Kensington Borough Council and central government in dealing with a major emergency; Module 5 deals with firefighting, evacuation and stay put, training, communications and equipment (Phase 1 only looked at the emergency services insofar as they dealt with the events on the night; Phase 2 is a much deeper dive into these issues); Module 6 examines the response by central government to previous incidents/reports including in respect of building regulations, fire and firefighting; Module 7 looks at experts' conclusions on results from testing on cladding materials, adequacy of current testing regime, an overview of conclusions to be drawn about the Grenfell disaster – lessons to be learned. Finally, Module 8 will present the evidence concerning the movements of the deceased on the night of the fire, as well as trying to answer the questions of who, where, when and how people met their death. Of those modules, I am actively involved as team lead on modules 4, 5, 6 and 8.

At the time of writing, Modules 1, 2, 3 and 5 have been completed. The other modules are due to conclude later in 2022. Scotland Yard continues to conduct a parallel criminal investigation examining possible offences including corporate manslaughter and health and safety breaches, but will not bring any criminal charges until the inquiry has been completed and its findings published.

Grenfell Tower victims: where they were found

FLOOR
23
22
21
20
19
18
17
16
15
14
13
12
11
10
9
8
7
6
5
4

Outside tower block
(fallen from building)
Mohammad al-Haj Ali (23)
Abufars Ibrahim (39)
Mohamed Amied Neda (57)
(pulled out by firefighters)
Ali Yawar Jafari (81)

Close to nearby leisure centre
Mohamednur Tuccu (44)
Khadija Khaloufi (52)

In hospital
Logan Gomes (stillborn)
Maria Del Pilar Burton (74)

23rd floor   AGE
Hania Hassan (3)
Amaya Tuccu-Ahmedin (3)
Fethia Hassan (4)
Biruk Haftom (12)
Jessica Urbano Ramirez (12)
Gloria Trevisan (26)
Mariem Elgwahry (27)
Marco Gottardi (27)
Amna Mahmud Idris (27)
Berkti Haftom (29)
Rania Ibrahim (31)
Isra Ibrahim (33)
Amal Ahmedin (35)
Deborah Lamprell (45)
Ernie Vital (50)
Gary Maunders (57)
Hesham Rahman (57)
Fatemeh Afrasiabi (59)
Hamid Kani (60)
Raymond Bernard (63)
Eslah Elgwahry (64)
Sakina Afrasehabi (65)
Majorie Vital (68)
Fathia Ahmed (71)

22nd floor
Zainab Choucair (3)
Yaqub Hashim (6)
Fatima Choucair (11)
Firdows Hashim (12)
Yahya Hashim (13)
Mierna Choucair (13)
Nadia Choucair (33)
Nura Jemal (35)
Bassem Choukair (40)
Hashim Kedir (44)
Sirria Choucair (60)
Anthony Disson (65)

21st floor
Mehdi El-Wahabi (8)
Nur Huda El-Wahabi (15)
Yasin El-Wahabi (20)
Faouzia El-Wahabi (41)
Abdulaziz El-Wahabi (52)
Ligaya Moore (78)

20th floor
Malak Belkadi (8)
Alexandra Atala (40)
Victoria King (71)

[Between floors 19 & 20]
Leena Belkadi (6 months)
Farah Hamdan (31)
Omar Belkadi (32)

17th floor
Husna Begum (22)
Mohammed Hanif (26)
Mohammed Hamid (27)
Vincent Chiejina (60)
Rabeya Begum (64)
Kamru Miah (79)

16th floor
Joseph Daniels (69)
Sheila (84)

15th floor
Steve Power (63)

14th floor
Jeremiah Deen (2)
Zainab Deen (32)
Denis Murphy (56)

13th floor
Isaac Paulos (5)
Mary Mendy (54)

11th floor
Abdeslam Sebbar (67)

9th floor
Khadija Saye (24)

2020: A GLOBAL PANDEMIC, THE BIRTH OF A DAUGHTER AND THE DEATH OF GEORGE FLOYD

'In the end we will remember not the words of our enemies but the silence of our friends.'

Martin Luther King Jr

Not long after the Brexit referendum in 2016, I met Milena, a Polish woman who is now my wife. Originally, we planned to live together with her daughter in the UK, but we had a change of heart. I felt a shift in Great Britain after the referendum. Up until that point I had embraced my life in London with its fantastic cosmopolitan mix of languages and people. After the Brexit vote, we were a divided country, separated by a schism that laid bare an ugly truth. I had been living in a bubble and London, I realised, was not representative of the wider UK at all. Across the country, people were being subjected to racist and ethnic abuse in a way that I hadn't heard of in years: in school playgrounds the children of Central and Eastern European immigrants were being told they were not welcome;

Black people on buses were being told to 'go home'. Go home to where? All that bile and prejudice had been there all along, but held just under the surface and now, fired up by the vile and divisive rhetoric of certain elements of the Leave Campaign, people were showing their true colours as their underlying prejudices rose to the surface. So, after Milena and I married, in summer 2018, we made our home together in Poland.

Then, in March 2020, the Covid-19 virus brought the world to a halt. During this unprecedented period in our history, therefore, I have been living in Gdansk. But while businesses pulled down the shutters, schools closed and the world stopped for most people, it continued for me. The British state continued to kill people: in our prisons, in psychiatric hospitals, detention centres and at the hands of the police. When lockdown restrictions have allowed, I commuted to the UK in order to attend hearings. On the whole, however, I spent 2020 and 2021 appearing in courts remotely, still representing the dead and their families, but sitting in front of a computer screen in my small home office in Poland.

During the first lockdown I also became a father again, when our daughter Alisa was born on 8 May 2020. Now an irrepressible and ebullient toddler, she is a force of nature and along with my other children, her older siblings Megan and Isaac, the greatest source of joy in my life.

Just over two weeks later, on 25 May, the world watched as George Floyd was murdered by a Minneapolis police officer called Derek Chauvin. I, too, watched the unarmed 46-year-old Black man calling out for his dead mother as he lay struggling to take his last desperate breaths before the world's eyes. Before he lost consciousness the video showed him repeatedly pleading, 'I can't breathe.'

I cried the first time I watched the footage, as much in rage and frustration as in grief. Because, for me, witnessing what happened to George Floyd was sadly nothing new. In the UK, we have just as shocking killings of Black men, and less often Black women, also at the hands of the police and also recorded on camera. It brought back memories of the first time I saw a man die on camera, namely Christopher Alder all those years ago. But because the police suppress the video footage of such incidents, the only people who ever see it are the interested parties at an inquest and they have to sign undertakings not to disclose or discuss it. It took Mr Floyd's murder to spark righteous outrage across the world simply because that painful footage of his death *could be watched on mobile phones across the globe.*

In the days after George Floyd's murder made the headlines, it led everyone to ask questions about race, discrimination and racism. I heard all too often the refrain that the UK is not as bad as the States, that we don't have such police brutality here, that people aren't treated in the same way. Well, I have been doing cases involving identical restraint-related deaths for thirty years. And many of the racist encounters with the police which I myself experienced when I was a young adult – being stopped by the police and questioned on my way home from school, being pulled up in my car with my first wife and child and accused of being an illegal taxi driver – Black people are still experiencing today.

In response, therefore, I took to Twitter. Below the rhetorical statement, 'So, you think the UK doesn't have a policing problem . . .' I listed just some of the young Black men who have died in police custody in England during the time I have been an inquest lawyer, men who have been restrained, who have also pleaded 'I can't breathe'. People were absolutely stunned by my posts, but they contained absolutely no new revelations. Essentially, I had simply retweeted my original posts about positional asphyxia cases I've been involved in since I first joined Twitter in 2012. I got to twenty-nine names of those who had died and then I stopped.

I remember an email discussion, two weeks after George Floyd died, in Garden Court about making a statement of solidarity with the anti-racist ethos of the Black Lives Matter movement. One barrister said he didn't think we should say anything that may influence the criminal trial. I responded by pointing out that, if there was ever a moment for a human rights set of chambers to step up and be counted, this was it. This wasn't about due process and the fair trial of Derek Chauvin: the issue here was that we saw a Black man brutally murdered before our eyes. George Floyd was given no due process: *that* is the point. And for us at Garden Court, to remain silent would be shameful. In the end, everyone agreed including the barrister who raised the issue.

As the Black Lives Matter campaign gained momentum, I watched with appalled fascination as major organisations suddenly became 'woke'. Despite the fact that endless reports have been published and any number of public inquiries have been held about discrimination and institutional racism, and that issues surrounding diversity, inclusion and equality have been known for decades, big business were finally scrabbling to get with the programme because a Black man in Minneapolis was killed by American police. *Come on!*

I found myself bombarded with media requests for comment and calls for advice from every direction. I was not alone. I have heard time and time again from friends and colleagues in all walks of life, that as Black professionals we are expected to be the spokespeople for anti-racism. I've heard stories about Black employees in predominately white organisations who are being tasked with writing the company's anti-racist policy documents – on top of their day jobs. I totally get it, but corporations shouldn't rely on their Black employees to do their work for them. Not to mention that it puts us under an inordinate amount of pressure – and just because we happen to be Black, it does not necessarily mean we are qualified to fulfil that role.

My response is to say that if having Black skin makes me an expert, then I'm qualified, but I am *not* a race expert. Just because I am Black doesn't mean that I have all the answers. Like everybody else, I have had to start educating myself in anti-racism literature and discrimination and equality policy. If you want to learn about how to be an anti-racist, pick up a book. There is a wealth of excellent literature and learning materials out there; it is not my job to educate you. In order to live and work in a truly anti-racist society, white people must put aside their guilt and take action. And for those who can't see there's a problem, that's because they are a part of it.

I'd like it recognised that in the legal profession, as in our society, we also have a problem with systemic racism. And this occurs on both sides of the bench. In spite of the 1999 Macpherson inquiry into the death of Stephen Lawrence the criminal justice system remains institutionally racist with huge disparity in the treatment of Black men at every stage. The law is far from colour blind. Nor is it just the criminal courts that have a race problem. In the immigration system judges sit in judgement on Black, Asian and Minority Ethnic (BAME) people every day. Some of these people are seeking asylum in the UK after experiencing horrific traumas in their home countries. Some are victims of human trafficking and similar abuses. Some are people who have lived here most of their lives, are British in all but name, and are now being ripped away from their homes and their families because of a criminal conviction. Sadly, if not surprisingly, the attitudes of the people who administer this system today can at times be as racist and colonialist as those who created it in the 1960s and 1970s. One barrister told me that a white immigration judge, having heard an appeal by a North African appellant, commented on how refreshing it was to see a North African person working. The same barrister, who is herself Black, was told by a different judge that it was nice to see her 'sitting on this side of the table', pointing to the side of the table where counsel sits. Another judge told her at a training event that she did not have 'negroid features'.

Racism can be more insidious than this, however. It is a flawed and outdated view to assume the racist is someone who consciously demeans those who don't look like them. We need to acknowledge that bias is implicit and often unconscious. When our profession recognises that racism doesn't necessarily come from individuals, doesn't need to be conscious, and doesn't need to be intentional, we will be moving in the right direction. Racial injustice and racism isn't a simple binary: the racist needn't simply be bad, ignorant, bigoted, prejudiced or old; the non-racist isn't necessarily the good person, educated, progressive, open- or fair-minded, well-intended or young. This discussion goes far deeper than these simplistic assumptions.

I only need point to my own experiences at the Bar – the instances where I have been mistaken for a client, the times when I have been treated dismissively or disrespectfully because I am Black, when I have been deliberately 'othered' or made to feel different, are not unique. Many of my colleagues from the BAME community have similar stories. And if I can be treated in this way as a member of a well-respected profession, it takes very little imagination to visualise how Black defendants are treated in the judicial system in this country.

I'm trying not to be too negative, however. Although it took the death of a Black man in Minneapolis to re-spark the Black Lives Matter protests globally and put the conversation back on the agenda in the UK, there is now, at last, a real discussion about race in the public discourse. Even if I am only one tiny cog, I am determined to bring change to our society.

In June 2020, Gresham College, the 400-year-old City institution that provides free public lectures, appointed me as their first Black Professor of Law. It was a proud moment; me, the Battersea County boy who barely scraped through his A levels, now an actual *professor*. In the wake of the outcry sparked by the death of George Floyd, I embraced the opportunity to deliver a lecture series on deaths at the hands of the state and how to regulate the use of police restraint.

Not long afterwards, in September 2020, my late-blooming academic credentials were boosted by an invitation to join Goldsmiths University as a visiting lecturer. No doubt, my mother, who has been shielding for the last two years of the Covid pandemic in the relative safety of Antigua, sent a postcard with the press cuttings of the announcements to Mr Jerry in his retirement.

That same month, I travelled back to London to represent the family of Kevin Clarke in the inquest into his death. A young Black man who was obviously mentally disturbed, Kevin was set upon by a number of Metropolitan police officers and restrained until he collapsed in the sports' field at my son's school, St Dunstan's College, five minutes from my house in Lewisham. Kevin said 'I can't breathe' as they squeezed the life out of him. And this was all captured on the body cams of the police officers involved.

The inquest jury returned a narrative verdict concluding that Kevin was treated inappropriately by the police and ambulance service and that police restraint contributed to his death. They gave a list of damning failings by these state agents including the fact that at least one police officer heard Kevin say more than once that he could not breathe. Every police officer had denied hearing this, but the jury obviously did not accept this. This was justice for his family, of course, yet the depressing thing for me is that Kevin's case was so similar to those of Wayne Douglas in the mid-nineties, Christopher Alder in 2000 and Sean Rigg in 2012; all cases involving Black men who were restrained by the police and who died from positional asphyxia. The lessons had been learned, so we were told, so why is it that the same issues *still* continue to arise time and again?

It is depressing.

Fast-forward to April 2021 and I represented the family at the inquest at Bradford coroner's court into the death of Andrew Hall in September 2016. Andrew, a Black man in his forties, lived with his partner and their two-year old daughter in Huddersfield. They were having financial difficulties and, possibly due to the stress he was under along with a painful arthritic condition, he was suffering from chronic insomnia. Consequently, along with his arthritis medication, Andrew was taking prescription sleeping pills. Still struggling with night after night of sleeplessness, on the night of his death, Andrew had drunk a couple of glasses of brandy. The combination of the alcohol and his medication effectively knocked him out and in panic, Andrew's partner called the emergency services. When Andrew regained consciousness in hospital, he was disoriented, became aggressive and slapped a nurse. As a result, there was an issue as to whether Andrew was discharged from hospital or whether he discharged himself; this was hotly disputed. The police were called and he was taken to Huddersfield police station. There followed the all-too familiar tragic story: Andrew, a Black man in custody, was unwell and confused, but sixteen police officers were involved in the arrest and restraint. Two hours later Andrew was dead.

Things went badly wrong in the Andrew Hall case. In fact, everything that could have gone wrong with the inquest did. I wanted to be at the hearing but I couldn't come to the UK due to travel restrictions and so I attended remotely. While everyone else was in court, I appeared in front of the jury on a big screen in the courtroom. I was at a clear disadvantage. I couldn't see what was happening in court; I didn't feel I had a relationship with the jury. It was, in retrospect, a huge mistake, but the family had waited long enough for the inquest and I had no other option.

We attempted to run race as an issue. I felt strongly that at the heart of Andrew's case and in his treatment at the hands of the police was the use of racist tropes in the language used to describe him; as in many of the restraint cases I have worked on was the notion that Andrew was a big, strong, powerful, essentially extremely dangerous, *Black* man. These tropes are generally used against Black men by the police in order to justify their excessive use of force. I tried to highlight these pernicious stereotypes during the inquest and I don't think I did it successfully. In 2017, the Angiolini Review of Deaths and Serious Incidents in Police Custody said:

> The stereotyping of young Black men as 'dangerous, violent and volatile' is a longstanding trope that is ingrained in the minds of many in our society. It is not uncommon to hear comments from police officers about a young Black man having 'superhuman strength' or being 'impervious to pain' and, often wholly inaccurately, as the 'biggest man I have ever encountered'. Such perceptions increase the likelihood

of force and restraint being used against an individual who may be unwell. The detainee is effectively dehumanised. In such circumstances the police officers may also use force and restraint in order to gain compliance to the exclusion of any focus on the wellbeing of the detainee which can ultimately lead to a medical crisis or death.

The sad reality is that the assumptions and biases that a police officer might hold about Black people are often not sufficiently probed by the IOPC; and past disciplinary records are not automatically investigated. When determining if officers have a case to answer, inadequate consideration is given to relevant statistical evidence of disproportionality by the IOPC. In my experience, there is undoubtedly also an entrenched discomfort among coroners about including race in inquests. We lawyers are sometimes complicit in this as we don't want to be accused of 'playing the race card'. There will often be less contentious arguments to run with so why risk damaging our client's case with such a disagreeable topic? Furthermore, in the absence of evidence of overt discrimination, coroners are nervous to consider the statistical context of a case i.e. disproportionate use of force.

If I had my time again, I would take on board that it is not just a jury that needs to be educated in relation to these issues, but sometimes everyone in court, lawyers and coroners too. And, as I have said, I am not a race expert. In the wake of the Andrew Hall case, I reflected that I was not sufficiently well-versed in these conversations to get the court to understand that to use a racist trope or to have unconscious stereotypical thoughts doesn't necessarily mean you are a bad person. But the content of what is being said can have a huge, and often fatal, impact on actions. If, as a result of the stereotypical tropes they have grown up with, police officers see someone they perceive to be *big* and *dangerous*, it might well have an impact on how they treat the people they arrest. That might be an explanation as to why police officers routinely use greater force when apprehending and restraining Black men than with the equivalent white counterpart.

The official statistics are subtle and complex, but when you begin to drill down and dig deep, you see a picture of differential treatment based on race in which the perception of skin colour is associated with greater danger. And when you look at the reasons as to why Black skin engenders such fear, well, this is a whole other story explored in books like Akala's *Natives* and Elijah Lawal's *The Clapback; Your Guide to Calling out Racist Stereotypes and Tropes*. The fear of the Black man that has been perpetuated over centuries has historic precedent. And it maintains the status quo.

The Andrew Hall case lasted just under ten weeks with eight solid weeks of evidence. The coroner summed up the evidence for three days with detailed submissions made to the jury. The jury were out for less than a couple of hours. They came back and exonerated the police in the death of Andrew Hall.

Ultimately, I will never know if the jury's decision would have been the same had I attended the inquest in person. One thing I am sure about, however, is that when it comes to the issue of Black men and women dying in custody, race cannot be ignored. And this leads me to conclude that these cases could benefit from having a race expert on board to explain why the use of such language and such tropes amounts to unconscious bias. And that unconscious bias can lead to the deaths of Black people at the hands of the police.

I have made a decision not to take on any more police restraint death cases. Too painful. Too stressful. Too heartbreaking. The mind is a wonderful thing, it can always be changed, but I do not want to become a punch-drunk boxer who does not know when to retire. It is time for me to step aside and let others pick up this particular baton.

When I started taking on these cases I was the only Black lawyer I knew of in this field. But now there is a new generation of young Black lawyers who are much more skilful than myself, many of whom I've had the pleasure to work with. And not just young BAME lawyers, there are any number of fantastic young men and women at the Bar, some of whom I trained at Garden Court, others with whom I have worked with as my juniors over the years, and who are all much brighter lawyers in terms of black letter law than I ever was. These young advocates have the passion and commitment to carry on and take up the mantle in this area of inquest law.

In the same way that I had role models that I could look up to when I was starting out, great lawyers and mentors such as Rudi Narayan, David Richardson, Tony Gifford QC, Ian Macdonald QC, and Courtenay Griffiths QC – all of whom shared with me their skillset, their techniques and skills of advocacy and cross examination – I feel that I am handing down my skillset to the next generation of lawyers who will follow in my footsteps.

In the meantime, I have other battles to fight. At the time of writing, Phase 2 of the Grenfell Inquiry is ongoing and I am now attending the hearings in person. I have just formed my Chambers in the Caribbean and I look forward to working somewhere where, although the violation of human rights is still very much a concern, race isn't a key issue.

Let me end where I started. In my introduction I wrote about impostor syndrome. I have said that I have sometimes felt that somehow I was not good enough and the problem was with me, whether that be as a child in the Cub Scouts, on the beach in the south of France as a teenager, dining in the Inner Temple in my early twenties, or appearing in court for the first time. For years I felt like a fraud and that I should not have a seat at the table. But after nearly fifty years of reflection, I now realise that impostor syndrome does not adequately describe how I was made to feel. So, now I prefer to use the term 'trespasser syndrome'. In other words, it is not *me* that has the problem, but others who feel that I *should not* be at the table. I hope in my lifetime that people who look like me will no longer be made to feel like outsiders, or trespassers. I hope that someday I will walk into a British court and no one will blink an eye when they are confronted with Black judges, Black men and Black women counsel.

I hope I live to see the day when skin colour is an irrelevance not worthy of comment.

ACKNOWLEDGEMENTS

I realise that when you write about your life, the saying 'no man is an island' could not be more apt. There are just so many people who made this book possible. Firstly, I want to pay tribute to my mum, Sheila Thomas, for directing me and for being the most resolutely consistent person in my life, even when she thought I was going wrong. My late father, Godfrey, for showing me what hard work and dedication to family means. To my sister Janet for being my trusted advisor. And to Angela, my friend and confidante, who was by my side for so many years as we grew from children into adults; to my children Megan and Isaac who were the making of me as a father. You both taught me so many lessons about what makes a good dad and what makes a bad dad. And now, of course, my Milena, her daughter Oliwia and our daughter the irrepressible Alisa, a constant source of joy and light in my life. I am truly enjoying fatherhood again.

I am indebted to my teachers and friends Linda Austin, Sue Boothroyd, Huguette Collie, Lynn Fletcher, Nick Gunning and Carolyn Lornie. And to my mentors in law the Honourable Sir Nicholas Blake, Louise Christian, Professor Chris Clarkson, Professor Penny Derbyshire, Lord Anthony Gifford QC, Dr

Courtenay Griffiths QC, Mark Houghton, the Honourable Sir Stephen Irwin, HHJ Jan Luba QC, HHJ David Richardson, David Watkinson, Elizabeth Woodcraft, James Wood QC and Professor Robert Upex. Further thanks are owed to all those friends, colleagues and fellow lawyers who have stood by my side, encouraged and supported me over the years: the late Nan Alban-Lloyd, Patrick Allen, Phil Bampfylde, James Bell, Fiona Borrill, Jonathan Bridge, Sarah Brown, Ruth Bundy, Melanie Carter, Paul Clark, Andre Clovis, Jocelyn Cockburn, Colin Cook, David Corrigan, Chez Cotton, Kelly Darlington, Liz Davies QC, Professor Jo Delahunty, Blani Dorrell, Emma Favata, the late Mike Fisher, the late Marc Foss, Andrew Guile, Kirsten Heaven, Alexandra Hill, Sean Horstead, Neil Hudgell, Sarah Johnson, Jo Kearsley, Jo Keeling, Judy Khan QC, Sadiq Khan, Shazia Khan, Cyrilia Knight, Jo Knorpel, Susie Labinjoh, Tanya Lappo, Gary Leonard, John Lodwick, Ann Lott, the late George Louison, Daniel Machover, Isabelle Maguire, Peter Mahy, Emma Manning, Michael Mansfield QC, Ifti Manzoor, Thalia Maragh, Nathaniel Mathews, Judith Maxwell, Kate Maynard, David de Menezes, Rajiv Menon QC, Allison Munroe QC, Una Morris, Suzie Gregson Murray, David Neale, Elaine Needham, Paddy O'Connor QC, Ifeanyi Odogwu, Nogah Ofer, Tim Owen QC, Lina Peteryte, Martin Robbins, Nick Scott, Howard Serr, Anita Sharma, Jemima Smith, Jane Talbot, Julian Theseira, Marc Willers QC, Marcia Willis Stewart (Hon. QC), Tom Stoate, Carol Storer, Adam Straw, Chris Topping, Lotta Walker QC, Pat Wilkins, Harriet Wistrich; and Deb Coles, the late Gilly Munday and Helen Shaw at INQUEST. And to the clients and their lost loved ones who made this incredibly journey for the pursuit of justice possible, I have shared your tears, pain, and at times joy.

Finally, this book would not have come into being but for

my wonderful agent Zoe Ross at United Agents. You are a stalwart, thank you. I must also thank the brilliant Rose Davidson who helped me enormously with this work; and my publisher and editor Suzanne Baboneau for her trust and guidance in shaping this book. I am further indebted to the entire publishing team at Simon & Schuster: Kat Ailes; my copy editor Victoria Godden, and proofreader Clare Sayer; my publicist Rhiannon Carroll, Hannah Paget in marketing, along with the rest of the marketing and publicity team; Matt Johnson for the eye-catching jacket design. It has been a pleasure to work with them all and the book would have been much the poorer without all their creative input and dedication.

INDEX

LT indicates Leslie Thomas.

Thomas, Trevor (brother of LT) 24,
    26, 28, 29, 42, 43–4, 46, 57, 252
Thompson, Claudette 156–7, 158
Thompson, Owen 254
Thornton QC, Peter 211, 211n, 378,
    379
Times, The 20, 157
Todd, Mark 279
Tooks Court 105, 191, 261, 307
trespasser syndrome 429
Trevisan, Gloria 407
25 Bedford Row 261
Twitter 419–20

Uganda 19, 20
Ulster Volunteer Force 384
unconscious bias 115, 164, 427
Underwood QC, Ashley 313
unemployment 63–5, 65n, 66, 97, 134,
    146, 174
United Nations: Universal Declaration
    of Human Rights (1948) 197–8,
    197n
unlawful killing 140, 148, 173, 174,
    192, 193, 194, 205, 220, 221, 225,
    227, 253, 273, 319, 366
Upex, Professor Bob 82–3
uplifts 160

Vagrancy Act (1824) 61

Wakefield Coroner's Court 363
Wales, devolved government of
    387–98
Walker, Andrew 310
Walker, John 370

Wallace, Mario 350, 352
Walthamstow Coroner's Court 191
Webster, Linda 104
Wellington Street Chambers 91–2,
    93–106, 156, 374, 375
Wesbecker, Joseph 239
West Midlands Police 373, 374, 377,
    378, 380, 386
Westminster County Court 102
West Yorkshire Police 289, 298, 361,
    363
White, Bob 47
white nationalism 43
White, Sergeant Paul 296, 297–9, 302
Whitfield, Colin 240, 241
Wilby, Eddie 30, 32, 33–4, 41, 48, 50,
    51–2, 71
Williams, Geraint 241, 277–8
Wilson, Harold 15, 41
Wilson, Detective Chief Inspector
    Terry 289
Winchester Coroner's Court 288
Windrush generation 13–14, 22
Winter of Discontent (1978–9) 48–9
Witness O 381–4
Woodcroft, Liz 102
Wood QC, James 99
Wood, Sharon 361, 362, 367
Woolf, Lord 148–9, 158
Worcestershire NHS Trust 278
World in Action 373, 377

Yerushalmi, Yosef xi
Yorkshire Metropolitan Ambulance
    Service 346–7
Young (née Ruddock), Dawn 271–3